Praise for *Innovation Passport*

"Finally! A book that lays out a thorough yet workable path to collaborative innovation! With a highly readable style and using great examples, Frederich and Andrews describe the process by which IBM makes collaborative innovation work from a process, company, and customer standpoint. By following the guidelines in this book, those with aspirations of collaborative innovation can learn from the lessons of IBM and maximize their probability of success. A+!"

Gregory S. Dawson, Ph.D.,
Assistant Professor at W.P. Carey School of Business
at Arizona State University and former Partner at PricewaterhouseCoopers

Innovation Passport goes directly to the heart of how companies can speed up the transition from research to revenue. This book's combination of insight and actionable detail—derived over a dozen years—provides a roadmap for companies to accelerate the commercialization of ideas and technologies. Moreover, this best practice is based on collaboration with external partners, an approach that is even more critical given strained economic times."

Keith O'Brien, VP,
Best Practices Research, Frost & Sullivan

"Read this book if you want to gain critical insights into what it takes to commercialize innovations. It contains the collective wisdom from more than a decade of IBM's experiences that are equally valid for conglomerates and entrepreneurs. However, if you want to know how to mitigate the risks of commercializing your innovations, adopt it as your guidebook."

Alex Todd, Founding CEO,
Trust Enablement Incorporated

"The pathways that usher innovative ideas to technologies that are practical and successful are many. They also are gutted with roadblocks, potholes, even sinkholes into which great and worthy ambitions can disappear.

Frederich and Andrews, in their chronicle of a long-time innovation-nursery at IBM to nurture collaborative efforts with both in-house and external stakeholders, provide what amounts to a valuable how-to manual for taking, as their subtitle says, 'research to reality.' For research managers and potential collaborators aiming to make their innovative ideas real, the book can serve as a stem-to-stern guide.

Sociologists and historians of science and others who study the process of innovation and technology development will find in this chronicle a fascinating strategic approach to fostering innovation and the sort of detailed case studies that can provide ground proof for theories about technology development."

Ivan Amato, Senior Correspondent,
Chemical & Engineering News

Related Books of Interest

Reaching the Goal
How Managers Improve a Services Business Using Goldratt's Theory of Constraints
by John Arthur Ricketts
ISBN: 0-13-233312-0

"Excellent writing...a beautiful piece of work. I consider it one of the best books on TOC to have emerged from outside my organization. In fact, I am so impressed that I've asked John Ricketts to be my coauthor for a series of books I plan to write on the concept of ever-flourishing companies."
—Eliyahu M. Goldratt, author of *The Goal* and founder of the Theory of Constraints (TOC)

Ricketts draws on Eli Goldratt's Theory of Constraints (TOC), one of this generation's most successful management methodologies...thoroughly adapting it to the needs of today's professional, scientific, and technical services businesses. He reveals how to identify the surprising constraints that limit your organization's performance, execute more effectively within those constraints, and then loosen or even eliminate them.

Eating the IT Elephant
Moving from Greenfield Development to Brownfield
by Richard Hopkins and Kevin Jenkins
ISBN: 0-13-713012-0

Most conventional approaches to IT development assume you're building entirely new systems. Today, Greenfield development is a rarity. Nearly every project exists in the context of existing, complex system landscapes—often poorly documented and poorly understood. Now, two of IBM's most experienced senior architects offer a new approach that is fully optimized for the unique realities of Brownfield development.

Richard Hopkins and Kevin Jenkins explain why accumulated business and IT complexity is the root cause of large-scale project failure and show how to overcome that complexity "one bite of the elephant at a time." You'll learn how to manage every phase of the Brownfield project, leveraging breakthrough collaboration, communication, and visualization tools—including Web 2.0, semantic software engineering, model-driven development and architecture, and even virtual worlds.

Listen to the author's podcast at:
ibmpressbooks.com/podcasts

Related Books of Interest

The Greening of IT
How Companies Can Make a Difference for the Environment

By John Lamb
ISBN: 0-13-715083-0

Drawing on leading-edge experience, John Lamb helps you realistically assess the business case for green IT, set priorities, and overcome internal and external challenges to make it work. He offers proven solutions for issues ranging from organization obstacles to executive motivation and discusses crucial issues ranging from utility rate incentives to metrics. Along the way, you'll discover energy-saving opportunities—from virtualization and consolidation to cloud and grid computing—and solutions that will improve business flexibility as they reduce environmental impact.

Lamb presents case studies, checklists, and more—all the practical guidance you need to drive maximum bottom-line value from your green IT initiative.

Implementing ITIL Change and Release Management

by Larry Klosterboer
ISBN: 0-13-815041-9

For the first time, there's a comprehensive best-practice guide to succeeding with two of the most crucial and challenging parts of ITIL: change and release management.

Leading IBM ITIL expert and author Larry Klosterboer shares solid expertise gained from real implementations across multiple industries. He helps you decide where to invest, avoid ITIL pitfalls, and build successful, long-term processes that deliver real return on investment. You'll find detailed guidance on each process, integrated into a comprehensive roadmap for planning, implementation, and operation—a roadmap available nowhere else.

Listen to the author's podcast at:
ibmpressbooks.com/podcasts

Innovation Passport

Innovation Passport
The IBM First-of-a-Kind (FOAK) Journey from Research to Reality

Mary Jo Frederich and
Peter Andrews

IBM Press
Pearson plc

Upper Saddle River, NJ • Boston • Indianapolis • San Francisco
New York • Toronto • Montreal • London • Munich • Paris • Madrid
Cape Town • Sydney • Tokyo • Singapore • Mexico City

ibmpressbooks.com

IBM Press Program Managers: Steven M. Stansel and Ellice Uffer
Cover design: IBM Corporation

Associate Publisher: Mark Taub
Marketing Manager: Kourtnaye Sturgeon
Publicist: Heather Fox
Acquisitions Editor: Bernard Goodwin
Development Editor: Michael Thurston
Managing Editor: Kristy Hart
Designer: Alan Clements
Project Editors: Jovana San Nicolas-Shirley and Julie Anderson
Copy Editor: Gayle Johnson
Indexer: Erika Millen
Compositor: Jake McFarland
Proofreader: Sheri Cain
Manufacturing Buyer: Dan Uhrig

Published by Pearson plc
Publishing as IBM Press

IBM Press offers excellent discounts on this book when ordered in quantity for bulk purchases or special sales, which may include electronic versions and/or custom covers and content particular to your business, training goals, marketing focus, and branding interests. For more information, please contact

U.S. Corporate and Government Sales
1-800-382-3419
corpsales@pearsontechgroup.com

For sales outside the U.S., please contact

International Sales
international@pearson.com

Library of Congress Cataloging-in-Publication Data

Frederich, Mary Jo (Mary Josephine), 1960–

    Innovation passport : the IBM First-of-a-Kind (FOAK) journey from research to reality / Mary Jo Frederich and Peter Andrews.

        p. cm.

    Includes bibliographical references.

    ISBN 978-0-13-239076-7 (hbk. : alk. paper)   1. Research and development projects.   2. Diffusion of innovations—Management.   3. New products.   4. International Business Machines Corporation—Management. I. Andrews, Peter, 1954–   II. Title.

    T175.5.F69   2010

    658.5'14—dc22

                          2009027745

ISBN-13: 978-0-13-239076-7

ISBN-10: 0-13-239076-0

Text printed in the United States on recycled paper at R.R. Donnelley in Crawfordsville, Indiana.

First printing September 2009

To my mom and dad, who worked so hard and sacrificed so much to provide us with the moral, social, and educational foundation to succeed in life, and to Mark, D.J., and Catalina for their patience, love, and support. Thank you.
—*Mary Jo Frederich*

With gratitude, I dedicate this book to my parents, George W. Andrews and Clare K. Andrews. Their example of love provides a model for relationships. Their quiet insistence on ethics and fair play illuminates the path to trust and integrity. Their patience and persistence inspire hope and commitment. None of what I've done would have been possible without them.
—*Peter Andrews*

Contents

Foreword

Innovation has been and always will be all about generating new real value.

It has more to do with putting deep insights into problems and challenges—be they business, government, education, or societal—together in a unique and facile manner with your knowledge and technology to unlock hidden value.

The 21st Century has certainly demanded this type of innovation from us in less than its first decade. All the signs point to even more demanding times ahead. So much has changed in such a short period of time. So much more will change in an even shorter period of time. Our future success in delivering against our hopes and dreams, aspirations, and expectations will be tightly linked to our ability to innovate at an ever-increasing rate.

The good news is that we—each and every one of us—can. Increasingly, innovation is less about invention, creation, and discovery and more about what you do with your knowledge of the problem and its potential answers. The best environment to do this in turns out to be one that supports open, collaborative, global, and multidisciplined thinking and action.

IBM's First-of-a-Kind (FOAK) program did all this and more long before it was deemed fashionable, understandable, or desirable.

As a result of the deep customer intimacy and insight into problems and challenges this program afforded, the innovation unleashed so many of IBM's researchers with their deep knowledge, expertise, and technologies, which is nothing short of remarkable.

Right from the beginning, it was clear to me that this program would not only be good for our clients but equally good for our company. It is hard to argue with a program that generates value for both parties short term as well as long term. Supporting and funding this effort also helped me develop my own views of innovation here at the start of the twenty-first century. We used these ideas and concepts to not only drive our company forward on its global agenda but also several economies of the world. In short, the FOAK program has been an amazing source of value, pride, and energy for the IBM company.

—Nicholas M. Donofrio
IBM Fellow Emeritus
IBM EVP Innovation and Technology (retired)

Preface

Collaborative innovation represents the best way forward, perhaps the *only* way forward, as we face the problems of the twenty-first century.

For the last 14 years, IBM has been exploring, developing, and extending one approach to collaborative innovation through the First-of-a-Kind (FOAK) program. Each project within the program brings ideas, technologies, and assets from IBM research to real-world problems and opportunities.

The scope of these projects is, by design, limited. Budgets are fixed. The duration of each is only a year, and the maturity of each innovation is such that milestones and deliverables can be defined before investment takes place. This is not to say that FOAK projects don't have their share of surprises, both good and bad. Any innovation project includes a level of uncertainty and risk. But FOAK is not about open-ended, blue-sky innovation.

Nonetheless, you'll find within this book examples that we hope will be informative and inspiring. We've learned a lot through the experience of FOAK, and many lessons, called out explicitly, might be more generally applicable to innovation programs. Finally, the challenges, discoveries, and insights from scores of projects have provided overall perspectives that might offer a reference point for critiquing or designing collaborative innovation programs across the spectrum of creativity and engagement.

Primarily, this book is intended for people who are involved in collaborative innovation. Those who plan and manage programs should find examples, guidance, and cautions. Those who participate should see some of the factors that are critical to success. There is also a point of view that innovation is a social activity and that success depends on communications that are systematic, empathetic, and focused. The excitement of discovery and rapidly evolving challenges seen by innovators make it easy to shortchange partners. But explaining, updating, consulting, and reminding partners of all sorts—

including those who will turn prototypes and early applications into broadly adopted offerings—is as essential as getting the numbers right, combing out bugs in a program, and integrating new applications into systems.

Besides collaborative innovators, our hope is that people will read this book to get a new perspective on how innovation might be made available to solve problems for businesses, governments, and nonprofits. We've peppered the text with mentions of specific projects with the hope that the broad scope of possibilities will become evident. And because it is often business leaders, administrators, and politicians who need to be engaged as full partners if innovations are to deliver on their promises, we hope that the information in these pages will help ready a wide variety of professionals to more effectively engage with the researchers and developers with whom they will need to collaborate.

This book is primarily organized according to the journey a project takes, from working out the possibilities to market adoption.

Chapter 1, "A Program That Works," provides a basic orientation to the program and some discussion of its origins.

Chapter 2, "The FOAK Process: Phase I," presents an overview of the initial steps of the FOAK process. It describes individuals coming together to explore client needs or the possible uses of particular assets, gathering input and support across different organizations, and submitting a proposal. This chapter also defines and explains a number of the essential roles and teams that participate in the process.

Chapter 3, "How Ideas Take Shape," gets specific about how the pieces of a strong proposal come together, refined by teams with different perspectives and reformulated to fit real-world opportunities and needs.

Chapter 4, "Getting the Most out of Partnerships," focuses on a major theme of the book—building relationships and commitment with a variety of stakeholders.

Chapter 5, "Choosing the Best Projects," describes the criteria for selecting projects for funding. It illustrates how proposals are investigated and explored, with an eye toward improving their odds of success.

Chapter 6, "The FOAK Process: Phases II and III," concludes the overview of the FOAK process. It describes project approval, engaging partners, execution, completion, and commitments that lead to marketplace adoption as products and services.

Chapter 7, "Clarifying Project Plans," digs into the ways in which different entities establish both how they will work together and what they will do to execute a project effectively.

Chapter 8, "Ensuring the Work Gets Done," details the sometimes difficult balancing act required for those who want to keep the flexibility needed for new ideas and approaches with the hard-nosed structure needed to fulfill the commitments of an innovation program.

Chapter 9, "Telling the Story: IBM's Industry Solutions Labs," goes into an area that is often overlooked in innovation books—the promotion of the results. While IBM presents the results of FOAK projects in many ways, here the focus is on one channel—the Industry Solutions Labs. It provides a number of concrete examples of the elements of successful promotion, including audience analysis, development of demonstrations, and clear articulation of value propositions.

Chapter 10, "Portfolio Management," provides a program-wide view of FOAK. It emphasizes trade-offs, maintaining support, and keeping the overall balance of projects vital and relevant.

Chapter 11, "Contracts and Intellectual Property," answers some of the questions about how different organizations make legal commitments that reduce the possibility of misunderstanding and make explicit how investments, work, and benefits will be shared.

Chapter 12, "A Guide for Creating Innovative Programs," abstracts and generalizes the experience of FOAK. The aim is to provide innovators at any organizational level with a reference that can be used to explore possible models or to validate the completeness of an existing collaborative innovation approach.

Chapter 13, "The Future of Collaborative Innovation," looks toward some of the dramatic changes that will create new options and challenges for those who are looking to partner for innovation.

To set the work in context, this book also includes some of the history of FOAK and a viewpoint on the future of collaborative innovation.

Day to day, FOAK continues to evolve. Any program needs to be flexible and open to new possibilities in a world that, at times, can be altered dramatically by new technologies, economic tsunamis, emerging business models, political surprises, and the changing roles of users, customers, and citizens. In addition, we've found that discussions of collaborative innovation have become richer and more informative as we've reached out more broadly to validate and explore the ideas in this book. With this in mind, we've established a Web site at www.ibm.com/research/FOAK so you can stay up to date on the challenges FOAK takes on and the paths to success it discovers. We also hope to have rich conversations with you if you have questions or if you want to share your own experiences and perspectives. Toward this end, we've also created a blog at http://innovationpassport.blogspot.com/. We hope you can join us there.

Acknowledgments

We'd like to thank our friends and families for their patience and understanding while we wrote this book, and our sponsors, Holly Unland and Cathy Lasser, for their never-ending encouragement and support. We could not have done this without you.

We'd also like to thank our reviewers Jim McGroddy, Eric Jens, Andrew Papageorge, Andy Schriever, and our colleagues Francoise Legoues, Angela Sullivan, Jenny Galitz McTighe, Tom Swett, and John Mackay, for their input and guidance. They provided great insights into how to make this book better.

We also appreciate all the researchers who have toiled in FOAK over the years—in particular, Larry DelSonno, Larry Lieberman, John Vergo, Laura Haas, Abderrahim Labbi, Kamal Bhattacharya, Julia Rubin, Michael Haley, Thomas Li, Ron Ambrosio, Maria Ebling, Steve Gates, Jin Dong, Sougata Mukherjea, Prasenjit Sarkar, Wei Lu, Vas Bala, Hendrik Hamann, Mukesh Mohania, Vova Soroka, and John Morar for their candid input to the book.

FOAK could not operate without its Board members and the Industry Research Relationship Managers (RRMs). Throughout the years, they've generously provided their guidance, perspectives, commitment, and support.

A book is always a team effort, and the people who helped us bring this to publication took on the task with patience and cheerfulness. Thanks to the IBM Press, Pearson, and IBM legal teams for guiding us through the book publishing process, especially Steve Stansel, Lou Percello, John Buckwalter, Michael Thurston, and Bernard Goodwin.

Mary Jo would like to extend her sincere appreciation to Sharon Nunes and Nick Donofrio for encouraging her to begin the journey of writing this book. And Peter is especially grateful to his wife, Susan, who put up with stacks of papers, pacing, rants, and many hours when he was in this world but not of it. And last but not least, a very special thanks to Alexis Bantel, whose dedication and tireless energy have enabled the FOAK program to continue to grow and transform over the years.

About the Authors

Mary Jo Frederich is the director of the IBM Industry Solutions Labs and First-of-a-Kind (FOAK) program. She has more than 25 years of experience in the IT industry, gained while holding positions such as principal of a Northeast networking and systems management consulting practice, portfolio manager for Global Industry Solutions, and systems engineering manager for telecommunications. Throughout her years at IBM, she has gained extensive business and technical management experience working with clients in the consumer packaged goods, communications, utilities, and financial services industries. She is credited with transforming the FOAK program over the last eight years to drive greater value for IBM and its clients.

Peter Andrews, currently an independent executive consultant and writer, coauthored this book when he was the innovation strategist for IBM's Executive Business Institute. While at IBM, he participated in corporation-wide studies into ad hoc innovation, innovation partnering, and the use of collaboration tools for virtual teaming. He has trained hundreds of IBM researchers in techniques for realizing the value of their inventions. He was honored by IBM as one of its "Pioneers of the Web." He is a popular speaker at conferences and has authored dozens of Executive Tech Reports, which explore innovation and emerging technologies.

Introduction

Innovation is a social activity. Without advocates, builders, critics, and developers, even the best ideas have no impact. Thomas Edison tacitly admitted this when he swore he'd never invent anything for which a market did not exist. Look at any innovation, and you will find partnerships, teams, and communities that worked together to realize the value of an idea or cluster of ideas.

The challenges of keeping an original idea alive and shepherding it along the full path to becoming a new product, service, or business model become more daunting every day. The greatest opportunities and the most urgent needs tend to be complex and work only within larger contexts. Many of the best ideas need to operate across different disciplines, industries, cultures, legal systems, and geographies.

If you invest time and resources in innovation for competitive advantage, higher margins, and the creation of new markets, meeting the new standard is difficult. The demands include the following:

- Looking more broadly at emerging opportunities
- Engaging in productive discussions with people who have different perspectives and needs

- Creating options that allow the sharing of benefits between organizations that traditionally have not worked together
- Coming to an understanding between the participants about the project's goals, its basic approach, and the value sought
- Agreeing on roles, responsibilities, and conditions of satisfaction against a matrix of rules, contracts, and laws that have their own histories and requirements

All of these challenges must be met in a consistent manner that delivers results regularly and quickly enough to provide real business benefits. Ideas must enter the pipeline, be evaluated, be acted on, and deliver on promises to the participants, time after time. Above all, communications need to be effective, and relationships must be maintained despite different points of view, enterprise requirements, cultures, and values.

IBM's First-of-a-Kind (FOAK) program has been at the leading edge of collaborative innovation for over 14 years. Each project has attempted to bring together the best of IBM to a creative client to produce real value for both partners. Together, IBM and its clients have experienced significant accomplishments, including finding ways of providing information for healthcare without compromising patient privacy, providing real-time speech translation capabilities to U.S. troops in Iraq, and driving down the cost of electricity by adding intelligence to power grids.

Scores of projects have achieved their objectives, both in terms of providing value to the partner and in terms of building stronger relationships between IBM and its clients. The operational scope of these successes in collaborative innovation is notable. Consider the following:

- IBM collaborated with clients in 17 different industries, including banking, retail, insurance, aerospace, automotive manufacturing, consumer electronics, and pharmaceutical. There were also more than 30 projects in the public sector.
- The size of clients ranged from small nonprofits such as the Department of Environment, Parks Canada Agency's Alexander Graham Bell National Historic Site of Canada in Nova Scotia to consortiums such as the Middle East Consortium on Infectious Disease Surveillance (MECIDS),[1] to large enterprises with huge market valuations such as TD Bank Financial Group, with over CDN $500 billion in assets.[2]
- FOAK projects brought together team members from numerous countries. All the IBM Research labs—in Switzerland, Japan, Israel, India,

China, and the U.S.—have contributed to FOAK efforts. And in recent years, the portfolio of projects has spread investments across continents: 46% in North America, 33% in Asia Pacific, and 21% in Europe.

Overall, IBM and its clients have completed over 250 projects, but not all have been successes. FOAK has had a fair share of missteps, misunderstandings, and projects that have just plain failed to launch. The problems have come from either side or both—or even from changes in circumstances in a rapidly evolving business climate. Sometimes, those on a project just drew the short straw. After all, innovation is an inherently risky business. Over the years, IBM has learned its lessons in collaboration the hard way, and we will share those with you in this book.

These collaborations faced demands not just in bridging the differences between IBM and its clients, but in getting organizations within IBM, and within clients, to work together effectively. While IBM has taken on technical and business challenges, it is the range of *cultural challenges*—in communications, values, leadership, and relationship building—where we probably have the most experience and knowledge to share. The sheer variety of opportunities and hard-won know-how has allowed IBM to evolve guidelines and advice that we hope will provide real benefit to those who are attempting to build more effective and constructive collaborations for innovation.

Finally, IBM has the examples. Seeing how insights in the lab get tempered by the reality of fussy users, hardheaded accountants, and ad hoc critiques will provide a reality check for those who have romantic ideas of lone inventors changing the world.

Who Will Benefit from This Book?

The new mantra of industry is "Everyone is an innovator," but this book is not for everyone. The primary intent of this book is to share the experiences of IBM's FOAK program with those who need to plan, manage, or participate in collaborative innovation projects so that they can take advantage of best practices we have found.

But we do hope that what we present here will be more broadly valuable so that those who are interested in emerging technologies, business trends, and examples of organizational behavior will also benefit from this book. We suspect that many of the practices we found to facilitate collaboration for innovation will also be applicable to those who are looking for ideas on how to team more effectively for other purposes, including organizational change, building client relationships, and sharing business intelligence.

Overall, this book will serve those who are curious about the future and how it is created. In most circumstances, it is more hard work than magic, more listening attentively than getting your own point of view across, and more building relationships than putting together prototypes.

Part of the impetus for this book was to answer the questions IBM gets directly from clients as they visit our Industry Solutions Labs (our display facilities for work in emerging solutions and technologies) or as they talk to us about how IBM does innovation. Typically, people ask these kinds of questions:

- Where do the ideas come from, and how are they validated and developed?
- How does IBM justify its investments in innovation?
- How do you prioritize FOAK proposals?
- How do you work across boundaries of organization, culture, language, and time zones?
- How do you handle concerns about the ownership of intellectual property?
- How do you find and select partners?
- How do you initiate and manage a project?
- What are the key roles and responsibilities in your innovation projects?
- How do you keep partners engaged?
- How do you measure success?
- How do you get full value from what you learn on a FOAK project?
- How do you manage a portfolio of diverse, complex projects?
- What are your best practices?
- How do you showcase innovation?

Our focus is on FOAK, so we won't address these questions globally. However, much of what we have learned can be extended beyond FOAK, and our hope is that these lessons can be adapted by many organizations that want to take the next step in innovation, bringing complex new solutions to the marketplace.

Our Approach

For many, the most interesting books on innovation are those that tell the story of how people came together to change the world, worked through all the obstacles, and ultimately triumphed. These heroes' tales can be engaging and inspiring, but they require a lot from any reader who wants to extract practical information.

IBM has heroes in the FOAK program and more than a few tales, but these did not become the basis for organizing the book. For one thing, we are not talking about a single success, but a series of successes that continue to this day. For another, we want to make this a useful document. We'll call out as lessons those best practices and processes that help ensure that FOAK remains ambitious, relevant, and productive. In many cases, these can easily serve as reminders or be adapted by other innovation initiatives.

However, recounting best practices and processes becomes meaningful only if they are tied to the critical success factors for innovation. Therefore, this book is centered on six key activities:

- Finding ways to clarify goals so that all participants understand why they are investing their time, ingenuity, and resources
- Systematically building trust and commitments between participants so that they give more than is asked of them
- Creating value propositions that resonate with all participants
- Creatively taking on the common obstacles of logistics, funding, failure, prioritization, and organizational loyalty that can derail the most promising projects
- Responding to change that inevitably emerges as the real world and the unexpected intrude upon well-defined processes
- Sharing success in fair and generous ways so that today's project experience inspires tomorrow's innovation

Chapter 1, "A Program That Works," provides an overview of the program's origins and development. This allows us to present historical context clearly while showing our evolution toward the practices we espouse. We believe this is a useful but not essential conceit. The chapters are written in a way that allows them to be read out of sequence by people with specific needs and interests.

We have highlighted advice and guidance throughout the text. We bring this all together in Chapter 12, "A Guide for Creating Innovative Programs," with hope that it will become a mini-handbook for innovation teams.

Finally, we must concede that this story continues. Those of us involved in FOAK are still learning new lessons, and the ever-changing world presents new challenges with each project IBM initiates. Chapter 13, "The Future of Collaborative Innovation," looks at the open questions, the unsatisfactory answers, and the indications of emerging requirements for success in innovation. We hope this chapter will become a starting point for continuing the conversation in the blog that is associated with this book, http://innovation-passport.blogspot.com/.

Endnotes

1. IBM press release: "New Data Sharing Technology Speeds International Collaboration to Identify and Respond to Infectious Diseases," June 2, 2008.

2. Source: http://www.td.com/profile.jsp.

I

A Program That Works

If you were tripping over uncut jewels and precious metal ores, you'd probably find a way to take advantage of it. IBM Research can feel like that some days. In the hallways, you hear conversations about computers that understand natural language, advanced analysis of streaming data, or "green" ideas for reducing power and waste. Around you are people who think for a living, hard at work—taking on intractable problems of securing bank records during disasters, optimizing supply chains, or building systems that can simulate drug interactions. Good things are happening. Exciting things.

But for years, reaching out to the real world for innovation partnerships was not an obvious choice for IBM Research. IBM has always had good, inventive minds at work, helping clients and creating the next generation of essential tools for business and the public sector. But IBM kept the jewels to itself. Researchers (that specialized role emerged in 1945) labored in what seemed to be splendid isolation. They managed to invent the disk drive, random-access memory, FORTRAN, RISC computing, and dozens of other technologies that helped create today's digital world.

Not incidentally, IBM made a lot of money during this period. IBM had first-class questions it needed to answer, and it did not need to look outside for expertise. Almost everything was proprietary, and everything that was needed for a complete solution happened within the company. Besides, IBM Research was modeled after Bell Labs, and the perception was that splendid isolation was both appropriate and necessary. The real world, with its budgets, deadlines, and messy problems, would only distract the best and the brightest. Naturally, there *were* ideas, problems, and relationships that kept IBM Research relevant. It wasn't a completely closed system, but that was the basic perspective.

Research Partners with the Rest of IBM

IBM Research had few formal ties beyond corporate headquarters until the 1970s. At that time, other IBM divisions were facing significant challenges, and they became restive about making contributions to IBM Research when they weren't getting any immediate benefits. In response to this, so-called "Joint Programs" were established. For the first time, other divisions of IBM, those that built and sold and struggled with client problems, began to directly impact the IBM Research agenda and its funding.

Rather than securing 100% of its budget through the corporation, now IBM Research was allocated only a portion of its annual funding. IBM Research needed to secure the remainder of its funding directly from the IBM brands. This was intended to align a portion of the research work with IBM brand strategies, while still providing IBM Research with the liberty to pursue pure, unconstrained exploration.

This funding model still exists today. Every year, each of the IBM brands allocates a portion of its budget to fund its Joint Program with IBM Research. For every dollar that a brand invests in its Joint Program, IBM Research matches it. This matching-of-funds approach has ensured that IBM Research focuses some of its work on areas strategic to the IBM brands. It also has provided an effective incentive for the brands to invest in their Joint Programs, because it is a mechanism for the brands to increase the number of people working on their products, while providing only half of the funding. Essentially, they get extra help at a discount rate.

With the advent of Joint Programs, a substantial and growing number of IBMers began to work shoulder to shoulder with colleagues from across IBM. The collaboration was deep, with brand division employees working at, and even directing, projects in the research labs. The responsibilities of researchers extended to the products themselves, and it was not unusual for the researchers to move their offices to a manufacturing or development site. And if a product did not come off the line with sufficient quality, or a client had a problem with an offering that a researcher had a hand in, that researcher could be called in. Firefighting and problem resolution became part of the job, and many researchers became familiar with the hotels in Burlington, Poughkeepsie, Endicott, Hursley, and Markham.

In 1993, IBM Research took another step toward becoming more externally focused with the introduction of the Services, Applications, and Solutions (SAS) program. SAS aimed to bring IBM Research expertise and technologies to a much larger number of clients who were struggling with business challenges that had no off-the-shelf solutions.

SAS recognized that researchers lived in the state of the art in many areas of science and technology. If they could apply the very best of what IBM Research had to real-world problems, they could drive significant value for clients and the IBM Corporation.

Beyond generating new revenue for IBM, SAS led researchers to confront many difficult business challenges. It also forced the researchers to think more deeply and creatively about the potential impact of their work beyond the laboratory. Looking back, one can see how SAS and the Joint Programs drove IBM Research to be more vital to IBM by guiding the researchers into areas that they might not have otherwise explored. Figure 1.1 shows the evolution of IBM Research from being internally focused to externally focused.

Although IBM Research didn't welcome these changes enthusiastically, the cloud had a silver lining. Beyond management questions and economic pressures, it became clear that more and more of the action was happening where people from different organizations worked together. Synergies, new perspectives, and fresh ideas drove advances such as parallel computing, object-oriented software, and everything that came with the advent of the Web. And with few exceptions, success in the marketplace depended on a complex array of partnerships. Today's competitor is always, potentially, tomorrow's collaborator.

Research Evolution

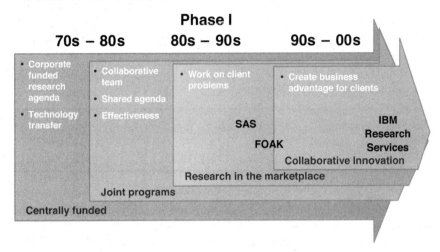

Figure 1.1   IBM Research goes from isolation to ever deeper partnering with other IBM organizations and clients.

IBM Creates FOAK

IBM's First-of-a-Kind (FOAK) program (so called because each of its projects creates the first marketplace example of a technical asset's use) was a natural outgrowth of the era and IBM Research's interest in reaching out further. IBM funded FOAK in 1995 as a way to differentiate IBM's solution offerings.

The very first FOAK, MedSpeak, was also the first commercially available continuous speech recognition application. A medical application seemed to be the perfect place to get going. Radiology reports are essential to patient care, but in 1995 they needed to be dictated to transcriptionists, typed, and returned for correction and signature. The process was expensive and time-consuming; it took 12 to 72 hours to turn around a report. Attempts to use existing, discrete transcriptions had failed because they were too awkward for most radiologists to adopt.

But what if an IBM Research asset, a continuous speech recognition engine, could be used to transcribe radiology reports? The MedSpeak

FOAK was set up to do just that. Furthermore, it made the asset more commercial-ready by building a prototype application. This ambitious project actually was done by working with three IBM clients to ensure that the asset and prototype would address real, important client pain points.

LESSON: Find a real need for innovation, and identify whose need is most acute.

Ultimately, MedSpeak became IBM MedSpeak/Radiology. It enabled radiologists to dictate reports directly and instantaneously into text and then correct, sign, and store reports for access by other physicians. The business value of this solution to the customer was fast turnaround of signed radiology reports and elimination or lowering of costs for transcription services. MedSpeak also garnered worldwide press coverage and accelerated IBM's development of continuous speech recognition.

But MedSpeak had an even more profound impact. It became a proof point for the whole idea of FOAK. With MedSpeak, the FOAK team was made up of researchers and contractors. When the FOAK project was completed, the contractors simply left IBM Research and moved with the technology to the delivery organization. MedSpeak demonstrated a new way to develop deep technical expertise on a solution and transfer it out of IBM Research.

With FOAK, IBM created a program dedicated to speeding the movement of great ideas and new technologies from the labs to the marketplace. This became a way for IBM, officially and systematically, to begin sharing the jewels with its clients. And, not incidentally, it has become a way to get these jewels out of the lab and provide value to IBM.

FOAK's Aim Is Leadership and Growth

FOAK has a 14-year track record of creating value. With, on average, 15 projects completed each year (out of about 20 to 25 approved for funding), FOAK successfully transfers assets for reuse from 70% of the FOAK projects completed.

In summary, the payoff for the partners working in this middle ground is the possibility of doing something that provides leadership and growth from the following:

- Early access to game-changing technologies
- First market adopter advantage
- Access to world-renowned researchers
- Skills and knowledge transfer
- Firsthand experience with emerging technologies and new business models
- Direct input into IBM's requirements process
- An investment funding model that minimizes the client's investment

IBM benefits from the following:

- Accelerated delivery of new technologies to the market:
  - New offerings
  - IBM Research Services engagements (described in Chapter 6, "The FOAK Process: Phases II and III")
  - Asset licensing
  - Enhancements to core technologies

- Accelerated solution sales:
  - References
  - Proof points
  - Reuse
  - Differentiation

- Linking IBM Research's strategic initiatives to real client problems
- Valuable experience and thought leadership
- Headlights into emerging market opportunities
- Mindshare in the innovation space

For these reasons, clients continue to line up to participate in FOAK projects, and IBM continues to provide the funding and strategic direction to make them happen.

The FOAK leadership (the FOAK Board, described in the next section) and the Program Management Team (described in Chapter 10, "Portfolio Management") have identified many best practices. Some criteria—especially those for tying the projects to strategic objectives and ensuring client commitment—have become part of how FOAK does business. But all these areas continue to be under review. In fact, 2001 became a turning point for FOAK (as discussed later in this chapter). The need for change was raised because the FOAK Board did regular, systematic evaluations of how those participating in the program did the work. As opposed to many other innovation programs, the FOAK leadership sees FOAK as unfinished, with plenty of opportunities for improvement remaining.

FOAK Gets Systematic: The FOAK Board

Early FOAK projects provided a strong starting point, but not a finished model. For instance, initially IBM Research had many assets lying around that could be cherry-picked for "hardening." This means taking a technology and providing the structure, training, and documentation needed for the technology to be used reliably in the marketplace. This availability of almost-ready assets couldn't last, and a crisis of sorts occurred when less mature and visible assets became central to FOAK engagements.

It became clear that FOAK needed to include more development activities—especially alignment with markets and current offerings—during projects. Today, careful consideration is given to the state of the initial assets that become the core of the FOAK project to ensure that they can be implemented, enhanced, and extended within a 12-month time period, which is the typical duration of a FOAK project.

In addition, it became clear that too many projects failed because they were being approved without sufficient attention to clear goals and roles. The program also did not provide enough guidance to those who in many cases were not used to working with clients and managing those relationships. The early projects also showed common weakness in project management.

In 1999, the concept of having an overall governing body for the program to manage its investments and help alleviate pain points in the processes emerged. The FOAK Board (described in Chapter 5, "Choosing the Best Projects") consists of a cross-IBM team of executives who meet quarterly to do the following:

- Review and approve investments
- Help innovation teams navigate obstacles
- Ensure that both IBM and its clients are realizing value from the program

Although the members change continuously, the concept of the FOAK Board and its purpose have remained consistent over the years.

Problems occurred on the client side as well. Clients are used to having IBM "jump" in response to their requirements. A FOAK is fundamentally different in that IBM pays the bulk of the bill and has an objective in mind that may not align perfectly with the client's objectives. For example, with one FOAK, the Enterprise Portfolio Management Hub, the client wanted special adaptors built to interface with its tools. These were one-off solutions that IBM was not interested in building. It was just too big a job. Ultimately, the IBM Project Team had to reset the client's expectations. A painful lesson was learned about the need to set expectations correctly from the beginning. This is discussed in more detail in Chapter 4, "Getting the Most out of Partnerships."

> *LESSON: Set expectations with stakeholders correctly from the beginning, and then validate that those expectations are understood and accepted.*

Setting client expectations goes well beyond the features and functions of a given FOAK project. Balancing the whole premise of exploratory prototypes versus commercialized offerings is difficult and continues to be a challenge for the program even today.

Retooling and Polishing the FOAK Approach

Although the FOAK program delivered value throughout its first five years of existence, the FOAK Board believed it could have an even greater impact on IBM and its clients. So in 2001, the program was reengineered to better align it with IBM's solution strategy, link it to more strategic markets, improve its asset transfer rate, strengthen client commitments, and have a better means of measuring the program's impact.

Alignment with the Solution Strategy

Part of the impetus for change came not from a realization that improvements were needed, but from a strategic change outside of FOAK. In the late '90s, IBM's solution strategy shifted away from building applications to one of partnering for applications. IBM wanted to provide industry-focused consultants and subject matter experts who could leverage the breadth of IBM hardware, software, and integration services. This meant that the types of assets being developed and tested on FOAK projects needed to shift as well.

Instead of large, application-based assets, IBM needed to invest in a wider variety of assets. Middleware, business models, methodologies, architectures (business, functional, and implementation), analytics engines, and more—extended by innovative technologies and thought leadership—became the focus of the program's investment strategy; it remains so today.

This fundamental shift from application-based assets to a broader range of assets being developed and piloted on FOAK projects cut the program's funding needs in half. In some ways, this enabled the program to survive during times when the company was focused on quarter-to-quarter financial performance.

In recent years, however, the focus has shifted back toward innovation and growing the FOAK program. This is supported by an almost 50% increase in FOAK program funding in recent years.

Linkage to Strategic Markets

Organizationally, the FOAK program is the teaming of IBM's research and sales divisions (Sales & Distribution (S&D)). This enables the sales teams to leapfrog IBM's traditional development cycle and helps guide research efforts toward strategic markets.

The value of S&D input was understood only over time. Prior to 2001, the majority of the FOAK projects presented to the FOAK Board were IBM Research-initiated, with limited involvement from the S&D industry teams. Yet S&D had a sophisticated market planning process in place to pinpoint strategic market segments likely to grow—something IBM Research did not have.

The FOAK Board wanted the IBM Research teams to leverage S&D's market planning process to ensure that the FOAK projects were well aligned with the industry-defined strategies and focused on their targeted market segments. This was a pivotal insight for FOAK, and drove greater value for S&D.

Today in the FOAK model, sales identifies strategic market segments and targets early-adopter clients and business partners to work side-by-side with IBM scientists, testing new ideas and innovative technologies. FOAK selects research that is too immature to be included in a brand product plan, but not so immature that it poses a substantial risk to the client's business. IBM funds researchers as they pilot their innovations in a real business environment. The FOAK client invests in the hardware, software, and services needed to fully participate in the project.

It might be surprising that a sales organization could have such interest in innovation and would provide funding and personnel to partner with a research organization. The personalities and values of sales and research typically don't intersect. Classically, the researcher is interested in satisfying curiosity, gaining the respect of peers, and doing something new. A sales person is interested in commissions, salary, and bonuses. Although these characterizations are a bit stereotypical, they contain enough truth to raise curiosity about why research and sales should work together.

The answer to why such different organizations choose to work together is one word: growth. For IBM, FOAK enables S&D to guide IBM Research efforts towards strategic emerging-market opportunities that sales people have identified as potential sources of new opportunity. IBM Research has an opportunity to create an organizational ally and demonstrate its contributions.

During the reassessment of FOAK, another practice was found to be ripe for change. Prior to 2001, the innovation teams tended to engage clients before they secured FOAK Board approval of their projects. The researchers believed that if they had a qualified client, their FOAK proposal would be stronger, and the risk of rejection would be minimized.

This practice often led to innovation teams securing FOAK clients who were in *nonstrategic* market segments, as defined by the industry's market planning process. This may have been fine for getting the project done, but it could be lethal to attempts at later asset adoption. Delaying such commitments and linking the FOAK program directly to the industry's market-planning process has better aligned it with S&D's strategies and has driven greater impact on the IBM Corporation as a whole.

LESSON: Find the sweet spot for your innovation program—what it can do that nothing else can.

Improved Asset Transfer

Once a FOAK project is completed, the intellectual property needs to be transferred to an owning organization, such as IBM Software Group, to enhance and commercialize the assets for broader market consumption. Prior to 2001, most innovation teams did not explore asset transfer until their projects were completed.

Asset transfer occurred too late in the overall FOAK project lifecycle to have an impact, because it provided little or no opportunity for the commercialization organization to understand the requirements or influence how the assets were developed. These asset *catchers*, as they are called in the program, are responsible for the assets' ongoing enhancement, maintenance, and support. These catchers can be in an IBM product brand organization, a services practice, or an external partner's organization.

Today, FOAK innovation teams must engage the targeted catching organization early in the process. They need to gain the organization's support and feedback on strategic and technical relevance to the catcher's future product plans. Beginning with the proposal phase, they actively discuss the project's merits with the potential catchers, and these relationships are nurtured throughout the project. And it doesn't end there. When a project is about three quarters of the way to completion, more detailed discussions occur about the actual plans for transferring each asset.

These early and regular discussions are crucial to ensuring the assets' broader market applicability. This up-front dialogue, coupled with the ongoing involvement of the catching organization in the FOAK projects, has proven to be widely successful in pushing the asset transfer rate of the FOAK program to 70%. It is important to note that this asset transfer rate is based only on projects that have successfully made it through the various project filters (described in Chapter 2, "The FOAK Process: Phase I") and the FOAK Board approval and the contract negotiation processes (described in Chapter 6).

Stronger Client Commitment

During the reevaluation of FOAK, another change was made, this one involving the client. When the FOAK program was introduced, projects were offered to clients for free. The thinking at the time was that, since IBM couldn't commit to a fully commercialized product at the start of the FOAK project, it shouldn't charge the client a fee for participation. But without a client's financial commitment to the FOAK project, it was often difficult for the FOAK innovation teams to keep the clients interested in the projects' success. And upon completion of the FOAK project, it was virtually impossible to gain the client's commitment to fully deploy the solution.

The FOAK Board hypothesized that if the program had a more clearly articulated value proposition, the clients would be willing to invest—both financially and with in-kind resources, such as personnel, data, process, and user groups—to participate in a FOAK project. (The FOAK client value proposition is discussed in Chapter 4.) Today, a modest client investment is required to participate in the FOAK program. This improvement in approach over the last nine years has had a tremendous impact on the level of client involvement in FOAK projects and the overall value realized by both the clients and IBM.

LESSON: All key stakeholders need to have some skin in the game.

Measuring Impact

Finally, measuring the impact of an experimental investment program is difficult. The traditional approaches used to measure businesses with existing markets don't necessarily make sense for experimental, unborn markets. Yet the FOAK program needed a way to prove its value to and impact on IBM and its clients. In 2001, a set of standard metrics was established and a scorecard tracking mechanism was created to measure and track the portfolio's performance at a glance. Not only does the FOAK Board use these metrics to manage the portfolio, but they have become critical in keeping the program funded. FOAK program metrics are discussed in detail in Chapter 10.

FOAK Proof Points

The goal of FOAK is simple and has remained consistent since its inception in 1995: to deliver innovative technologies and thought leadership to the marketplace. By accomplishing this goal, the research labs at IBM can generate opportunities for growth for IBM and its clients.

Is it working? The question isn't academic. Investments, careers, and credibility are at stake. While FOAK is far from the only path for externally influenced innovation—acquisitions and mergers bring new products and services into IBM and its clients' business regularly—FOAK is a serious initiative, intended to be an important route to innovation.

FOAK is an important bet from a public relations and client relationship point of view as well. If the program does not deliver thought leadership, the IBM brand—currently worth $59 billion—is put at risk.

Finally, recognizing and acting on emerging opportunities and challenges is what creates the future. If FOAK does not provide a means of identifying, understanding, and responding to change in the world, IBM will not be taking advantage of the chances that come its way to develop and grow. FOAK itself continues to change, expanding the range of disciplines it involves itself with and reaching ever further into different organizations and cultures to find the best talent and ideas. For example, the program has seen a 60% increase in the amount of FOAK activity in the growth markets, reflecting the change in global markets, such as China and India.

Luckily, there is plenty of evidence that FOAK is working in an effective and productive manner. Here's a small sample:

- One FOAK project, MASTOR, achieved near-real-time translation for the military in combat zones. According to Admiral Edmund Giambastiani, Vice Chair of the Joint Chiefs of Staff, "This type of technology can help to improve communication for U.S. and coalition personnel with Iraqi citizens and aid organizations serving in Iraq."[1]

- In the Middle East, a FOAK project is helping to better predict and avoid the spread of pandemics. Public Health Information Affinity Domain (PHIAD) is a standards-based, interoperable infrastructure that leverages IBM inventions to enable scientists and public health officials to query clinics, hospitals, lab systems, and other stakeholders for anonymous data, categorized by disease. They can then create and use models of infectious diseases to paint a picture of the health of a population with real-time information.[2]

- With end-of-life legislation and recycling requirements becoming effective worldwide, a Japanese automaker needed a better way to track parts from their creation to their ultimate disposal or recycling. Researchers worked with the firm to create a global parts traceability system framework and data architecture (TraceSphere) to enable distributed, accurate, and dynamic bill-of-materials tracking throughout the entire vehicle life cycle. As a result, the client can comply with new laws while reducing its manufacturing costs and improving quality levels and customer satisfaction.

Of course, the value provided to clients does not tell the whole story. IBM also benefits from the solutions it creates for its clients. For example, a scheduler that balances workloads and allocates resources for a bank can find uses in other firms. A framework that combines requirements for engineering, conceptual design, and analytical models for a carmaker may be beneficial for IBM manufacturing. A security solution that uses analytical tools to index digital video recordings and issue real-time alerts for a government agency may find its way into a retail or educational environment.

In each case, IBM builds relationships and gets a better understanding of how banks, manufacturers, governments, and other organizations work, and what they may need next. These relationships are key to building the trust necessary to open the door for new partnerships and megadeals. Understanding the industry provides an important way to prepare for what is coming in the future and to be ready with the next solution.

This specific know-how is useful for many IBM endeavors that go forward long after a FOAK project has finished its last task. Just as valuable to IBM are the contacts and trusting relationships that are established through successful implementation of a new and challenging solution.

FOAK's Distinctive Model for Innovation

On any given day, hundreds of individual projects are under way in IBM Research. It would be misleading to imagine that FOAK is the only route to innovation at IBM. IBM's methodical, tested approaches to developing most of its market-ready offerings remain essential because they reduce risk for both IBM and clients. Many clients either can't afford to take chances or choose not to. They buy the IBM brand, in part, because of a reputation for reliability that has been earned through rigorous development processes.

IBM also goes down exploratory paths in innovation. Some projects are aimed more at new knowledge or proofs of concepts than at creating new products and services. A high percentage of these may never lead directly to bottom-line results, but they provide an essential context and culture for ensuring that innovation occurs at the highest levels. These efforts also add to IBM's credibility and help recruit the best minds.

IBM has many programs that foster client collaboration. It's the combination of clients and researchers applying new technologies and know-how in ways never seen before that makes FOAK client collaborations so different.

The success of a FOAK project takes different forms:

- Knowledge gained from early in-market experiences with new technologies
- Development of a working prototype of a solution not yet available in the marketplace
- Know-how to improve a client's business
- Software components, methodologies, and tools for reuse in IBM products and services

The program aims to demonstrate market-proven success with the first client so that the innovations can be made available on a larger scale through commercialized offerings from IBM's brands and strategic business partners.

FOAK is intended to exploit the middle ground between risk and potential that often is ignored. The funding, time investment, and contractual requirements are all intermediate. It has as a premise that you can get richer innovation collaboration if you make the trust between partners one of the key criteria for working together. As demonstrated by their investments, the people who take part in FOAK are willing to take measured risks. There is a chance that a FOAK project will not yield value; there are no guarantees. Partners need to have expectations that fit the program—neither so low that commitment is unnecessary nor so high that specific results are demanded. In other words, they need to have the experience in innovation and partnering that allows them to be realistic.

> *LESSON: Make trust an important criterion for choosing partners, sponsors, and other key stakeholders.*

Summary

IBM's approach to innovation has evolved with the times. Originally, the IBM Research division operated as a separate entity, patterned after Bell Labs. Competitive and economic pressures led to its collaborating with other

IBM divisions in the form of highly successful Joint Programs that included a new funding mechanism. The emergence of the SAS program upped IBM Research's ante in the growth areas of the '90s, and the FOAK program was a natural extension of this outreach, which connected researchers with S&D and its clients. This became a catalyst to further transform the culture of IBM Research and a powerful way to take advantage of IBM Research's assets to show leadership, build mindshare, create new markets, solve client problems, and deepen relationships.

Engaging with a wider world provided an important step forward, but the journey was just beginning. In 2001, IBM shifted its solution strategy. This made a large portion of the projects that FOAK grew up on irrelevant. The FOAK Board needed to respond to this first by retrenching and then by taking a new look at the kinds of projects that might make sense. As difficult as this challenge was, however, the FOAK Board used that moment of transformation to take on persistent problems around guidance of FOAK, clarity of goals and roles, alignment with sponsoring organizations, client expectations, commercialization, and measurement.

Today, the FOAK program's management system is in a continuous state of transformation. Early each year, the FOAK Board meets to discuss program improvements and alignment with IBM's strategic initiatives and priorities. Additionally, time is allocated during each Board meeting to discuss what is working with the program and what is not so that the processes can be tweaked and tuned throughout the year.

FOAK has many successes it can build on. The examples provide inspiration and guidance for innovators. They also are a ready set of proof points for new partners and IBM sponsors. Through planning, adaptation, and a bit of trial and error, FOAK has put together a pathway that supports succeeding time and again. We'll explore Phase I of the FOAK process in Chapter 2.

Endnotes

1. IBM press release: "IBM Donates Speech Translation Technology to Foster Better Communication and Humanitarian Efforts in Iraq," April 2, 2007.

2. IBM press release: "New Data Sharing Technology Speeds International Collaboration to Identify and Respond to Infectious Diseases," June 2, 2008.

2

The FOAK Process:
Phase I

The way things get done, especially the sequence and timing, is important to the success of any project. People need to understand when to jump in and lend a hand. They need milestones, appointments, and due dates marked off on their calendars. They need checklists and approvals. In other words, they need process.

For some, process equals bureaucracy, and that translates into a Circle of Hell. Especially for creative people who like to wing it. But process is about doing the right things at the right time. It is also about helping people coordinate their efforts and avoid rework. Process makes stakeholders calmer by helping ensure completion and quality.

The FOAK process has evolved over years, and it continues to evolve, but the basic stages persist. Each project goes through three phases. Phase I includes all the up-front steps: generating the idea, defining the project, and gaining the appropriate support needed to submit a project to the FOAK Board for review. Phase II begins with an approved proposal and contains all the steps taken to secure an optimal partner and perform the project. Phase III deals with the transition of the assets to the catcher (a person responsible for the ongoing enhancement, maintenance, and support) of the assets for commercialization.

We'll deal with Phases II and III in detail in Chapter 6, "The FOAK Process: Phases II and III." (A quick overview of the process as a whole can be found in the Appendix, "FOAK Process Overview.") Before digging into the specifics of Phase I, let's look at the various players who are called on to contribute their perspectives, support, resources, and commitments.

The Key Players

The players identify, articulate, validate, clarify, and perform. They provide resources and skills and they take responsibility for various aspects of the project. Some players remain constant throughout the entire process while others are called upon at various points within the process.

- **Research Team:** Researchers who work together on an idea that the industry has not yet formally accepted as a FOAK candidate. The Industry Research Relationship Manager (RRM), described in detail later in this chapter, is a core member of this team.
- **Industry Team:** The Industry RRM and the marketing, sales, and services professionals assigned to the industry segment targeted by the FOAK project. The Industry Team has an Industry Solution Board that manages their portfolio of solutions. It is chaired by Sales & Distribution (S&D) and Global Business Services (GBS) executives.
- **Proposal Team:** Industry RRM, lead researcher for area proposed, sales and services leaders for the industry or solution areas to be explored and optimally, the catching organization.
- **IBM Project Team:** Researchers, services professionals, and client representatives for the selected account, and optimally a resource from the planned catching organization. The players on this team are identified once the project has been approved.
- **Client Team:** Resources identified and allocated by the FOAK partner. This team is identified during the contract negotiation process.
- **Joint Project Team:** Combined resources from the Client Team and the IBM Project Team brought into action upon contract signing.
- **FOAK Board:** A cross team of IBM executives responsible for the oversight of the FOAK portfolio.
- **Program Management Team (PMT):** A small team from IBM Research and S&D who manage the FOAK program and provide

guidance to the IBM Project Teams. The PMT performs quarterly
reviews with each IBM Project Team.

Phase I

Phase I, shown in Figure 2.1, consists of 11 steps that ensure that a
FOAK project is innovative, well-aligned with market needs, and positioned for replication within an industry.

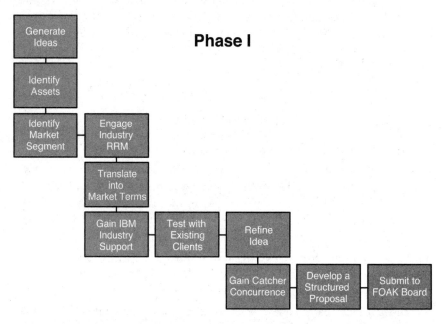

Figure 2.1   FOAK process, Phase I

Generate Ideas

Ideas for innovation can come from a variety of places: a flash of
genius, a suggestion from a client, a recognized need, or a new perspective. Many companies put a major focus on new ideas through training
in creativity and the establishment of suggestion programs. IBM is no
exception. In fact, it has a collaborative application called Thinkplace,
which is responsible for thousands of new ideas annually.

Creativity and idea programs *do* support and feed into FOAK proposals, but they are not properly their starting points. Many people generate new FOAK ideas: researchers, product developers, industry marketing, sales teams, IBM executives, and clients. However, the majority of FOAK ideas come from the industry sales teams and the researchers themselves.

In contrast to many innovation programs, which may begin by brainstorming ideas in general or doing a *de novo* exploration of answers to emerging-market problems, FOAK is much more match-and-adapt. That is, FOAK participants look for assets that might match a need, and then they investigate how they might be adapted to meet that need in a real circumstance.

A specific, well-described problem or opportunity is brought to IBM Research, and the treasure chest of possibilities is sorted through and qualified. For example, one FOAK project was brought to IBM Research by a telecommunications company that was struggling with the flood of mobile message spam. This was an annoyance not only to end consumers, but also to the mobile operators and their infrastructures. IBM Research pulled together pieces of existing intellectual property to build an online analytics system to filter out mobile messages from senders of spam.

Since the IBM Research inventions that are in play on FOAK projects have gone beyond the basic idea stage—often to the point of having working prototypes—FOAK can also go in the other direction. Instead of creating a project to find the right asset for a need, it can find a need for an asset. Here, the researcher brings an idea to someone with client knowledge who understands market trends and the industry's portfolio of solutions. This is often the Industry Research Relationship Manager (RRM). These Industry RRMs are seasoned researchers who, in addition to performing research in their fields of expertise, take on the added responsibility of working with a particular Industry Team. By working with the Industry Teams, the Industry RRMs become industry experts and valued members of those Industry Teams. Through the Industry RRM, the researcher can explore how much of an impact his or her research work might have in answering these identified business needs.

For example, an idea arose for a Contact Agent Buddies (CABs) FOAK—"listening" to conversations between agents and a customers and making suggestions to the agents in real time about how to solve the customers' problem. It originated with an IBM Research manager who believed the market opportunity for innovative contact center solutions was huge and that IBM Research could have a real impact.

The researchers hosted a cross-IBM company workshop on the Contact Center of the Future. As part of this workshop, they interviewed a number of people within IBM who had some level of contact center involvement or experience. One person was about to work with a large automotive manufacturer on an IBM project, and he identified the key challenge as agent productivity (a cost). The researchers then thought about how they could apply their text analytics innovations to this problem.

They concluded that a solution involving speech analytics from IBM Research was probably the right idea. They approached the Automotive Industry RRM to see if the CABs idea would align with the automotive industry's solution portfolio. Drawing on his industry knowledge, the RRM was able to find the right spot for the asset and position it within the strategy.

Identify Assets

Conceptually, most people understand the core ideas behind the FOAK projects. However, many times it is difficult to understand which assets are actually being created and which assets are being enhanced by the projects. It is not uncommon for the FOAK Board to ask, "So what's new here?" or "What will we have available to sell at the end of this project?" So, as part of the FOAK proposal template (described later in this chapter), the Board asks for a listing of the assets (existing and new) and the planned catchers for each.

In some instances, assets from a project need to be transferred to multiple organizations. For instance, in the CABs example, the IBM Project Team developed a new asset—a diagnostic system to automatically analyze call types and employ virtual agents to quickly assist contact center agents in addressing a customer's inquiries and issues. The IBM Project Team ended up transferring the decision making tool developed for the FOAK to GTS and its diagnostic tool to Global Business Services (GBS).

Since the completion of the project, new clients seeking a solution similar to the CABs FOAK have been offered contracts that combine these services offerings to deliver a complete solution.

LESSON: Systematically explore and document options for the commercialization of the innovation.

Clarity from day one around what the assets are and who will commercialize and sell them sets the stage for ongoing discussions. This ensures that proper expectations are established, and facilitates the overall commercialization process.

Identify the Appropriate Market Segment

Once an idea is born, it needs to be transformed from an abstract thought to a concrete instantiation that creates value for IBM and the client. For this to happen, technology and context (everything around where it fits in to create value) must come together seamlessly.

For example, the energy and utilities industry identified a gap in its portfolio that led to the Intelligent Power Grids FOAK project. Working with its Industry RRM, it was able to pull together components from IBM Research and build a solution that met the market need to perform real-time, event-driven analytics and optimization of power grids. So, on one hand, if an idea is born in the industry, it inherently has a market context and needs the technical underpinnings to become something that is tangible.

On the other hand, if an idea is born in IBM Research, it needs an industry context to define how the idea addresses a specific pain point or uncovers totally new opportunities for an industry. An example is the Smart Surveillance Solution (SSS) FOAK project.

With SSS, clients can do effective data analysis of video clips, either in real time or by using recordings. Clients can capture and analyze critical information across multiple sources such as cameras and radar sensors. By applying metadata search parameters (which could be attributes of the data, such as name, size, position, or owner) and event prioritization criteria, they can reduce costs and reduce the time it takes to analyze and act on the data.

So far, the SSS innovation has been applied to multiple industries—not just in government for antiterrorism, but also in retail for fraud detection and effectiveness of store design and in-store promotions. In each instance, the Research Team worked with the Industry Team to position SSS to address a specific pain point of the industry and develop a value proposition for the project that would resonate with clients in that industry.

It is bringing forward the raw ideas and getting input from various participants—the researchers, Industry Teams, and brand teams—that gives form to the ideas and places them on trajectories toward specific market segments. Of course, IBM Market Intelligence experts are brought in to provide assistance as well. During this step in the FOAK process, Market Intelligence helps the IBM Proposal Teams identify the potential addressable market opportunities for FOAK assets. With a potential industry identified, the researcher can pursue support from the industry.

Engage the Industry Research Relationship Manager (RRM)

Industry RRMs play two key roles. First, they serve industry strategy, strengthening and differentiating IBM's offerings by injecting thinking from across IBM's research labs. Second, they bring the industry insights, brand messaging, and requirements (such as technical standards and infrastructure specifications) into the labs. This influences how researchers view their work and encourages them to transform their inventions into IBM line-of-business solutions.

No matter where an idea originates, the Industry RRM must support it if it is to get any traction. For ideas coming from outside of IBM Research, the Industry RRM can help the idea take shape and guide the idea owner to subject matter experts who can help develop the idea into a FOAK project. For ideas born within Research, the Industry RRMs can help the researchers identify the optimal industry for their FOAK project and help gather support for the idea from the appropriate Industry Team. They are key players in the innovation socialization process, so the owners of ideas may need to sell their concepts repeatedly to the Industry RRMs.

When IBM researchers developed an advanced data-mining and content-management tool to convert video and audio material into digital files that could be queried for patterns and objects, they went looking for the right Industry RRM. The so-called Media Analytics for Actionable Intelligence FOAK project could be applied to many industries. But after discussions with multiple Industry RRMs, the IBM Project Team found the *right* partner in the government. Local law enforcement had a pain point of having a huge backlog of crimes to solve because of the manual processes they employed to search through various forms of evidence.

IBM researchers developed an application designed to help law enforcement solve crimes more quickly by enabling efficient and timely analysis of wiretaps, interrogations, and surveillance tapes, and text-based evidence such as interview notes and witness statements.

The Industry RRM and the Government Industry Team worked with the researchers to develop a value proposition for the application and presented it to the FOAK client, Cape Breton University, which engaged a police end user in the Cape Breton Regional Police Services.

> **LESSON: *Don't be afraid to engage the experts to help form projects and steer them toward market needs.***

Here, the Industry RRMs provided an important filter to the Generate Idea step. Many ideas will make their way to these Industry RRMs, but only the ones that are technically innovative and business-relevant will make their way to the next step.

In addition to Industry RRMs validating ideas from researchers, they can bring ideas to researchers to see if holes in the industry's portfolio can be filled by IBM Research assets. For example, in the automotive industry, the Industry RRM was instrumental in collaborating with the marketing and sales teams to drive three FOAK projects:

- A Cognitive Early Warning System to monitor, measure, analyze, correlate, and predict key vehicle behaviors in real time to better manage warranty coverage and help auto manufacturers adhere to government regulations
- An Automotive Parts Traceability Solution to enable on-demand traceability of parts to specific vehicles to improve warranty processing and vehicle recall business processes
- A Common Quality Framework to streamline quality processes for software, electronics, and electrical components during the design and engineering phases of a vehicle's lifecycle

The Industry RRM brought these project possibilities to light by reflecting on the industry's solution portfolio. Then it recommended IBM Research assets and capabilities to fill gaps and build bridges between business needs and technology innovations. Figure 2.2 shows how these FOAK projects (the box on the left) directly align with the industry's solution portfolio (the box on right).

Industry marketing teams, industry sales teams, and clients with new ideas for FOAK projects work with the Industry RRMs to identify the appropriate researchers who can respond with their contributions: innovative new technologies and thought leadership. These contributions are then molded into FOAK proposals.

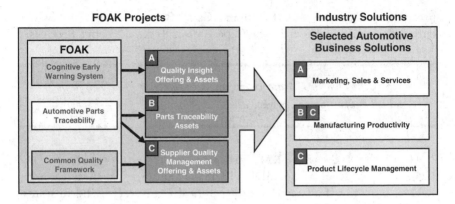

Figure 2.2 Automotive industry example of FOAK alignment with the Industry Solutions portfolio

The Industry RRM is intimately involved in building the industry strategy and has firsthand knowledge of the industry pain points, priorities, and portfolio of offerings. The Industry RRM must approve and sponsor all ideas in both directions (such as an idea coming from the industry into Research or an idea coming out of Research into the industry). If the Industry RRM does not believe the idea has merit, it cannot move forward. The Industry RRMs are the first idea filters for the FOAK program.

Translate into Market Terms

All good businesses have well-developed strategies, and within these is a view of what the future will look like and what that business's role will be—the vision. If a FOAK project is to make a difference in the market, it must make sense within an industry's vision, usually in how information technology (IT) will help clients realize their goals.

How the project makes a contribution is usually expressed in a well-articulated value proposition: If this project is completed in a specific way, these will be the benefits. Fit the vision, and understand how the innovation can be introduced into it.

With the Industry Team and Industry RRM sponsorship, each FOAK idea needs a value proposition that will resonate in the marketplace. That value proposition needs to detail the impact that the project will have within a specific segment of a client's business. Furthermore, it must contribute in one of the traditional areas of business focus by increasing profits, lowering costs, providing competitive advantage, and so on.

Preferably a FOAK project's impact will be within a line of business that is both influential and visible in the marketplace (since this will help provide the attention needed for further adoption of the innovation). For example, the Core Banking Transformation FOAK project aimed to move low-cost deposits through optimized processes for faster results, providing banks with increased margins within a shorter payback period. This value proposition was easy to understand and resonated well in the marketplace. It set this project proposal on a firm *business* foundation for further development. Once the value proposition is defined, the idea can be presented to the Industry Team for prioritization and sponsorship.

Gain IBM Industry Support

With the support of the Industry RRM and a strong value proposition in hand, the FOAK Proposal Team can present their idea to the Industry Team for sponsorship, taking an important step toward eventual commercialization. The presentation must be in terms that are clear and persuasive to the executives on the Industry Team. This means that the Industry RRM must translate the technical ideas into business terms.

> *LESSON: Sell an innovation on its business value, not just its technical function, and get market validation early.*

For the Effective Large-Scale Fingerprint Identification FOAK, this meant translating the value of complex image indexing techniques beyond what excited the researchers: higher accuracy, scalability, and lower-cost fingerprint identification. It meant identifying specific applications for the technology from the following points of view: forensic (criminal and missing-persons identification), government (national ID card, driver's license, social security, passport, border control), and commercial (computer logon, cellular phones, medical records management, credit card and ATM access). Then the potential impact of the technology on these different segments was discussed. Working with the Industry RRM, the Proposal Team was able to present the technical merits of their research within these segments and positioned the proposed FOAK project within the Government Industry's solution portfolio. This enabled the Proposal Team to secure the Government Industry Solution Board's sponsorship for the project.

The Industry Solution Board acts as the second idea filter for the FOAK program (and one more step into the real world). All FOAK ideas must have industry sponsorship—in the form of written endorsements—in order to move forward (a sample letter is included in Chapter 5, "Choosing the Best Projects"). This is not an easy requirement to fulfill. Researchers need to get onto busy calendars, answer probing questions, and build relationships with people who have different perspectives. Proposal Teams need to give special attention to this part of the process because the Industry Solution Board and executive schedules can be a gating factor, pushing the job further into the future. More delays can come when rework is required, and sometimes this step can take months to complete. Since proposals need to be pulled together in time for already-scheduled FOAK Board meetings, delays here can make or break a project. Potential FOAK Proposal Teams are cautioned not to underestimate the time it takes to secure industry support.

Test with Existing Clients

Lots of good things are going on in IBM Research, but which ones are interesting explorations in science, and which ones are innovations that will have a business impact in the near term? Industry Teams bring pre-FOAK ideas to existing clients with whom IBM has daily interactions and well-established relationships. This way, the teams can better formulate their ideas into projects that will be attractive both within and outside of IBM. A good idea that has no relevance to a client's needs and priorities isn't really a good idea for FOAK innovation. It is a good idea for FOAK only when clear business value exists.

During early, pre-FOAK client discussions, the researchers and Industry Teams tease out the requirements and test the market's readiness for the FOAK innovations. These discussions can take place practically anywhere: in the client's office, at an IT or industry conference, at one of the Industry Solutions Labs (ISLs), on an airplane, or even over the backyard fence. In fact, by going to allies and partners in ways that are most comfortable to them, the researchers are forced to see their work in a new context, and the response from Industry Teams is more authentic.

Client discussions pay off. They were pivotal to redirecting the Grid for Financial Services FOAK project. Thanks to those conversations, the FOAK Proposal Team came to address a key requirement of financial institutions—a better way to schedule jobs on computers in a grid. It provided for shorter, high-volume, faster transaction processing based on a *real*-world approach rather than the one that the researchers originally conceived.

An up-and-down, hierarchical approach to scheduling made so much sense to the researchers that they didn't seriously consider alternatives. The real system used a resource scheduler that sat above the hierarchy of operating systems and that could schedule transactions *across* the operating systems. Ultimately, this project went on to improve the FOAK client's processing time on its retirement planning application from more than 4 minutes to just 15 seconds—a 94% improvement.

Refine the Idea

After discussions with clients, Industry Teams, potential catchers, and other researchers, the IBM Project Team has the combined insights of a broad community. They need contributions from all these people to refine their idea and to position their project for the market. With this input, the idea has enough details to allow the Proposal Team to explore the idea in new ways. They can discover potential barriers and put the work into a context that can add function, make usage easier, or otherwise enhance the concept.

Idea refinement is an iterative process that eventually evolves into the Refine the Scope step in Phase II of the process, which is discussed in Chapter 6.

Gain Catcher Concurrence

FOAK participants and leaders are never quite sure what the results will be until a FOAK project is completed. Therefore, FOAK leaders can't ask potential catching organizations for a full commitment to commercialization of the assets before the project kicks off. However, what the Proposal Team *can* do at this step in the process is gain concurrence on the idea, the segment, the approach, and the alignment with the catcher's strategy and priorities. This discussion enables the Proposal Team to educate the catcher on the project and gain additional input into how they might craft the project to ensure synergy with the catcher's plans, alerting the Proposal Team to potential problems and paving the way for a smoother transition of the assets upon successful completion of the project.

Sometimes this early check yields a pleasant surprise. With the Grid for Financial Services FOAK described earlier, the Proposal Team learned during the discussions with the IBM Software Group that an opportunity existed to be a part of a full product offering the following year if they built the FOAK on a specific platform. Knowing that there was an actual plan for a future product made the platform decision clear and easy.

> **LESSON:** *Make sure that an innovation as it evolves continues to be relevant and important to the plans and strategy of the intended commercialization organization.*

But to connect this way, the Proposal Team must be able to articulate to the potential catcher the anticipated state of the assets upon completion of the project. That way, the catcher can estimate what level of additional investment will be required to commercialize the assets. For example, the investment needed to commercialize an asset within an existing product is likely to be less than that of an asset that goes to market as a totally new product or solution.

For each asset, the FOAK Proposal Team needs to do three things:

- Identify the catcher.
- Determine what additional effort will be required on the part of the catcher to commercialize the asset.
- Gain the catcher's sponsorship, support, and firm commitment to commercialization.

Although not a formal idea filter for the FOAK program, these early asset commercialization discussions do serve at times to eliminate FOAK ideas.

Develop a Structured Proposal

The prototypes from IBM Research never neatly fit into the situations that the client-facing IBMer or the Industry RRM have identified. The Proposal Team must investigate how the proper elements might be put together and modified to create a project that fits the specific needs while fitting within the time and resource constraints of the FOAK program. While the approach to doing this is never quite the same, the Proposal Team does take advantage of standard forms and procedures to

QUESTIONS TO ASK ABOUT AN ASSET

One of the best ways to think through the potential catchers of FOAK assets is to ask questions such as the following with regard to each asset:

- How big is the job? For instance, assets with lots of lines of code generally need a commercialization organization that has the systems and processes in place to manage large code bases. So this question tests the proposal's practicality and points to who might need to participate.

- How much customization will the asset require? Assets that require lots of customization generally need a services engagement to deliver the asset's full value and thus lend themselves more toward a services practice.

- How broad a marketplace will the asset serve? Assets with very broad applicability are appealing to product commercialization organizations, while assets with a more specialized market focus tend to appeal to industry-focused services organizations. Additionally, the level of localization required to make the assets fit the needs of broader markets, such as other geographies, also needs to be considered.

- What is the state of the asset? How mature is it, really? Assets requiring a significant amount of rework or enhancements need a commercialization organization that has the development resources to take on large development efforts. Those requiring little effort can be made available on services engagements fairly quickly.

- Does the asset logically enhance or extend an existing product or service offering? If so, the asset will make sense for the existing offering organization to catch. This will make it easier to provide a context and will make it more attractive to offering owners.

- Is this a capability in the catcher's road map and long-term strategy? If so, the probability of asset commercialization increases. If not, additional meetings and levels of sponsorship will be required to position the assets within the catcher's road map.

- Proposal Title
- Sponsors
- Project Team
- Problem / Opportunity Statement
- Solution Description
- Technical / Business Innovation
- Business Value
- Solution Diagram
- Intellectual Capital / Assets
- Strategy

- Market / Solution Opportunity
- Competition
- Targeted Clients / Business Partners
- Commercialization
- Path to Market
- Related Contract Information
- Project Funding (IBM, Client, Brand)
- Milestones
- Industry Solutions Lab Demonstration

Figure 2.3   FOAK proposal template

look at a full set of considerations as they go forward. Figure 2.3 summarizes the FOAK proposal template.

Standard procedures and the use of such templates, especially when experienced innovators are on the Proposal Team, provide a distinct advantage over more ad hoc approaches often used by inventors because they reduce the probability of surprises that can derail a project. This also makes analysis and comparison easier for the FOAK Board. At the same time, these approaches are not as constrained as the approaches product brand development teams use. They allow more opportunity for FOAK projects to move into white spaces and provide leadership.

Ultimately, the Proposal Team must put limits and structure around the FOAK project in such a way that it will provide the tangible value promised to IBM and its client. This is assured even before the Proposal Team brings the proposal forward for formal approval by the FOAK Board. In addition to completing the application, the Proposal Team must meet with experts and gather recommendations that bolster arguments for their approach. Some go the extra mile and review their proposal with FOAK Board members prior to the FOAK Board meetings, which reduces friction, increases credibility, and creates allies.

LESSON: Make innovation communications to stakeholders easy to evaluate by using common formats, instructions, and designs.

Submit to the FOAK Board

Phase I is coming to an end now. The Proposal Team is hopeful that their proposal will be approved. The pieces have come together, at least on paper.

Four weeks prior to the FOAK Board meeting, an outline of the combined Research and Industry Team's idea needs to be submitted to the FOAK PMT so that they can begin to build the calendar for the meeting. The outline is a simple description of what the proposed project is all about. Some Proposal Teams are more verbose than others, and some choose presentation format over document format. Figure 2.4 is a sample project outline.

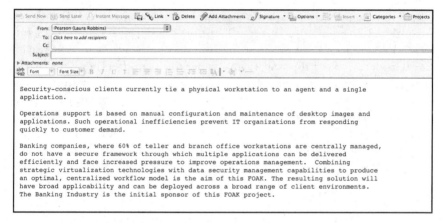

Figure 2.4   Sample project outline

FOAK Proposal Teams must submit their completed proposals to the FOAK PMT early enough to allow time for the FOAK Board members to read the proposals. This is usually two weeks prior to the meeting.

The FOAK PMT does a preliminary review of all the FOAK proposals during this time, filtering out any proposals that do not meet the program requirements or that are just not ready for FOAK Board review. Here are some examples of showstoppers:

- Lack of sponsorship
- Too narrow or too broad a scope
- Weak asset commercialization plans
- Not aligned with a market segment or solution area

These are problematic for the Proposal Team, but they provide "teachable moments" for the PMT. Proposal Teams that fall short in these areas get guidance that is personal, specific, and relevant. They are unlikely to make a submission with similar problems in the future.

The FOAK PMT also provides the stronger Proposal Teams without these flaws with input on how to improve their proposals, the types of questions the FOAK Board might have, and guidance on their "chartmanship." The pressure is always on to get it right because the opportunity to go before the FOAK Board is limited. This PMT review serves as the third idea filter for the program.

And then it's showtime. FOAK Board meetings generally are only one day long. Each Proposal Team is given 30 minutes to present. The FOAK Board presentation has a standard template. Proposal Teams are encouraged to plan to talk for 20 minutes and leave 10 minutes for Q&A. Experience has shown that, with proper preparation and the use of the templates, the Proposal Teams generally can effectively and efficiently present their proposals within the allocated 30 minutes. Of course, some Proposal Teams have to be managed, but for the most part the Proposal Teams have planned and practiced their proposal content so that they can get through their proposals within the allotted time.

The FOAK Board presentation template contains the following (see Figure 2.5).

- Proposal Top Sheet
- Problem / Opportunity Statement
- Industry Point of View
- Solution Roadmap
- Solution Diagram / Assets Highlighted
- Deliverables
- Commercialization Organization
- Sponsors and Supporters
- Market Opportunity
- Path to Market
- Target Clients
- Funding Requirements
- Why Is This a FOAK?
- Project Team

Figure 2.5   FOAK Board presentation template summary

After reviewing all the projects presented, the FOAK Board moves into a closed session where they select the projects that are the most compelling. This process is discussed in detail in Chapter 5. Decisions are communicated back to the Proposal Teams within 24 hours of the meeting. The FOAK Board is the fourth and final idea filter for the FOAK program.

Summary

FOAK projects are positioned to create results from innovations that are in the space between exploration and development. Although the FOAK process continues to evolve, the basic steps aimed at getting together the right partners to take on new but practical projects have remained essentially the same over the years. The biggest change has been stricter commitment to goals, such as doing projects that have strategic importance and that show leadership. Another major change has been tighter adherence to practices that facilitate success, such as including a project manager and engaging early on with a catcher.

The devil is in the details, so *how* all this is accomplished is the subject of subsequent chapters. However, the description of Phase I of the process provides a perspective that creates a context for a clearer understanding of the specifics that follow. Chapter 3, "How Ideas Take Shape," explores how the FOAK ideas that fuel Phase I surface and take shape.

3

How Ideas Take Shape

Idea people—writers, composers, inventors, researchers—love their private time—those moments when they have a pad of paper, a piano, or a lab full of toys that they can use to satisfy their curiosity. Unfortunately, ideas, manuscripts, and inventions don't make an impact (don't become innovations) until they go beyond the idea person. Inventors who want to move from ideas to innovation must maintain a delicate balance between overprotection and abandonment. They must continue to support their ideas and guide their development while letting the world transform them. This chapter explores how FOAK ideas surface and are molded into proposals for real projects.

Where Do Ideas Come From?

Despite IBM's buttoned-down reputation, ideas—sometimes crazy ideas—have long been a part of its lifeblood. Even in the dark days of the 1990s, when IBM was losing billions of dollars, it continued to invest billions in its IBM Research Division. The starting point for innovation in its many forms, including FOAK, is a culture that values ideas: big ideas, small ideas, incremental ideas, and outlandish ideas.

Thomas Watson Jr., the IBM CEO who brought the company into the Computer Age, once said: "You can make wild ducks tame, but you can never make tame ducks wild again. One might also add that the duck who is tamed will never go anywhere anymore. We are convinced that any business needs its wild ducks. And in IBM, we try not to tame them."

IBMers bounce ideas back and forth with peers not just in the research labs, but everywhere. Thousands of ideas pour into Thinkplace, a global suggestion box where colleagues can rate, critique, improve, and collaborate to help realize an idea. The IBM Academy, which brings together select IBM innovators, takes on knotty problems that sit at the intersection of business and emerging technologies. Then the Academy forms teams from across IBM to come up with answers that participants develop on their own time. And IBMers can sharpen their creative capabilities by selecting from dozens of courses—most available online at no charge to the business unit—on ideation and innovation.

It's no surprise that such a culture has no shortage of ideas and that those ideas are listened to. An idea for a FOAK proposal may come from a researcher, but it may also come from someone in a client-facing role. The germ of an idea may be developed by an executive, a salesperson, a manager, or even a client. Let's look at some ways in which an idea might begin its path to FOAK.

An Invention in the Lab

In the past, a project emerged when researchers working on assets in the lab began to see how they might be applied and become an innovation for a particular industry. This was the approach that led to the first FOAK project, MedSpeak, described in Chapter 1, "A Program That Works." IBM Research had an asset, the speech recognition engine, and they went looking for a likely application. They found a market opportunity in transcribing radiology reports, which was an expensive and time-consuming operation. Today, the researcher's search is likely to begin with the Industry Research Relationship Managers (RRMs), who can present many possibilities to the researchers because they are experts in their specific industries.

But the researchers also make use of their networks of trusted individuals with whom they can test notions and validate facts about the marketplace or industry. Along with these allies, they explore whether there is a fit for the asset:

- Does the idea provide a solution for a known pain point, such as reducing the cost of customer service in retail or optimizing a supply chain in manufacturing?
- Does the innovation create a new opportunity by, for instance, providing a reason why telecommunications customers would use more bandwidth?
- Can the innovation help position a firm strategically by enabling a business model that disadvantages the industry leader?

This matching of technology to the most promising opportunity, rather than the most obvious one, has become a hallmark of FOAK. And working with the right client increases the probability that the asset and the prototype innovation will lead to addressing real and important client pain points.

A Gap in the Portfolio

Alternatively, the idea might come from one of the Industry Solution Boards. These Boards continuously review their portfolios of solutions, taking advantage, again, of market intelligence to manage their investments. Significantly, the Industry Solution Boards use the comments, questions, and requests of client-facing personnel or clients themselves as input into their process. Part of the reason they do these reviews of their portfolios is to identify offerings that need updating or that may even be obsolete. In doing these reviews, an Industry Solution Board may identify a gap in its portfolio. If this gap represents a real opportunity for providing additional value to clients, the Industry Solution Board actively seeks out a solution from IBM Research to address the gap.

For example, in 2005, IBM completed a market intelligence study on retail trends and retailers' pain points in China and the global market. This study found that in the highly competitive retail market—especially with frequent mergers and acquisitions and fragmented customer expectations—*where* stores are located is crucial for retailers who want to increase their profitability, improve customer satisfaction, and sustain growth. Retailers need their stores in the right sites, with the right merchandise available and service capacity in place to serve their targeted customer segments. This was a difficult challenge for retailers, but it was a delight to researchers at IBM's China Research Lab, because it triggered new topics in their fields of analytics and optimization.

After the researchers worked through preliminary ideas, they held brainstorming meetings with IBM retail consultants in China. As they collaborated, the consultants grew excited about the proposal that was being developed, so the researchers built a prototype based on a previous IBM Research asset that was developed to select banking branch sites and optimize networks. Thanks to the consultants, the retail prototype delivered by the researchers reflected industry knowledge. The proposal was strong, and ultimately the FOAK project delivered a solution that satisfied the client partner, the Chinese retailer Jia Jia Yue. The resulting offering currently is being rolled out worldwide.

Looking for Ideas from Outside IBM

Since researchers tend to maintain strong ties with academia, it is not surprising that at times the ideas will surface from academic relationships or conferences. The Social Network Analysis project came to life this way. It analyzed telephone call detail records to enable a telecommunications company to learn more about its customers so that it could retain high-value customers and perform more sophisticated marketing campaign management. The idea was sparked during a conversation with a visiting professor on assignment at the India Research Lab. After maturing the idea, the researchers presented it to the IBM client-facing team (these are the sales and services people who work with clients on a daily basis) for a telecommunications client. The client subsequently opened the door for client discussions, which resulted in a match.

A Client Request

Perhaps the most exciting starting point for ideas is when a client brings up the need to someone who is associated with FOAK. These instances generally happen during one of our collaborative sessions with a client at one of the Industry Solutions Labs (ISLs). The ISLs are IBM client centers that showcase solutions available from IBM today along with the solutions from IBM Research for tomorrow. They provide a stimulating backdrop for client collaborations and conversations that naturally lead to "Could you also do this?" or "I wonder if you considered...?." The ISLs are described in detail in Chapter 9, "Telling the Story: IBM's Industry Solutions Labs."

The High-Performance Stream Processing Platform project surfaced this way. Many financial institutions have built automated trading systems that consume high-volume market data feeds. Their business success depends on millisecond-level responses to approximately a half-million messages per second. They typically have a homegrown purpose-built solution with hundreds of servers. This worked at that time, but market data providers were projecting traffic increases of more than five-fold during the next two years. Their current systems could not cost-effectively scale to handle the anticipated load.

As a client facing this problem watched and listened, a researcher at the ISL explained how real-time, high volume data could be converted into useful information on the spot. Because this capability could scale, it showed promise in addressing the growing workloads of the financial services industry.

Fortuitously, the FOAK Board was at the ISL, reviewing the High-Performance Steam Processing Platform project, even as the client was visiting the ISL. This created an unusual opportunity for the Board to directly deliver the good news to the client that the project had been approved.

> **LESSON:** *Be creative about developing and using many opportunities to engage clients with innovation and gain their input.*

Developing Ideas

No idea goes very far in its raw form. It needs to be socialized across all the stakeholders. It needs to be looked at closely, for both problems and hidden value. It needs to be compared to the competition. It needs to be tested against the realities of what is technically possible, economically sensible, and acceptable to decision makers.

Clearly Expressing Ideas

Because FOAK projects are executed across different disciplines and organizations, it is essential that the discussions begin with clear statements of capability, value, and potential use. This means that all parties involved need to become more aware of their assumptions and the professional jargon they are prone to using. Analogies, use cases, and diagrams may help get the concept across, but the starting point needs to be mutual respect and patience. What is obvious to one party might not be obvious to his or her collaborators. People need to be able to ask basic questions without fear of being judged. Those giving answers need to have a genuine interest in communicating, even if that involves rephrasing and repetition.

Uncovering Problems

Quite a bit of the idea development work gets done during the client discussions. You can always count on clients to take a critical look. They are essentially the primary buyers of the idea, with dollars, work hours, and reputations at stake. They ask probing questions, kick the tires, and work to imagine an end result that isn't just elegant, but also works for them and produces real results for the enterprise.

A good example of this is the process that the Smart Customer Interaction FOAK went through. Here, the whole intent of the project was redirected—with terrific results—by a shrewd client. The researchers were originally thinking that the client would apply the innovation to the end consumer. That is, a consumer working from his or her Web browser would use the guidance from the Smart Customer Interaction engine to diagnose his or her problems and find a solution. However, for the targeted FOAK client, who listened to the researchers' use case respectfully, a lot of the story didn't add up. Would the value be obvious to the consumers? Would they put in the effort? How would anyone make money from it?

This sort of questioning forced the researchers to take a more critical view of what they had created. Not incidentally, it also engaged the client, who appreciated being listened to. He took seriously his role in exploring the innovation's potential—a potential that was not obvious to those who had created the technology.

What emerged was an approach more in line with how the market actually works. The client advised the researchers to apply the new technology to their customer-facing agents instead of to the consumers themselves—and that's where they redirected the project. In fact, this model turned out to be correct for other markets. Subsequently, the researchers brought their technology to IBM's own online marketplace, ibm.com, where it was piloted with the agents supporting customers. During the pilot, ibm.com realized a twofold increase in opportunity identification and a 55% increase in closed sales using the Smart Customer Interaction solution.

This is not to say that only clients identify problems and concerns. All those involved try to take an objective view of potential drawbacks in a project. But the FOAK leadership (FOAK Board and Program Management Team (PMT)) found that the client perspective is vital.

SHARING BIG IDEAS

Whatever an idea is and wherever it originates, its value comes from clearly communicating it to other people. Four steps can help an innovator methodically move a big idea from the concept stage to the point of engaging others in its development:

1. Avoid the seduction. Ideas and dreams have a lot in common. They both are unexpected, and they both may create excitement bordering on passion for the owner. Both imply more than they say. Dreams and initial ideas are rarely complete. They are starting points, no matter how compelling they may be to us personally. They are sparks of inspiration. Fiction writers know this. They may put their ideas into journals, but the stories they sell are almost always built and reworked with an audience in mind.

2. Determine what kind of inspiration you have. Here are eight possibilities:

   - **Good question:** Curiosity often begins with questions. For an innovator, the question itself may have resonance because it takes on a new topic, explores something in a new way, or, if answered, would have profound consequences.

   - **Rich problem:** A well-articulated client problem often can catch your imagination and create a brainstorm of ideas for its solution.

   - **Analogy:** Especially for processes and ways of doing things, working through relevant comparisons often leads to good starting points for investigation.

   - **Bright light:** Sometimes the "aha" experience comes from a new perspective or sudden insight. You see a piece of the puzzle you haven't seen before.

   - **Use:** An unexpected application of something that is already out there or a function enabled by something new.

   - **Pattern:** This may be an intuitive recognition of underlying mathematics, but it could also be as simple as "This usually follows that."

- **Oddity:** An anomaly. A quirk. One of the best things to hear a scientist say is "That can't be true!"
- **Natural extension:** The future, often the next step, for something that is familiar.

3. Use the list of inspirations to augment and complete your idea. For instance, the Wright brothers were fascinated by the good question of how to make heavier-than-air flight possible. They found a pattern in nature by observing how birds' wings change shape and came to a deeper understanding of lift. Their explanation, or natural extension, of the not-very-useful working models attracted the U.S. military as a sponsor for development.

4. Test the defined idea with colleagues. Here, going to a diverse group pays off in a few ways. It forces you to work from fewer assumptions as you describe your idea (so it must be clearer), the fresh perspective is likely to enhance your idea and make it fuller at an earlier state, and it may force you to ask tougher questions because your colleagues aren't enamored with your idea.

The earlier in the FOAK process that clients share concerns, ideas, and other input, the more effective the project becomes.

LESSON: When it is feasible, try it their way, even though you know your way is right.

Using Scenarios

Stories, such as those shared on the floor of the ISL, have always been good conversation starters. Although FOAK has not made scenarios and use cases a standard part of its process, this approach has been used successfully and has proven to be valuable in communicating ideas, so it is recommended. As the participants in innovation become more diverse, it is often a story—not a checklist of functions—that helps communicate a unified vision of possibilities.

In fact, one of the more recent investments that some of the ISLs have made is in creating unified displays in banking, retail, insurance, and healthcare, complete with characters that represent the needs and attitudes of real consumers. These scenarios help IBM's clients understand how other industries are finding new ways to give their customers better experiences. This also helps the clients see ways to carry these concepts and ideas into their own industries. Figure 3.1 shows the healthcare section of the Customer Experience Center at the Hawthorne ISL.

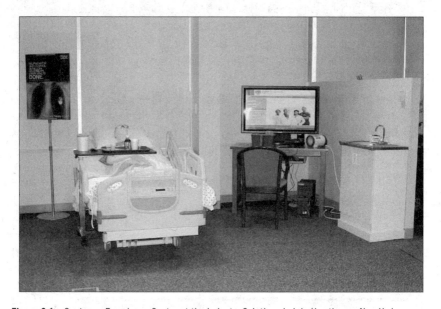

Figure 3.1   Customer Experience Center at the Industry Solutions Lab in Hawthorne, New York

The ideal scenarios are those that include real-world problems that need to be solved. This both provides credibility and suggests starting points for conversations. A too-perfect scenario does not give the audience opportunities to engage. No scenario should cleanly solve all the characters' problems or be photorealistic. By leaving holes and not polishing the story too much, it becomes easier to stimulate productive conversations. "That doesn't make sense" or "It doesn't work that way" can be starting points for discussions that make proposals more down-to-earth. Scenarios can also help the participants develop trust and understanding.

Another important success factor for scenarios is developing good, probing questions. "Tell me about how you handle this kind of challenge today" can be the beginning of insight from the client's perspective. It can help the FOAK Proposal Teams firm up their ideas and understand how a project targeted to one industry can play a role in another industry. Throughout, it is important that clients are listened to and given proper air time in these discussions.

But scenarios don't work for everyone. Operational executives or those who are always asking for "net-net" may not have the patience for storytelling. Scenarios are tools for the imagination. Ideally, innovators will find them useful, but some participants may have other approaches that are more in their comfort zones. A use case, a briefing, a demo, or a traditional listing of functions and characteristics of a technology may, at times, better serve the purpose of catalyzing productive conversations.

Prioritizing Ideas

No one can do everything. The to-do list for FOAK has a tendency to grow, so FOAK program participants need to be rigorous about moving the best ideas to the top so that they receive the attention they deserve.

Testing for Value and Impact

Ideas get prioritized in a few places during the FOAK process—first by the Industry RRMs, who take a hard look at ideas coming from the researchers. At this point, our Industry RRMs can spot the flaws quickly: vague descriptions, no indication of competition or context, no clear explanation of needs or value delivered. Some ideas simply go away at this point.

Others are so compelling—because of their clarity and relevance—that they rise to the top of the list. Then the Industry Solution Boards for all ideas (research, industry, and client-initiated) take the projects that look good and test them against their knowledge of the real world.

Finally, the FOAK Board and PMT look at the ideas, now fleshed out as projects, in terms of real companies that might be interested. Which of these clients are likely to be receptive? Can the ideas be used in multiple industries and geographies? How will conducting a FOAK project with any of these organizations benefit IBM? Ultimately, analysis and prioritization expose not just a project's value, but also who that value is for. This provides the best hope for success: enthusiastic stakeholders.

Getting the Timing Right

Everyone knows that timing can make all the difference to the success of an innovation. Move too early, and the context (such as the proper infrastructure) or the value (such as compelling need) may not be obvious to customers and other stakeholders. Move too late, and the innovation becomes a "me-too." Timing can also take advantage of or avoid problems with leadership, the economy, and other environmental factors.

The FOAK Board often considers timing in their discussions about which projects to fund. When reviewing projects that do not meet expectations, one remark often heard at a FOAK Board meeting is "We were too early on that." The sense here is not that the technology is not ready. In almost every case, the technology worked. But sometimes the economic justification isn't clear. Or the Board is not yet convinced that the world is headed in the direction that will make the technology pay off. Or the odd alchemy of buzz, urgency, and luck has not come together to make an idea inevitable.

The FOAK and Industry Solution Boards look at emerging market conditions as a starting point. If the interest is high now but might evaporate before the project is done, there is no sense in starting. Competition is also a major factor. Most technologies need to fit into an ecosystem of applications, processes, and standards that offer opportunities for first movers. Getting there first is important. Another key element of timing is the "If this works..." concept. If the project succeeds in its own right, will the follow-on work of market development, scaling up, and partnering be doable within a reasonable amount of time? Can everything that is necessary be accomplished within the window of opportunity?

According to Charles Foster, director of The Chestnut Hill Institute in Boston, a research and consulting firm focusing on the psychology of business success, good decisions "are habit-forming. Each time you make the right decision, you gain the necessary self-confidence to keep making good decisions."[1]

If this is true, a natural consequence is that successful innovators are experienced in making good decisions in the rough-and-tumble world of innovation. With more than 14 years of experience, our FOAK Boards have made a good many choices on when the time is right to take action with a project. This is reflected in the projects' impact, such as seeing 70% of completed projects successfully transfer assets to commercialization organizations. This and other metrics of the FOAK program are described in Chapter 10, "Portfolio Management."

Ultimately, know-how in the area of timing is not easily codified, but it can be shared in stories. These stories bring their own contexts, and often the lessons become the basis for helping others make their own best decision.

In one case, timing was the deciding factor for a FOAK project. A researcher developed an accurate, convenient, and nonintrusive voice-based authentication system, and this became the basis for the Conversational Biometrics for Credit Card Security FOAK project. The system combines text-independent voiceprint matching with knowledge matching. Questions are asked of the user, and they must be answered correctly in order to access sensitive information. Adding the knowledge match to the voiceprint match improved the accuracy and enabled a higher level of security.

The obvious industry was banking, but the Banking Industry Solution Board would not prioritize this project over other projects they were considering. It wasn't until a couple of years later that the Banking Industry Solution Board decided that credit card fraud was a priority. The project was eventually performed with a credit card company; however, it could easily have been done with a number of other industries, such as retail or healthcare. Finding the right industry at the right time with the right client is the trick. Looking more broadly increases the odds of getting the best start and increases the odds of reuse and commercialization.

> **LESSON:** *The wrong timing for one industry might be the right timing for another.*

In addition, having a diverse, knowledgeable network improves the chances that the best alternatives are considered and that those with little or no chance are eliminated. This is because people with different perspectives—working in different areas and paying attention to the changes in the environment that matters to them—usually provide a more accurate view of possibilities and trends than an outsider can develop alone. It appears that good timing decisions, based on FOAK's network, is a case of the Wisdom of Crowds. This means pulling together information from people with different perspectives to arrive at choices that are better than could have been made by any single expert.

Supporting Networks

Timing isn't the only way a network helps. The various FOAK Proposal Teams and boards can't do it all alone. Any given project may have people far from the center of the work with ideas, criticisms, facts, capabilities, and questions whose contributions are essential to improving the odds of success and the quality of the ultimate deliverable. The best innovators are those with broad and diverse connections.

For an innovation to provide value, people need to be enlisted to fulfill a variety of roles. Their advice, perspectives, insights, advocacy contacts, and ability to enable the ideas must be put to work, often without much in the way of financial incentives. Building a good personal network is an essential key to successful innovation.

Most networking advice revolves around finding a job—selling yourself. For innovation, you also create trust and confidence in yourself. But innovation networking creates an additional focus on taking a journey into the unknown. Here are some suggestions:

- **Be genuinely interested in other people:** Since innovators are naturally curious, most can develop this interest. But in order to meet people, they need conversation skills. They need to know when to let the other person talk. And they need to know when to put aside their egos and ideas until the trust is developed.

- **Listen:** Not just to the content, but to the needs, interests, passions, and emotions. When face-to-face, innovators should listen with all their senses and ask good questions. An innovator never knows how someone might be of help. It may mean listening through several layers of discussion before anything is obvious. Nobel Laureate Linus Pauling once said that the reason he had so many good ideas was because he had so many ideas. The reason great innovators have so many powerful relationships is because they have so many relationships.

- **Get their card—don't push your card:** A card you receive is a token of a successful meeting and good conversation. It means your investment of time is showing potential. If you have their cards, you have permission to contact them.

- **Keep in contact:** Contact management requires being systematic. Put things on the calendar, and create an inventory of touch points. Then methodically work them. A good rule of thumb is if you haven't provided people with value in 90 days, they are no longer in your network. Don't expect people to join the team spontaneously. Ask for help.

- **Do favors:** The best networkers are generous, sharing knowledge, contacts, and resources. They graciously accept favors, advice, and offers of help—even when they could do it better.

- **Be a connector:** Share valuable contacts. If you are the person who knows the answer and can get things done, or you know who to go to, you are golden, and the phone will ring. And people will want to help you succeed.

- **Keep commitments, and be honest:** For the innovator, this includes answering that difficult question, "So how far along are you with this idea?" Or, "Has anyone else succeeded in doing this?" The most effective members of an innovation team are those who have the straight story and know the risks.

- **Find projects of mutual benefit:** The former president of a college was being interviewed about a novel she coauthored. The interviewer asked, "Why did you work together?" Her answer: "To be sure we'd stay in touch." The more you can go beyond words in relationships to actions, the stronger your network will be.

Three steps can help innovators establish a network:

1. Honestly evaluate your people skills, and make an effort to improve them.
2. Take an inventory of your network. Start with folks who can provide advice, perspectives, insights, promotion, access, and enablement for your innovation. But don't stop there. Remember, everyone is a potential ally.
3. Get out there. Be accessible and visible. This means going beyond glad-handing people at parties and conferences. You need to find online opportunities, such as social networking sites, blogs, wikis, and perhaps your own website. As Woody Allen said, 90% of success is showing up. And remember, networking is a two-way street. Don't just find opportunities for yourself. Actively develop them for others.

Creating Project Value Propositions

Value propositions are created and presented by the FOAK Proposal Teams as part of their submissions to the FOAK Board. That is, if this FOAK project is completed in a specific way, these will be the benefits to IBM, the client, or other stakeholders. This is a vital step in reshaping the idea, because it begins the process of making it fit the partners' needs.

The term "value proposition" used here is more general than that used by marketers. FOAK innovators aren't just looking for money. They are looking for executive leadership, insights, advocacy, questions, uses, criticisms, relevant data, and more. For each person who can contribute, a case must be made to them that demonstrates why they should. What do they get out of it personally? A good use case also talks about trade-offs and alternatives. And, of course, every value proposition has an expiration date. (When you have a project that must be completed in 12 to 18 months, those expiration dates are approximately the same as a gallon of milk.)

The marketing view of value propositions is finding its way into FOAK in one way. The FOAK PMT has found that many of the projects lack the clear, attractive charts that can really help drive the value propositions to higher levels and make them easier to grasp. So last year the FOAK program piloted funding resources in India to weed through all the documents on a handful of projects (proposals, presentations, patents, papers, demos) and build stronger, more focused collateral for value propositions. The feedback has been positive, but the FOAK leadership is still exploring this approach.

Socializing Ideas

It is an axiom that people buy the salesman, not the product. For FOAK, this means that an innovator's greatest advantage in gaining acceptance for a new idea from partners and clients is strong relationships. These relationships occur at many levels: longstanding contracts between IBM and clients, experience working on a past FOAK, professional ties, and simply having met face-to-face under pleasant circumstances.

Mutual knowledge, respect, and trust, as well as a history of shared successes and seeing commitments fulfilled, all feed into a good relationship. It is best if things work on a personal level as well. Treating people as people, not just as a source of needed resources, can make a big difference.

> *LESSON: Developing strong relationships with partners provides an edge in ultimately getting an innovation accepted.*

With the basis of strong relationships, the responsibility for which falls mostly to the client-facing teams and Industry RRMs, the targeted value propositions just described can be put to work. But there is one more piece: a clear understanding of FOAK itself. As stated earlier, FOAK does not provide clients with a finished, predictable offering. For those on the IBM Project Team who have experience and training, the setting of expectations is known to be a key job. The team looks around the circle and tries to make sure everyone has the message. However, as with any successful endeavor, FOAK has gathered peripheral participants, and these people may not understand the program's processes and limits.

After all, *who* is telling you the idea and what you can expect of them is a critical frame to any discussion about it. When the *who* is client-facing IBMers with misconceptions about FOAK, the clients may end up with the wrong expectations, especially about costs and intellectual property rights. Having faced the painful consequences of getting "help" from these people, the FOAK PMT has taken action. They publish the guidelines and review them at the kickoff meetings. This doesn't help, of course, if people don't read the guidelines or don't take part in the kickoff call. Taking it a step further, guidance is now included in the funding letters, both internally and externally. Essentially, this gets the correct message to partners (internal and external), even if the message bearer has more enthusiasm than clarity. The lesson here is to communicate on many levels, multiple times.

Summary

There is never a shortage of raw ideas for FOAK projects, and they come from a variety of participants with different perspectives. The processing of these ideas depends on engaging a network of people from different disciplines. In particular, client views are actively solicited. IBM's clients become partners in grounding ideas even before proposals are drafted. Often those who provide early guidance point to eventual partners or become partners in FOAK projects themselves.

The shaping of ideas is absolutely dependent on establishing and maintaining strong, positive relationships. Collateral, value propositions, and systematic approaches to improving and socializing the ideas contribute to getting the best ideas and getting the best from any given idea. Consistency in forms and procedures helps make the process easier for all involved.

Of course, ideas mean nothing without people—the right people engaged correctly. Because FOAK is fundamentally about collaborative innovation, having the right partnerships makes the difference between success and failure. Chapter 4, "Getting the Most out of Partnerships," explores how the FOAK IBM Project Teams identify and engage their clients.

Endnote

1. Forrester, Charles, PhD. "Simple Laws for Making Good Decisions from Good Decision Makers." http://www.bottomlinesecrets.com/article.html?article_id=27567.

4

Getting the Most out of Partnerships

In the mid-90s, a mind shift occurred within IBM regarding how the IBM Research Division was viewed. Instead of trying to confine research to the labs for fear of leaking secrets to the marketplace, IBM decided to open its research laboratory doors to clients. In fact, to leverage its investment in research and to influence sales while bringing valuable market insights into IBM Research, IBM created both FOAK and a showcase in the form of its Industry Solutions Labs (ISLs). These programs enabled researchers to gain immediate marketplace feedback: Was their research merely an interesting science project? Or was it an innovation that could have real business impact?

FOAK and the ISLs also enabled clients and IBM's delivery organizations to gain early insights into emerging technologies that, if not planned for and exploited ahead of the competition, could disrupt their businesses.

This business rationale drove the need for better, more facilitated ways of partnering. For the first time, funding was available to support partnering in a systematic way. But how do you find and qualify partners? How do you engage with them? How do you align your interests and keep the partnership strong? Processes for partnering, both internal and external, needed to be developed almost from scratch.

The Partners

What characteristics make good FOAK participants (both within IBM and within client organizations)? From the very beginning, they must be people who can imagine how technologies might be used. They must be able to consolidate ideas, capabilities, and resources in ways that provide natural synergies. They must be flexible when new opportunities arise and persistent when things don't go as planned. And they must have people skills so that they can keep discussions going, smooth out the differences between organizations and perspectives, and maintain a positive attitude. Client-facing IBM participants must possess the additional characteristic of being able to look outward, toward potential clients in a variety of industries.

So candidates for a FOAK Joint Project Team (IBM and client) should have the following qualities:

- **Creative:** When ideas arrive, they are not fully formed. They need to be explored, combined with other ideas, and adapted to real-world circumstances. FOAK participants need to generate a variety of options to go forward.

- **Analytical:** While no innovation is completely understood, the team needs to bring an array of questions, measurements, and validation tools that they can put to use from the proposal development stage all the way to project completion.

- **Curious:** Intense interest is the beginning of passion, discovery, and doubt. All of these lead to pursuit and appreciation of new facts.

- **Flexible:** No innovation project ends as it begins. Redirection is forced on a team because of emerging opportunities, failure, and operational change. If team members stick to exact definitions and specified roles, it is unlikely that the work can continue to move forward.

- **Persistent:** New directions meet barriers, inspire resistance, and, at times, lead to failures, large and small. They put innovators at risk, in terms of both their careers and their reputations. Without determination, commitment, and confidence, challenges will defeat an innovation team.

- **Passionate:** Ultimately, innovation does not promise an easy, sure path. It requires hard work, fortitude, and courage, and that must translate into an emotional as well as intellectual steadfastness.

In addition, FOAK Joint Project Team members should be able to listen, weigh options, make decisions, and inspire. It doesn't hurt if they also are in a position to make things happen within an organization. Few if any people are strong in all these areas, but it is possible to put together an effective team that brings together these characteristics in a way that makes innovation happen.

LESSON: Successful innovation depends on having the right people—those with a commitment to innovation and the skills to help move an idea into the marketplace.

Setting Expectations So That Partners Aren't Disappointed

The first days of the FOAK program were filled with enthusiasm for all the possibilities. Both IBM and clients brought high expectations to the program. Some of these were right on target, but in some cases the goals were not aligned or clear. In many instances, IBM did not know in detail what it wanted from a FOAK relationship and, as a result, was often shy about directly stating what it expected. So, each FOAK contract was negotiated differently, various project approaches were employed, and good client selection was often a result of serendipity. It took about five years of trial and error for FOAK leadership (the FOAK Board and the Program Management Team) to fully articulate what it wanted from the FOAK program:

- Every FOAK will have the potential for creating significant intellectual property (IP).
- Clients will contribute financially and with resources (data, market knowledge, access) that are not available to IBM.
- The goals of a FOAK project will be achievable within one year.

- FOAK will deepen the relationship with clients, and the impact on the relationship will be measured.
- FOAK project successes will be publicized to enhance the reputations of IBM and our FOAK partners.
- Projects will be First-of-a-Kind, not One-of-a-Kind.

But before these criteria could be met and the right processes could be put into effect, FOAK's leadership needed to determine who needed to be on the team to ensure success.

The Key Players

While good processes improve the chances of success, it is the people involved who make or break a project. Naturally, they need to know their fields, have experience, and have status that will encourage their ideas to be heard and adopted. But the right resumes don't necessarily create the right team members on an innovation project.

Softer skills in persuasion, listening, judgment, and even courtesy will keep participants engaged through the inevitable tough times. The right combination of flexibility and persistence helps guarantee that an innovation is reworked to meet the demands of the real world without sacrificing its essence. Patience and courage are needed in the face of opponents and naysayers. Trust, loyalty, and commitment form the foundation that allows innovation team members to respond to opportunities with daring and answer challenges with courage.

On top of all these characteristics, the members of the innovation team must have passion and enthusiasm. This is the fuel for discovery and execution. Here are some quotes from FOAK IBM Project Team members that exhibit the kind of passion that FOAK team members have:

- "It's the lure of creating world-class breakthrough solutions. FOAK generally allows us to work with the best companies in the world. It's a great proving ground!"
- "FOAK has always had a big positive effect on the researcher to stimulate them—and to appreciate the often untidy way requirements emerge in real business."
- "FOAK enables fabulous learning opportunities, and they really energize our researchers by giving them the opportunity to work with a client."

People on an innovation team need to make adjustments, deal with the unexpected, take chances, and handle failure. If the work itself remains abstract, if there is no emotional pull, the chances of success are diminished. If all the members of a team have a positive attitude, they are difficult to stop. Let's look at the various players on the FOAK projects.

Researchers

These are the creative catalysts of FOAK: no researchers, no projects. Why shouldn't others clamor to partner with *them* and, presumably, adapt to their styles and mannerisms? Here, it is good to recall a quote from Machiavelli:

> *There is nothing more difficult to take in hand, more perilous to conduct, or more uncertain in its success, than to take the lead in the introduction of a new order of things. For the reformer has enemies in all those who profit by the old order, and only lukewarm defenders in all those who would profit by the new order, this lukewarmness arising partly from fear of their adversaries . . . and partly from the incredulity of mankind, who do not truly believe in anything new until they have had actual experience of it.*
>
> —Niccolo Machiavelli

Unless they are desperate, potential partners for innovation—clients, sales people, and consultants—don't tend to seek out researchers and accommodate themselves to their peculiar ways. Added to this is the fact that IBM Research is an organizational wallflower. Sales organizations bring verbal finesse and revenue. Manufacturers have the goods. Accountants and lawyers always have partners, because no one has a choice.

For a research organization, value is often hidden. Revenue? Limited. Great patter? Only if you have a taste for the abstract and complex. And no one forces you to come to IBM Research. Researchers, on the other hand, are not a natural at putting themselves forward. While there are important exceptions, as individuals, researchers tend to be focused and cerebral. They are not slick sales people; they sometimes say things without finesse, and many times they dress differently.

When researchers first began working directly with clients, things didn't always work smoothly. They sometimes asked controversial questions, spoke unfamiliar languages and didn't always connect with client concerns. However, over the years, they have become far more business-savvy, tactful, and clear. Training has helped, as have FOAK experience, IBM Research Services engagements (described in Chapter 6, "The FOAK Process: Phases II and III"), and ISL interactions.

LESSON: *Invest in helping technical people develop people skills.*

Client Leads

With the advent of FOAK, IBM was in new territory. For the first time, researchers, in significant numbers, needed to work with IBM's client-facing teams (Client Leads) to identify potential partners, make an assessment, and then make the relationship work.

Usually, the IBM Client Lead is either the Sales & Distribution (S&D) Client Representative assigned to the account or a services Consultant for the specific industry, technology, or solution area being explored on the FOAK project. The Client Leads who first brought their clients to IBM Research were a mixed bag. Some seemed to think that researchers were salespeople with cool technologies. Others were desperate, hoping that a damaged relationship could be repaired by the allure of IBM Research and success in an area remote from their day-to-day travails.

FOAK came to see the contributions of an effective Client Lead as essential to the success of an innovation partnership. The perfect Client Lead has the following characteristics:

- **Knowledge:** The Client Lead knows the business and the people. He or she also understands the relevant problem or opportunity.

- **Perception:** In many cases, taking steps into new territory distorts the view with unexamined elements and inappropriate emphasis. The good Client Lead doesn't miss what is important and isn't distracted by that which is not.

- **Imagination:** Many client-facing people have an excellent grasp of what is. A Client Lead needs to reach beyond this and be able to envision, and even contribute to, a view of what might be.

- **Communications skills:** The Client Lead is often put into a position of explaining, justifying, and advocating on behalf of the project. He or she must support the IBM Project Team in setting client expectations correctly. This must be done effectively, with a keen understanding of the audience and the desired outcome of any communication. Just as important, the Client Lead must be an excellent listener.

- **Judgment:** The choices made in the course of innovation impact both the achievement of value and the sense of fairness and trust among team members. The decisions of the Client Lead must take both into account and create an environment that is consistent in the face of change.

- **Leadership:** The Client Lead needs to keep people engaged and on track while providing participants with a sense of responsibility.

- **Persistence:** As with all participants, the Client Lead must keep working in the face of adversity.

- **Integrity:** Since trust is so vital for an innovative enterprise, the Client Lead must be honest and consistent. He or she must keep commitments and make sure that participants get appropriate credit and benefits.

The absence of a strong leader in the Client Lead role makes it virtually impossible to engage a FOAK client. In most cases, when a FOAK project is terminated for lack of securing an appropriate client, it is because a strong Client Lead had not been identified and engaged in the client selection and contract negotiation process.

The Client

As mentioned, the Client Lead plays a critical role in collaborative innovation, and a part of this is getting a good understanding of the client. But FOAK is not for everyone. In practice, *many* IBM clients are not a good fit, and many of those who express interest are filtered out early in the process.

Of course, the development of contracts is a critical part of building a relationship with the client. Contract negotiation is covered in Chapter 11, "Contracts and Intellectual Property," but some danger signs are worth noting here:

- The client is reluctant to share the costs or even asks to be paid to participate.

- The client does not see value in "softer" outcomes, such as skills transfer or new knowledge.
- The client is uncomfortable with the measurements of success (and often is happy only with return on investment (ROI)).
- The area of investigation is not central to the client's concerns and interests.
- Presentations are met with skepticism and without enthusiasm and become a "hard sell."
- The people on the client side don't show up for meetings or don't have appropriate expertise or influence.

The best clients can provide evidence that supports the approach that will be taken for innovation. They already understand how the capabilities that might be developed on the FOAK project would meet real market needs, often making suggestions that make the work more relevant. They already appreciate the value of working with IBM Research and can easily identify related people and projects within their own organizations.

Client Sponsors

Having a committed and passionate sponsor for any project is important. Having one for an innovation project is absolutely necessary. The FOAK Client Sponsor needs to be in a position of authority in the client organization and have the credibility within that organization to persuade the business to assume some risk and participate in the FOAK project. He or she must be able to initially drive a positive FOAK decision and then promote the value of the project across the entire organization throughout the project's duration.

A FOAK Client Sponsor needs to recognize the value of early investment in emerging technologies and new approaches. They can aid the FOAK Joint Project Team in articulating the project's potential business impact and strategically position the organization to take swift action to deploy the FOAK concepts if they are proven.

FOAK projects, although practical and managed, do not have neat and pretty business cases with clearly defined ROIs. For instance, if a FOAK project goes through the standard procurement process for review and approval, it will fail to meet the financial criteria. An effective FOAK Client Sponsor will personally shepherd the FOAK project through an exception process to avoid procurement roadblocks, exhaustive business case reviews, and knotty terms and conditions (T&Cs),

which are nonstandard and will never fit into a standard procurement template.

In essence, on the client side, the Client Sponsor has three important jobs: He or she must

- Provide the go-ahead for the project and assume responsibility for it.
- Promote the value of the project continuously by articulating its business impact, defending it against inappropriate measures, and maintaining enthusiasm and focus.
- Ensure that successes are deployed effectively so that they can deliver the promised business impact.

Since real innovation is inherently risky, the Client Sponsor must have the position, credibility, and courage to take a chance on failure. The perfect Client Sponsor has the following characteristics:

- **The ability to say yes:** The intent must be approved, and resources must be made available.
- **Appreciation of the value of IBM Research:** If the benefit of working with researchers is not recognized, the value proposition (and commitment to the project) can be fatally weakened.
- **Commitment:** The unexpected can happen, and it isn't always pretty. Client Sponsors need to help keep things moving forward in the face of doubt and disappointment.
- **Integrity:** Trust is so central to innovation that any breach can be fatal.
- **Sphere of influence:** Projects gain attention from other organizations, and often these need to be brought on board or, if they are obstructive, neutralized.

Internal Partners

For the most part, IBM Research is not a client-facing organization. This means that for virtually every FOAK project, another organization is part of the partnership. This introduces a level of complication that other research organizations might not face. Even though two IBM organizations are both on the same "side," things can and do go wrong.

Partnering may occur between the various research labs. These relationships can stem from numerous sources, such as casual acquaintances, connections made by the IBM Research management team, and match-making by ISL staff members. This level of partnering is solely driven by the need for qualified skills and relevant IP.

Next, partnering occurs between the researchers and the client-facing team(s). Here the qualifying attributes are access to viable clients and commitment to securing signed agreements. The FOAK IBM Project Teams are under tremendous pressure to find and sign a qualified client partner within three months of project approval. (This is discussed in more detail in the section "Contract Negotiations.") So it is not surprising that they are looking for client-facing partners who have access to clients (preferably multiple) at the right levels in the organizations and that they are committed to making the FOAK contract signing a priority. The commitment to the contract signing is crucial. Some client-facing teams are focused on their annual sales objectives and are only minimally interested in investing time in negotiating a FOAK project that will not yield benefits until the longer term. These are not good candidates for internal partnerships.

Partnering also occurs with the services organization. They provide the project manager and any consulting and system integration services required for the FOAK project. Generally this level of partnering is driven by the client-facing team and is based on skills, availability, and client relationships. The connection generally is made by the resource manager of the specific services area.

Finally, partnering occurs with the catcher organization(s). Are they really interested in the project and its deliverables? Are they at the right level in the organization to allocate resources to the project when needed and make a commitment to commercializing the assets upon completion of the project? This level of partnering can be complex when multiple catching organizations are involved.

Sometimes, one of the partner organizations shifts its priorities, precluding the organization from being as fully involved in the FOAK project as it had planned. Other times, a change in executive leadership occurs, requiring a resell of the idea and confirmation of the business unit's commitment. And acquisitions can create a whole new set of issues, with new players who need to be explored and sold on the merits of the FOAK project.

It is just as important to set expectations and define roles, responsibilities, measures, and rights with an internal organization as it is with an external organization. A FOAK project has lots of internal partnerships.

> *LESSON: Because innovation may be difficult to explain, may pay off only in the long term, and may carry higher risk, setting expectations with partners is a critical success factor.*

Finding the Client

One of the strengths of the FOAK program has been identifying good partners. Naturally, these partners must be working in a relevant industry and have a budget, capabilities, and the ability to say yes. But that's not enough. Trust and real commitment are also essential to getting results that benefit both parties.

How do you find the right people to partner with? In FOAK, the IBM Project Team has the ultimate responsibility for finding an appropriate client. They take five basic approaches to do this:

- The character of the project itself points to a likely client set for the project. For instance, research related to processing large amounts of data from a video surveillance system suggested government and security applications.

- Market intelligence indicates an emerging need within a specific industry. This may, in fact, have been the starting point for the underlying research activities.

- Partners walk in the door. IBM showcases its emerging technologies. A great example of this is the exhibits within the ISLs. Many IBM clients come by to see what is new, to be inspired, and to gain insights. The connections made during these visits have led directly to FOAK partnerships.

- Client-facing IBMers, listening to their clients, tap researchers on the shoulder. In trying to find a solution to especially tricky problems, many of these clients find their way to the IBM FOAK Project Teams.

- Social networks are put into play. Typically, those involved in FOAK are well-connected, both internally and externally. They know how to get the word out that they are looking for collaborators, and they are effective at helping their colleagues recognize appropriate candidates.

Of course, although the IBM Project Team is responsible for finding potential partners, its members don't really stand alone. Client-facing

IBMers bring the ideas into conversations, as do executives. The members of the Industry Solution Board and the FOAK Board, as well as colleagues with FOAK experience, are also tapped to identify candidates.

Qualifying the Client Organization

Over the years, the FOAK IBM Project Teams have entered into literally hundreds of discussions with potential FOAK clients. Many of these discussions led the way to successful projects, but others never matured beyond the initial conversations or got caught up in the contract negotiation process. Through these interactions with clients from across the industries and around the world, the FOAK Program Management Team (PMT) has developed a set of key attributes that describe clients who have proven to be a good fit for the FOAK program. These attributes are shared with each of the FOAK IBM Project Teams during their project kickoff meetings to help guide and facilitate their client selection process.

Value Research

One of the client value propositions discussed earlier is the access to IBM's researchers and the skills transfer that takes place when working shoulder-to-shoulder, day-to-day with them. If a client does not perceive value in this basic design point or suggests payment for their participation in a FOAK project, the IBM Project Team either is dealing with a client that is not a fit for the FOAK program or is not dealing with the right level of Client Sponsor within the organization. Another bad sign is when a Client Sponsor gets pushback from someone (such as procurement or legal) and does not run interference for the project team. Conversely, executives who push for FOAK indicate that the team is in the right place.

> *LESSON: Hard-selling partners leads to bad partnerships.*

Moreover, when the IBM Project Team finds itself having to apply hard-sell techniques to gain a client's interest in doing a FOAK project, they are likely not dealing with an optimal partner. In fact, these types of reactions to the FOAK project are early warning signs of an uncommitted FOAK client. When a FOAK client is not fully committed to the project, the researchers struggle, and the value realized by both organizations is significantly diminished.

Alignment of Interests

For a FOAK project to be a success, both the potential FOAK client and IBM must have some level of alignment of interests in the FOAK project and its outcome. To determine alignment of interests, IBM Project Teams (and eventually the FOAK Board) look for either a direct match or an indication that this is something that would have been on the potential partner's list if it had been seen as viable. (And the IBM Project Team needs to be cautious if the client's list is highly tactical and they appear to see this as a demo project.)

Clients who have initiatives under way in areas consistent with or adjacent to the FOAK project's areas of focus are optimal because they have already established some level of priority in the area to be explored.

There is flexibility, however, in the level of alignment required between the client and the proposed FOAK project. During the client selection process, the researchers have early discussions with multiple potential FOAK clients. This makes it easier for them to confirm the market needs, validate their approaches, and identify some direction as to how and where to apply their technologies and thought leadership. Such knowledge helps them maximize the impact of their innovations in a client environment.

If an exact match is not found, but interests clearly align, the relationship is definitely worth pursuing. It can guide and direct the researchers to areas they had not considered that may actually be of greater value to the client and the marketplace. The Grid for Financial Services project (described in Chapter 2, "The FOAK Process: Phase I") and the Smart Customer Interaction project (described in Chapter 3, "How Ideas Take Shape") are good examples of this. In both instances, early client discussions helped the researchers redirect the focus of their work to applications that were of greater value to the client. This form of client interaction and immediate market requirements input is the essence of the FOAK program.

Although the program allows clients to redirect the FOAK research to address a pressing market need or opportunity, at times too much of a disconnect occurs for collaboration to take place. Ultimately, the researcher needs to be certain that his or her inventions will be fully tried and tested on the FOAK engagement with the selected client.

Potential for Impact

A FOAK project must align with the overall IT vision of the client and have a value proposition that drives real impact to at least one highly visible business unit. If the client does not view the FOAK project as a direct enabler of their overall business and IT vision, it is highly unlikely that the FOAK project will receive the right level of client focus.

Working with the FOAK Client Sponsor, the IBM Project Team needs to identify the specific business unit and process that will yield the greatest benefits from the FOAK innovations. This is a critical step in maximizing the FOAK project's impact, gaining visibility across the organization, and securing broader acceptance of the resulting solution.

Perhaps the strongest indication of real impact for the client is how they play it back to their business unit. For example, at a large retailer the FOAK Client Sponsor convened a two-day workshop with the specific objective of homing in on the right process to apply an innovative new approach to rapidly transform and deploy business processes called Model-Driven Business Transformation (MDBT). As a result, they prioritized their collaborative flow forecasting process—a highly visible function that touched many people—to be the focus of the FOAK project. The project went on to be widely successful by reducing the application development time by an estimated two-thirds and had visibility throughout the executive suite.

Having an early, open dialog with the FOAK Client Sponsor is key. The Client Sponsor can help determine that the FOAK project is well grounded in a business unit that can recognize the project's value and become an advocate for broader deployment across the enterprise.

Working Relationship

A solid working relationship is fundamental, and FOAK experience shows that it directly correlates to the level of value realized by both companies on a FOAK project. Clients who truly view IBM as their partner and have an existing relationship based on mutual trust generally are the best FOAK clients.

It is IBM's intent when entering into FOAK engagements to find ways to commercialize the assets tested on the projects. But since there is no way to know for sure the what, when, or how until after the work has been completed, the relationship needs to fortify the agreements. Clients who understand this and view IBM as their trusted partner are energized by the notion of being first and are willing to assume the associated risks along with IBM. A base level of mutual trust and partnership must exist.

Contract Negotiations

The FOAK program uses nonstandard IBM T&Cs. These always require detailed discussions and negotiations to determine that all parties understand and agree to the parameters that bound the project execution and deliverables before any collaboration can take place between the two companies. Since most FOAK projects last only one year, the time invested in identifying and securing the right client needs to be well spent.

A client who historically has had a prolonged contract signing process is likely not to be the best FOAK partner due to the program's carefully managed project schedules. For example, during negotiations with a large global financial services firm, the contract process began to take an inordinate amount of time. During an internal IBM review of the situation, one of the IBM lawyers noted that IBM had a history of long and drawn-out contract negotiations with the client. Had the IBM Project Team known this earlier, they would have gone after a different candidate client. Additionally, clients who cannot work with contracts that use nonstandard IBM T&Cs may not be a good fit for FOAK either. They should be avoided until the assets are a bit more mature and can be made available using more standard IBM terms.

Geographic Location

IBM has research labs in eight locations: New York, Almaden, Austin, Beijing, Zurich, Haifa, Delhi, and Tokyo. Since the sun never sets on IBM Research, it is common practice on internal projects for the researchers to collaborate across geographies, time zones, and languages. This capability extends itself to the FOAK projects. It is not uncommon for some researchers on a FOAK project to be located outside the external client's geography. In some instances, the entire IBM Project Team is located remotely from the client.

Many organizations have concerns about working with virtual teams and working across different time zones. Here, IBM may be different. Distance, and differences in time zones and languages, do complicate the process. Engaging a FOAK client in the same geography as the primary Research Team performing the FOAK project work is desirable and facilitates the project. But teaming across geographies, time zones, and cultures has been handled effectively on many FOAK projects, so being within the same geography is not a requirement of the FOAK program.

Frequent communication has enabled teams working across different regions to succeed. Regularly scheduled project checkpoints and, where possible, face-to-face meetings at key milestones—such as project kick-off, implementation, training, and executive reviews—have helped. In situations where a project member (usually the project manager) was local to the client, he or she served as the client interface and ensured that all client input was communicated back to the remote IBM Project Team members. In situations where there was no IBM Project Team member in the client's locale, the daily interface to the client was either the Client Lead or the Consultant. And, of course, plenty of e-mails were exchanged and conference calls held.

Confining the FOAK client selection process to the immediate research lab geography can actually prevent an IBM FOAK Project Team from successfully engaging a client and even force a FOAK project into early termination. Taking a global view is a far more effective approach.

Skills and Expertise

The FOAK Proposal Team knows what skills are needed from both IBM and the client to pave the way to a successful FOAK project. Therefore, they actively seek clients with skills in the areas most critical to the FOAK project. For example, one FOAK IBM Project Team might be looking for Java resources, another may be interested in Linux skills, and still other FOAK IBM Project Teams may be looking for totally different sets of skills from their FOAK clients. However, in many cases, the technologies are so new that the skills required cannot be realistically found at a client. In these situations, the researchers look for a base set of skills that would lend themselves to those required by the FOAK project in the hope of extending and enhancing them throughout the FOAK project.

LESSON: While not every skill may be available, basic resources and capabilities should be in place before an innovation project begins.

Since IBM is looking for daily, direct client input throughout the entire FOAK project, access to the right expertise (business and IT) in the client organization is fundamental. In the past, many FOAK projects suffered from clients reprioritizing human resources not long after the projects began. This left IBM researchers literally working on FOAK projects by themselves, and it minimized the value of the project to both the client and IBM.

Domain experts and knowledge of the client's IT systems and processes are key ingredients of a successful FOAK project. On one FOAK project, the lack of availability of the client's domain experts and annotated data delayed the FOAK project. The client acknowledged their impact on the FOAK project schedule, and a project extension to the contract funded by the client had to be negotiated. The FOAK project was successfully completed, as was a subsequent follow-on services engagement. Today, all FOAK projects have a services Statement of Work (SOW), which specifically includes timely access to experts as a standard term.

Installed Platforms

To facilitate the partnership, each FOAK project requires a specific IT environment at the client location. Finding a client who already has an installed IT environment that is similar to that of the proposed FOAK project is yet another consideration when searching for the optimal FOAK client. If the FOAK IBM Project Team is lucky enough to identify a FOAK client with not only the appropriate business environment but also the required IT platforms already installed, they can dramatically accelerate their FOAK project schedules by avoiding the time required to install and customize new hardware and software and training the clients on new platforms.

At times, however, a FOAK project may be an incentive for a client to move to an IBM platform. Generally, to be chosen for FOAK, these clients must

- Be an exact match on the business side.
- Be viewed as strategic to IBM.
- Have the right level of line of business and IT sponsorship.
- Have brand name recognition that could significantly add value in the marketplace as a FOAK reference.

This compensates for the expected project delays in migrating the client's platforms and training their staff on the FOAK project.

Client Reference and Investment

References are a critical deliverable of the FOAK program. FOAK clients must be willing to be a reference upon completion of a successful FOAK project in order to be selected. This is one of the terms of the FOAK contractual agreement between the two companies. The extent of the reference is negotiated during the contracts and negotiation process to meet the combined needs of both organizations. The various levels of client references are described in Chapter 6 in the section "Create Joint Press Publicity."

In addition, as stated earlier in this chapter, for a client to be a good candidate for a FOAK partnership, the organization must be willing to financially invest in the necessary hardware, software, and services to enable it to actively participate in the project.

The Process of Partnering

The actual process of partnering in any context—be it business, community, government, or just plain ordinary people—is never easy to define, much less document. Partnering is more art than science, more passion than intellect, and, ideally, more oriented toward giving than getting. Like a good marriage, it begins with knowing the fundamental values, characteristics, and goals of each partner.

FOAK is no different. As mentioned earlier, each IBM Project Team is given guidance on how to select a client during the internal project kickoff meeting using the criteria just mentioned. In essence, these are the characteristics that work well based on IBM's values, characteristics, and goals. (Whether they work well for your organization and your partners depends on your own organization's culture and needs.)

The FOAK IBM Project Teams are also provided with a summary of the FOAK T&Cs and a presentation template for use in setting client expectations. But in the end, the process of establishing partnerships lies in the hands of all the FOAK Joint Project Team members, because partnerships are needed across all levels in both organizations in order to ensure success.

With more than 200 projects completed with organizations of all sizes and shapes, one might wonder how the FOAK program can productively work across such diverse environments. FOAK doesn't employ any special algorithm to manage these partnerships. But IBM's heritage has diversity at its roots. The following IBM Workforce Diversity

Imperatives demonstrate the broad reach and range of our diversity programs:

- Global marketplace
- Commitment to equal opportunity
- Advancement of women
- Diversity of leadership team
- Cultural awareness/acceptance
    - Ethnic minorities
    - Multilingualism
    - Individual differences

- Integrating the workplace and the marketplace
    - People with disabilities
    - Gay, lesbian, bisexual, transgender

- Work/life balance
    - Culture
    - Flexibility
    - Dependent care

This culture of diversity and the globalization of IBM and its clients has helped the FOAK program operate across industry and geographic boundaries for years. Of course, language issues arise (both business and cultural), and collaborations need to be scheduled around multiple time zones, but these are not seen as showstoppers or even major obstacles. Despite challenges, the teams get the job done.

> **LESSON:** *Full access to talent and diverse perspectives is contingent upon having a welcoming culture.*

One recent FOAK project brought together a client from Korea and IBM researchers from the Haifa Research Lab. The Joint Project Team set out to employ a standard modeling language to enable consumer electronics companies to integrate smarter processes into their development cycle. The goal was to accelerate the time-to-market for new products while lowering software development costs.

The lead researcher, Julia Rubin, commented, "All of us found it fascinating to exchange different cultural ways. We enjoyed a complete sharing of knowledge. They brought know-how about the development process for manufacturing actual consumer products, and we brought a strong background in model-driven research. The combination gave both parties a lot of insight into how things work and which directions would be optimal for our solution."

Value Propositions for the Program's Stakeholders

One of the cornerstones of a good partnership is ensuring that there is a value proposition that resonates well with each partner. Some of the FOAK value propositions, such as mindshare (how a company is viewed in its chosen markets), are shared between the client and IBM. Others, such as competitive advantage and growth, may differ for each party, according to how they are put into practice. In fact, the main focus may be entirely different for each party. A client may want to be an early market adopter, while IBM may want the FOAK project to validate market requirements. The value propositions at the project level are discussed in Chapter 3, but let's look at the value propositions of the FOAK program for each party more closely here.

The Value of FOAK to Clients

The range of value for clients participating in FOAK projects is broad. Some clients have a specific business challenge that they are struggling with, and submitting product requirements to IBM is their main driver of value. Other clients feel competitive pressures and are seeking game-changing plays through an early market adopter position. Still others are looking for ways to experiment with innovations as part of their ongoing strategic planning cycle, and being a FOAK partner affords them that opportunity.

Early Market Adopter Advantage
Through early, firsthand experiences with new technologies and business models, clients are better positioned to exploit an early market adopter advantage. This position can enable an enterprise to find new,

more efficient ways of performing core tasks or drive fundamental changes that enable them to enter or create new markets that drive new growth.

Knowledge Transfer

The daily interaction between the client's personnel and IBM's researchers doesn't just facilitate the transfer of valuable skills and knowledge. It also establishes relationships and networks that can be leveraged well beyond the FOAK project. These relationships can lead to collaboration in new areas of technology and business innovation. They also can facilitate the extension of the existing FOAK project innovations into totally new areas of the business. For other clients, the appeal of FOAK is the experience, discipline, structure, and leadership perspective that IBM can bring to the partnership.

Influence on Product Directions

Another aspect of the FOAK client value proposition is the ability of clients to influence IBM's products. Although IBM makes no commitment to a commercialized product as a result of a FOAK project, IBM's intent is clearly to gather market requirements, test the market's readiness, and feed the information, proven assets, and know-how back into the IBM product-planning process. Many clients see value in having their business needs directly influence IBM's product strategies and plans. The FOAK program provides this opportunity.

Contained Investment

The Foak Program's investment funding model eases the financial burden for clients and encourages them to explore new and emerging areas of technology that they might not otherwise have considered. FOAK clients gain early access to potentially game-changing technologies and approaches without having to bear the full financial responsibility traditionally associated with performing experimental work. The client's financial commitment to a FOAK project varies, based on the scope of the specific project. The client is responsible for funding the hardware, software, and services required to complete the project. IBM funds the research labor only. (This is discussed in Chapter 11.)

Creating Mindshare

With the heightened buzz in the marketplace around innovation, more and more companies are looking for ways to differentiate themselves as innovators with their partners and customers. A joint press release or cosponsored media event around a FOAK project provides a great platform for gaining market recognition as an innovator.

Business Impact

Perhaps the greatest value realized by FOAK clients is the business impact a project has on their operations and markets. The business impact of FOAK projects goes well beyond information technology (IT) innovation of making things go faster, adding more resiliency, or reducing the total cost of ownership. They extend into true line-of-business impact statements that help bridge the gap in value between IT and business. Here are some examples:

- Going live with eight major banking applications in just six months, leveraging IBM middleware and realizing a 30% productivity improvement at a large bank
- Achieving a 13-fold improvement in the processing speeds for a 10,000-simulation scenario and reducing the processing time from 10 hours to just 44 minutes at an insurance industry research center
- Realizing a 10% savings in energy costs by using 3-D images of datacenters to pinpoint hot spots, air leakage, and other inefficiencies
- Achieving a 21-fold improvement in the volume of data consumed by financial trading systems

Because the FOAK portfolio of investments aims to explore new ideas across a varied spectrum, the business impact for each client that participates in the FOAK program also varies widely. Overall, although the technical accomplishments are real, it is the business impact that persuades clients to partner on FOAK projects.

LESSON: For each partner, identify and articulate compelling business reasons to participate.

The Value of FOAK to IBM

For IBM, the value of the FOAK program goes well beyond the obvious enhancements to its existing core technologies or the delivery of new technologies to the marketplace. It extends to the acceleration of the solution sales process and to providing powerful headlights into emerging markets and creating valuable mindshare for the IBM Corporation.

Rich Portfolio of Intellectual Property

At the conclusion of each FOAK project, IBM has a collection of tried and tested IP at various states of maturity. That collection of IP spans all industries, geographies, and areas of technology and solutions. Some of the IP is laser-focused on a single industry business process or problem. One example is intelligent oil fields for chemicals and petroleum, which provided data analytics software for intelligent well data analysis. Other IP applies across multiple industries, such as the Contact Agent Buddies (CABs) project described in Chapter 2. The types of IP vary from algorithms, to business models, to connector code, to analytic engines, to language translators and speech interfaces and beyond. As previously mentioned, the objective is to create first-of-a-kind, not one-of-a-kind, solutions. Thus, it is critical when defining a project's scope that the IP is relevant enough to have impact and reusability beyond the FOAK client.

Validated Market Requirements

Most companies, whether they are product- or service-oriented, agree that testing new offerings in the marketplace is vital to delivering successful offerings. FOAK projects put innovations into real environments where they face realistic demands for performance, integration, and realization of value. They provide a venue for deep understanding of the actual needs of clients and parameters of success in the marketplace.

Industry Experience

Working in a lab environment enables the researchers to be headsdown and focused. Working on a FOAK project with a client enables the researchers to be heads-up and market-focused. This provides the researchers with valuable experience in how a client might actually apply their inventions to business.

In other IBM programs, a researcher may work on projects that are in direct response to requirements set forth by the IBM brands. These innovations generally make their way into product and service offerings, because they are directly commissioned by the brand and planned for within their specific strategic plans. In such instances, although the inventions are delivered to the market, the researchers generally do not get direct insight into how the clients are employing them to improve their businesses.

By contrast, in the FOAK model, the researchers gain a firsthand view of how their invention can impact a business. This fuels a sense of pride as the researchers see clients excited about their work and eager to embrace it. Moreover, when the results of their FOAK projects are on display at the ISLs or included in press and media coverage, it provides the researchers with a whole new appreciation of their work and capabilities. These FOAK experiences and the industry knowledge gained can then be leveraged by the researchers on other projects. More importantly, the researchers can inject a more market-driven approach into their future research assignments.

Accelerating and Influencing Solution Sales

As mentioned earlier, the FOAK program advances the Industry Teams' ability to deliver new solutions to the marketplace. FOAK accelerates the overall solutions development and sales process. In addition, the base components of the FOAK prototypes and the know-how can be reused to jumpstart the development of a new solution or enhance an existing solution to be sold to multiple follow-on clients. Using the FOAK IP as the core, hardware, software, and services can be wrapped around it to build out an end-to-end solution.

For example, the Advanced Analytics Platform for Telcos and Cables Operators FOAK delivered an analytics system that provides end-to-end visibility of key services offered to customers of telecommunications and cable operators. It accomplished this by ingesting and correlating event data from various sources in the network, including applications, networks, servers, hardware devices, third-party monitoring applications, and problem management and tracking systems. The result was faster problem resolution, reduced service downtime, and improved revenue through customer retention.

Today, the platform is delivered to clients as a service offering and includes service models, analytics rules, and service model consulting. The FOAK client proof points, which are focused on communications industry concerns, present tangible examples of how a technology can reduce operational costs, provide critical service assurance, and increase revenue through customer retention. FOAK results like these provide salespeople with the kind of references that help close deals.

Insights into Emerging Markets

Over the years, the FOAK portfolio has seen a collection of good ideas with successfully completed FOAK projects fail to evolve into tangible products due to a lack of market interest and readiness to accept them. In some instances, these innovations were mothballed and then unwrapped when the market developed an appetite for them years later. In other instances, the IP is still on the shelf waiting. The FOAK portfolio contains several examples of projects attempting to drive innovation into marketplaces not yet ready to accept them or marketplaces that have not yet come to fruition.

FOAK validates market requirements, but collecting these requirements is only half of the story. The market needs to be *ready* to accept and embrace the new innovations as well. This lesson has been hard-won.

One of the hidden value propositions of the FOAK program for IBM is the valuable headlights it provides into new- and emerging-market opportunities. Gaining early experiences and developing thought leadership that can be leveraged once new markets emerge provides IBM with a first market adopter advantage, just as it does for clients.

The FOAK program is a valuable source of market input for IBM Research to consider when validating and prioritizing inventions from its eight worldwide labs. Market data gathered from the FOAK program can help place inventions on a timeline for possible market adoption and aid IBM Research in making investment trade-off decisions.

Creating Mindshare

Finally, the value of the mindshare created by the program cannot be overstated. Mindshare translates into favorable decisions by clients, influence in market direction, and brand value. Whether it is through showcasing the FOAK prototypes at one of the ISLs, collaborating on joint press releases with clients, providing demonstrations at shareholder meetings, or featuring FOAK projects in IBM's annual reports, the marketplace has a thirst for innovation and wants to learn how to harness it to gain market leadership. The FOAK program is a rich source of examples for the IBM Corporation.

Summary

The FOAK client selection process is the single most critical component of the FOAK program. It is also the most time-consuming activity of the FOAK process. The search for good innovation partners is complicated and difficult, but it is essential. Having the right people with the right skills and characteristics is required. The needs of the partnering organizations must be clear and complementary. The climate must be positive, and all sides must accept risk and uncertainty. If any of these are missing, the project undertaken may be of limited success or even an outright failure.

Some challenges can be overcome and even lead to greater success. Although there are advantages to having all the participants in the same geographic region, accessing talent worldwide has created unexpected opportunities. In general, a common IT platform enables a faster start and quicker execution of a project, but FOAK projects can also catalyze the building of more appropriate and effective platforms for clients. And while it is always prudent to identify the availability of all essential skills and resources at the beginning of a conventional project, FOAK projects can proceed where the exact needs aren't completely known and where the people involved, by necessity, grow and develop their capabilities.

Of course, the project itself must be aligned with real business value and must be of the appropriate scale. In fact, much of the success of the FOAK program is contingent upon project selection. The process both creates competition that causes the best projects to rise to the top and provides an opportunity for learning that helps naïve innovators become more effective. This is the subject of Chapter 5, "Choosing the Best Projects."

5

Choosing the Best Projects

Since the FOAK program funds only 20 to 25 new projects each year, it is extremely competitive and has an investment strategy that is carefully monitored and managed (but dynamic, based on changing marketplace needs). Although the FOAK program aims to be light on process, it needs structure to make the most of its limited resources.

Throughout the FOAK program's history, its leadership (the FOAK Board and its supporting Program Management Team (PMT)) has needed to balance process and discipline with creativity and entrepreneurship. Too much process could discourage creativity and deter the researchers from participating in the program. Proposals that have made it through the Industry Research Relationship Manager (RRM), Industry Solution Board, and FOAK PMT filters finally make their way to the FOAK Board for review and a decision on approval (or rejection). This chapter discusses how the FOAK Board applies an IBM-wide perspective and prioritizes the proposals submitted by using a practical set of selection criteria.

FOAK Board Responsibilities

The primary obligation of the FOAK Board is to ensure that proposals have the elements that lead to success:

- A new idea that is mature enough to test in the real world
- Team members who are committed and capable
- A plan that is doable within the time and funding limits of scope
- Support (including a catcher) and a strategic outlook that will encourage adoption
- Potential clients that show the characteristics of good partners

But the Board is more than just one more checkpoint in the process. The FOAK Board has fiscal responsibility and makes decisions regarding funding. In addition, the FOAK Board is a source of suggestions on content and design that can improve the probability of success and increase the project's ultimate value.

With all this in mind, the FOAK Board is designed to include participants who represent the intellectual, strategic, business, and political perspectives of the key stakeholders.

The FOAK Board has 11 seats, with a chair from the Sales & Distribution (S&D) organization. Three seats are allocated to each of the funding organizations (Research and S&D), and one seat is allocated to each of the following business units: Corporate Strategy, Global Business Services (GBS), Software Group (SWG), Global Technology Services (GTS), and Systems Technology Group (STG). This executive team meets quarterly to review and approve FOAK proposals. Here is a sampling of the titles of executives who have occupied FOAK Board seats over the last few years:

- Vice President, Industry Solutions and Emerging Business Opportunities, Research
- Director, China Research Lab
- Director, Zurich Research Lab
- Vice President, Marketing, Industrial Sector, S&D
- Vice President, Chief Technology Office, Distribution Sector S&D
- Vice President, Strategy, S&D

- Vice President, Emerging Business Opportunities, Corporate Strategy
- Vice President, Infrastructure Solutions, STG
- Vice President, Infrastructure Access Architecture, GTS
- Vice President, Industry Solutions, SWG
- Vice President, Business Solutions, GBS

As is apparent, the representation on the FOAK Board reflects both experience in thinking about technology and in facing the market realities of client-facing organizations. This balances the projects' intellectual integrity so that they have research value while creating natural advocates (of both FOAK and specific projects) among those who deliver products and services.

As with other aspects of FOAK, the passion of participants is important. It's worth noting that all the Board members are volunteers. What do they get out of it? For the executives occupying the FOAK Board seats, the experience provides an opportunity to influence and shape the next generation of IBM offerings. Some Board members will directly impact their business units, of course, but for these executives, it is more important that the investments drive value for the IBM Corporation as a whole.

With FOAK, they can invest one day each quarter hearing innovative new ideas, learning about industry pain points and opportunities, aiding Proposal Teams in making connections within and outside their business units, and networking with their colleagues from across the business. Just as the FOAK projects provide IBM's clients with an opportunity to explore innovations beyond day-to-day solutions, the FOAK Board gives IBM executives the chance to also explore the innovations outside their immediate business units.

Here are some characteristics of an optimal FOAK Board member:

- **Committed:** Willing to spend the necessary time and energy to help the FOAK program and individual projects that face challenges
- **Well connected:** Able to talk to executives and clients who are needed to promote success in projects and the program
- **Forward-thinking:** Able to imagine and give priority to possibilities beyond the next few quarters
- **Has a broad perspective:** Aware of different industries, perspectives, cultures, and disciplines
- **Occupies an influential position:** Can lend prestige to FOAK and encourage cooperation within their organizations

- **Willing to guide struggling teams when needed:** Has a bent toward mentoring and an understanding of the educational role of the FOAK program
- **Passionate:** Conveys enthusiasm and acts with courage

The appeal of FOAK Board membership is such that there never has been a lack of volunteers to fill the positions. FOAK Board members demonstrate their commitment through active involvement in reading documentation, working with the PMT, and engaging with those who are involved in proposals and projects. However, it is not surprising that people with these qualifications sometimes have trouble finding time to serve. Occasionally, a Board member is gently asked to vacate his or her seat due to lack of attendance at the meetings. Although this is a somewhat difficult conversation to have, they always seem to understand and agree with the decision.

The players change not because of fixed terms but because, over time, the executive FOAK Board members have a shift in responsibilities or move on to pursue new career opportunities. Seats vacated by the industry marketing and research labs rotate across the industries and research labs, respectively. This rotation not only ensures that the various industries and labs have the opportunity to participate in the FOAK investment decision process, but it also injects broader insights into the program.

FOAK Board Meetings

FOAK Board meetings are convened once a quarter and are put on the calendar in December of the prior year. This gives sufficient advance notice to those submitting FOAK proposals, as well as the FOAK Board members. FOAK Proposal Teams must send a proposal outline (a short paragraph describing their motivation for the project, how IBM Research can participate, the planned approach, and deliverables) to the FOAK PMT four weeks before the Board meeting. (Refer to Figure 2.4 for an example of a FOAK outline.) This enables the FOAK PMT to manage the pipeline of proposals and plan the FOAK Board meeting agendas.

The actual proposals are not due until two weeks prior to the FOAK Board meeting. They are posted in a FOAK Board "team room." This is a self-service computer network tool that allows colleagues, often in different locations, to share and organize ideas, documents, and tasks in one place. This allows adequate time for the FOAK Board members to read the proposals. Proposal Teams who are late in delivering their proposals run the risk that the FOAK Board members won't read their proposals before the meeting.

A vital part of assessing proposals is a packet of letters supporting the idea. The Proposal Team solicits these letters from key stakeholders, including potential catchers, relevant executives, and subject matter experts. The ideal support letter has three elements:

- An indication of the innovation's potential and value
- Expressions of enthusiasm and a willingness to help realize the value
- An indication of how the innovation would fit within the current offerings and/or strategy

Since FOAK Board members can't be expected to have a 360-degree view of every proposal, the letters help broaden their view and provide new perspectives. Not incidentally, they also are an important mechanism for the Proposal Team to validate and socialize their ideas.

Often, no individual letter has all the elements of a perfect recommendation. Instead, the package of letters comes together to demonstrate each element and overall support for the proposal. Figure 5.1 shows an example of a good support letter. It is based on a real letter, but the data and names have been changed.

> *LESSON: Decision makers should get input from other experts and stakeholders, both for the value of a broader view and for creating opportunities to socializing an innovation.*

A typical FOAK Board meeting agenda begins with a 30- to 60-minute closed business meeting. Here, the FOAK Board receives updates on any program news and issues, as well as a view of current available funding and the funding requests for each new proposal. Next, the Proposal Teams make their presentations. Generally, eight to ten projects are on the agenda. When scheduling the proposal presentations, the FOAK PMT tries to accommodate time zones (sometimes this means starting the meeting with a proposal from Japan, for example, even before the business session) and the natural grouping of proposals by industries.

To: The FOAK Board,

This note is to indicate my enthusiastic support for the FOAK proposal titled "Management of Real-Time, Sensor-Based Data for Energy Systems," or "SeeAll, TellAll."

Within the petroleum industry, the topic of real-time data has been identified as one of strategic importance to our clients and to our solution development. Deepening the solution related to this area will provide a chance to differentiate IBM with energy industry clients by offering them visibility to the status of feedstocks and safety systems.
Today there is:

- Limited real-time data visibility due to a lack of data from dependable sensing devices

- Inadequate analytical tools to analyze the available data

- Recognition by leading manufacturers of the importance of providing value-added insights and actions that drive efficiencies and reduce hazards

The approach of the proposed FOAK is to help clients develop their agility using feedstock and production signals, by achieving full visibility from the final product back to the wellhead. The petroleum industry has a current and growing need for this solution, as evidenced by a March 2008 BVI Study that revealed the following proof points:

- 64% of clients are looking for ways to boost efficiency.

- 45% of clients plan to spend more than $70 million within the next five years on better sensing and real-time data management.

Worldwide, government regulations for better safety standards are creating requirements for more real-time monitoring of systems. Our need to develop this solution in a timely manner is imperative, since competition is growing quickly. For example, other service providers are currently doing the following:

- Grasshopper Perceptions has launched an initiative to shrink a suite of sensors and improve reliability by adopting advanced networking strategies.

- OBoy Detection has presented a strategic pathway that is centered around the processing of real-time data for the manufacturing industry.

- Potential Energy Advisors recently announced that it was teaming with Your Own Devices to provide a real-time solution for the petroleum industry.

We have also identified three clients–Ice Cap Energy, Process Clean, and Dig Deep Petroleum–that are reasonable targets for partnering with our FOAK project. Note that we are already working on a proof of concept, based on a data feed from Dig Deep Petroleum, that has provided much insight into and experience with the design requirements.

In summary, I support the "SeeAll, TellAll" FOAK proposal, and I am excited about the opportunity to partner with the IBM Research division on this important project. We foresee a solution that will have broad appeal for petroleum industry clients and related manufacturers.

Signed: Jerry Carboni, Industry General Manager, petroleum industry

Figure 5.1   Sample FOAK project support letter

The PMT allocates time on each FOAK Board agenda to present the results of at least one completed FOAK project to the FOAK Board. This gives the FOAK Board the opportunity to actually see how their investment decisions impacted both the client and IBM and gives them input into the lessons learned by the FOAK IBM Project Teams. It also affords the FOAK IBM Project Team the opportunity to thank the Board for their support and, if necessary, ask for their assistance in transferring the assets since each IBM brand is represented on the FOAK Board.

> **LESSON:** *Don't limit feedback just to data; tell decision makers the stories.*

During the meeting, the FOAK Board deliberates on two levels. First, a preliminary discussion of the proposals takes place. This is done to capture FOAK Board members' reactions to the proposals while they are still fresh in their minds and to help manage time on the agenda. The second level of deliberations takes place at the end of the day. Here there are deeper discussions of each proposal.

Selection Criteria

The FOAK Board learned the hard way that traditional business approaches to project selection were counterproductive. Originally, FOAK Proposal Teams were expected to use complex proposal templates that contained detailed business cases with broad market opportunity statements and complicated return on investment (ROI) analyses. The Proposal Teams would spend hours searching for data to create and justify market opportunity statements for emerging technologies and solutions that didn't have well-defined or existing marketplaces to pull data from. Often, there was really no market data for them to base their cases on, so Creative Proposal Teams basically invented their data and ROIs to fulfill the template requirement. In fact, during one FOAK Board meeting, two FOAK Proposal Teams submitted the exact same market opportunity data for two totally different markets because the teams were in essence reusing the same previously edited FOAK proposal template.

FLY ON THE WALL

Twenty minutes of preparation has occurred: greetings, coffee, testing the phone and Internet connections. Everyone is ready. Agendas are at hand, pens poised. A map of Beijing, marked with retail outlets, is on the projector. The meeting begins on time with a greeting to researchers in China.

The Chinese barely introduce the project before they begin a demonstration. Board meetings include successes. In this case, scads of data is presented to support decisions on store locations. As the demo proceeds, you can hear a child in the background. It is evening in China; one researcher is finishing a long day.

After brief exchanges on progress toward adoption of the technology, the call ends. The meeting moves to the introduction of new Board members. This would have been the starting point, but people in faraway time zones get first consideration.

This is a private session, and the Board takes on challenging issues: executive support, streamlining terms and conditions (T&Cs), measurements, and publicity. They run through the agenda, setting up the day's work—choosing projects.

The first Proposal Team is called in. They begin their introduction, working from standardized charts, already loaded. The clock is ticking, and the presenter moves quickly. Nonetheless, questions fly at him each time he takes a breath:

- How different is this from what's being done now?
- The list of catchers is long. Are these people committed?
- This feels more like a development project. Is it really new?

One Board member suggests that this project needs rightsizing. The Proposal Team gets suggestions on others to talk to. There are questions about the supporting letters, which could be stronger. Then "thank you."

Grouping proposals facilitates comparison. We are now looking at the first, in healthcare. The presentation follows the same pattern, except that the leader is in Haifa.

- Is the proposed catching organization really where the assets are likely to end up?

- Are the right people on the team?
- How does the business model work?

Board members provide advice on how to firm up catcher relationships.

The next Proposal Team seems confident. This is their second shot, a "comeback." The trip through their charts is rapid, with little discussion. The time is spent examining their comeback answers. The Board members seem excited. After probing other options, the Proposal Team is dismissed.

Two more proposals are presented, and then lunch. Normal chitchat takes place as members fill their plates, but it is back to business when they sit down. The discussion isn't formal, but all the talk is about the morning's presentations. Some Board members refer to their Project Selection Worksheet between bites.

Three hours later, just one more proposal is left before the Board goes into closed session. The discussion is businesslike, but passionate:

- "I like the broad, global potential."
- "Shouldn't Software Group just do this themselves?"
- "These guys have a terrific road map."
- "They can do it, but the assets will be orphaned."
- "Did *anybody* like this proposal?"

Some proposals are obviously winners. Others are intriguing. The biggest debate is about which to ask for comebacks on. And what are the comeback questions?

Deliberations last an hour. Some members rush off, but others linger. Their conversations are one part emotional response to the proposals and one part catching up with friends. They'll see each other again in a few months. It's already on their calendars.

During the FOAK program's transformation in 2001 (discussed in Chapter 1, "A Program That Works"), the FOAK Board decided it would be far more productive for the Proposal Teams to focus their energies on addressing less complex but more thoughtful criteria. Today, the FOAK Board members are given a Project Selection Worksheet, shown in Figure 5.2. It is essentially a matrix with each proposal down the left side of the page and the selection criteria across the top. It is basic, but it's a handy tool for the FOAK Board members to keep track of their thoughts on each proposal.

Project Selection Worksheet

Project Proposal	Strategic Fit	Content	Market Planning	Innovation	Path to Market	Asset Catchers	Deliverables
E&U: Smart Interaction (5.5 Head Count)							
Healthcare Biomarker (~5 Head Count)							
Healthcare Business Integrity (4 Head Count)							
Govt Contextual Mashup (5 Head Count)							
Telco: Intelligence for Telcos (4 Head Count)							

Figure 5.2 Project Selection Worksheet

Going through the chart column by column may provide a sense of what FOAK Board members are focused on during their approval meetings. It also reflects many of the program's hard-won lessons.

Strategic Fit

When the FOAK Board evaluates a proposal's strategic fit, it must do so from multiple points of view. First, they look at how the FOAK proposal fits within the industry's overall solution strategy:

- Does it fill a gap or provide an extension to an existing solution that will differentiate IBM in the marketplace?
- Does it resonate with a priority industry, or will it serve multiple industries?
- How serious is the Industry Solution Board?
- How committed are they to funding the asset commercialization of the proposed FOAK deliverables? Will they actively promote the project and its results to the sales teams to drive reuse?

■ Is there clear evidence of how the FOAK project will enhance and extend the industry's portfolio?

Next, how does the FOAK proposal fit within the industry's point of view? Each industry within IBM has a formal point of view that outlines a three- to ten-year industry outlook highlighting key business trends and imperatives, along with the potential implications to businesses. These points of view, created by IBM's Institute for Business Value (the research arm of IBM services—for more information, go to www-935. ibm.com/services/us/gbs/bus/html/bcs_whatwethink.html), provide both IBM and its clients with a foundation on which to build action-oriented road maps. For example, telecommunications faces a challenge in satisfying consumers with greater demands for content creation. Its road map includes details of the emerging consumer segments and how they make their buying decisions.

The strategic fit extends to the capabilities and qualifications of the proposed membership of the IBM Project Team. Do they have a FOAK track record? Can they really do what is being proposed? It's not surprising that proposals without a clear strategic fit are generally winnowed out of the process quickly and many times don't even make it to the FOAK Board.

Of course, a corporation like IBM has room for outliers. These are clever projects that do not fit the strategic plan but offer potential for future value. IBM continuously probes the future in many ways. Research projects, collaborations with academia, and grassroots projects with no formal support (but lots of encouragement) are some ways in which more speculative and curiosity-based initiatives are explored. These endeavors are appropriate and healthy for the IBM organization, but FOAK is not a proper home for them.

Content

Since FOAK proposals span a broad set of client challenges, opportunities, and industries, proposal content varies widely. Examples include new methodologies and approaches, software components, application programming interfaces, business and IT tooling, reengineered processes, and algorithms. When reviewing proposals, the FOAK Board looks at how broad and deep the content is to determine if there is enough value to have a significant impact for IBM and the client. For example, in response to one FOAK proposal that wasn't funded, the FOAK Board stated, "We believe that there is little new innovation in the project and that it would be difficult to sell the platform and integration framework presented without a significant investment in a portfolio of applications that could leverage it in the marketplace."

On the flip side, the FOAK Board may decide that the Proposal Team is being too aggressive in its planned use of content or that too much invention is required because the core components are either too immature or incomplete. Then the Board asks the Proposal Team to either scale it down or identify alternatives for portions of the content. This may be accomplished by connecting with other research or product development teams to identify preexisting components to source portions of the proposed FOAK project functions and features. Or it might mean restructuring the FOAK project to get it down to a more manageable scope.

In one case, a Proposal Team was seeking to develop a way for rich client devices (such as cell phones and Personal Digital Assistants) to access services with context-aware features. Their goal was to enhance the retail shopping and customer service experience by, for instance, providing on-the-spot demos of products. This Proposal Team was asked to go back to the drawing board. They needed to break the project into smaller pieces and consider ways of scaling down the project to fit within a more manageable scope of work.

In all cases, the FOAK Board is evaluating how complete the solution being proposed will be and how much reuse of existing IBM intellectual property (IP) is planned by the Proposal Team to optimize IBM resources.

> *LESSON: Make sure a review board's feedback includes advice, not just a yes/no decision.*

Market Planning

To maximize FOAK value, the FOAK Board qualifies proposals based on the opportunity size and readiness of the market segment (a key area of business) being targeted by the Proposal Team. A segment can be a geography experiencing rapid growth, such as China, a new pain point, such as Sarbanes-Oxley, or a new market, such as life sciences. Will the project be performed in a segment that is rich with opportunity and ready to accept innovative approaches?

IBM has a market planning process that uses a rigorous approach to analyze market trends, client wants and needs, opportunity prioritizations, and business plans. It begins with understanding the marketplace and ends with managing the business plan and assessing the performance of revenue, profit, market participation, client satisfaction, and loyalty. This process links to the IBM brands' offerings development process, Integrated Product Development. Linking FOAK to these planning processes ensures that the project is strategic and that the results will have a role in the brand portfolios.

Once the market segment is selected, a client partner needs to be identified. Candidates are usually nominated by marketing or one of the client-facing teams, but anyone can bring forward a potential FOAK partner. (Client selection was discussed in detail in Chapter 4, "Getting the Most out of Partnerships.")

Innovation

A less tangible benefit of FOAK is its impact on mindshare—how IBM is viewed in its chosen markets. Each year, the program delivers a stream of proof points (evidence of the validity of innovative concepts) for new technologies and thought leadership (recognition for innovative thinking and insights) applied to real business scenarios. Each project must demonstrate how it is a "first" and what mindshare it will generate for IBM.

Take the case of the Public Health Information Affinity Domain (PHIAD) FOAK project, briefly described in Chapter 1. It creates and uses models of infectious diseases to paint a picture of the health of a population with real-time information. When this project was presented to the FOAK Board, there was discussion about the business impact and time to market for a full-blown solution to pandemics. Although many agreed that the time to business value could not be determined, all agreed that the innovation and mindshare were significant enough to justify investment. The innovation value tipped the balance for approving the proposal. Currently, the FOAK asset is still in the pilot stage with the FOAK client and two other partners.

Path to Market

The Proposal Team makes an initial determination of the path to market for the assets. They validate this with sponsors and catchers in Phase I (see Chapter 2, "The FOAK Process: Phase I"). The FOAK Board makes a point of checking this early in the process, because looking at and testing the paths to market now helps set them on the course of achieving a key FOAK goal—commercializing the assets. The FOAK Board knows that the path identified in the proposal is not final. The IBM Project Team later confirms or redirects the path based on the learnings from the FOAK client. And, in Phase III (see Chapter 6, "The FOAK Process: Phases II and III"), ascertaining the path to market may often become complicated, because it needs to be determined at the asset level rather than at the project level. For each asset, the Proposal Team, and then subsequently the IBM Project Team, needs to consider which path will provide the greatest market exposure while providing for future enhancements, maintenance, and support.

Asset Catchers

The Proposal Team must show evidence of catcher support to the FOAK Board in their proposals. This is a hot-button issue for Board members. The institutional memory is long, and catcher problems bedeviled FOAK in the early days. Did they do the job here? Is their attitude toward catchers too casual? Do they get it?

As mentioned earlier, in the past, many Proposal Teams and IBM Project Teams did not explore their asset transfer options until their projects were complete. But this proved way too late in the overall project life cycle to have impact. It provided little or no opportunity for the intended commercialization organization to gain a deep understanding of the technology, gain insights into the market requirements, and influence the technical direction of the FOAK assets. Without this level of interaction, it became difficult and at times impossible for the intended commercialization business unit to accept the assets on the back end of a FOAK project.

That is why Proposal Teams must engage the targeted commercialization organization early in the process to gain their support and feedback as to whether the project has strategic and technical relevance to their future plans. Beginning with the initial Phase I discussions with potential catchers, the relationship is continuously nurtured throughout the project.

As mentioned, ensuring that the FOAK assets can be commercialized for broader market consumption is the end goal of the FOAK program. Identifying a suitable asset commercialization business unit that can provide the ongoing enhancement, maintenance, and support of the assets takes work.

Deliverables

The final criterion used by the FOAK Board is ascertaining the exact planned deliverables and their potential significance to IBM and its clients. The FOAK Board needs to explore multiple dimensions of the deliverables, such as:

- The depth and breadth of the IP
- How easily the IP can be reused
- What level of localization is required to reach global markets
- The relevance of the IP to multiple industries
- How much effort it would take to position assets within other market segments

The FOAK Board also wants to test the deliverables to ensure that they are not unwieldy or overly ambitious. Will the IBM Project Team be able to deliver the project with the head count requested and within the time frames proposed? Since most FOAK projects are one year in duration, at times the FOAK Board is skeptical about what it concludes can realistically be created and tested while working in a client environment.

Deliberations

Many questions surface from outsiders about how the actual FOAK deliberations take place. Some wish for complicated spreadsheets with weighted evaluation criteria. Others dream of a democratic voting process. Some seem to imagine heated, knock-down, drag-out debates. The truth is that the deliberation portion of the FOAK Board meetings is a forum in which all FOAK Board members voice their opinions on what they liked or disliked about each proposal.

It is as simple as a round-robin, weighing in on each proposal, followed by a quick straw poll to see where an emerging consensus exists. (Consensus is not the decision process for FOAK; it is more of a majority ruling.) Then a second round of detailed discussions takes place regarding the controversial proposals. Interestingly enough, over the last eight years there have been only a handful of situations where a FOAK Board member has not concurred with a FOAK Board decision. And in one case, a FOAK Board member was so opposed to his colleagues' decision that he officially went on the record to say that he did not approve the project. In most instances, FOAK Board members in disagreement go with the majority after voicing their concerns.

As soon as a reasonable level of deliberation across all proposals has occurred, the funding filter is applied. This is the filter that may prevent even a good project from being funded (generally because the Board prioritized it lower than others).

In some instances, proposal decisions are deferred until the Proposal Team can provide more clarity on scope, provide support from catchers or sponsors, explore areas of overlap with other IBM initiatives under way, or a host of other points. Although these decisions are put aside, a conscious effort is made to ensure that funding would be available if these Proposal Teams came back with compelling responses to these points of clarity. (It is important to note that it is not the intent of the FOAK Board to have teams come back to the Board multiple times to reach a decision, but rather to ensure that potentially good ideas are not passed over because of missing components.) Here are some of the FOAK Board responses to Proposal Teams that were not approved:

- We are not convinced that consumers would adopt the solution. Nor are we confident that the business model presented would gain traction within the time horizon that the FOAK program is focused on.
- This project was prioritized lower than the five projects approved for funding at the meeting because the value proposition was not clear, and the connections to the services organizations were not fully developed.
- It was not clear how IBM would make money in this space if the client value proposition could not extend beyond Asia Pacific and who the optimal catchers of the assets would be upon successful project completion.
- We need a firmer commitment from the catcher and more clarity on project scope before we can make a final funding decision.
- Unfortunately, with limited funding available, we needed to make some tough decisions. This project was prioritized lower than the five projects approved for funding at the meeting because the market opportunity presented was limited compared to other projects proposed at the meeting.

LESSON: Deferring decisions on innovation proposals, with clear direction on what would be needed for approval, helps raise the level of proposals and educate the innovators.

Decisions are communicated to the Proposal Teams within 24 hours of the FOAK Board meeting. Seeing the dreaded "Thank you for submitting a quality proposal at the FOAK Board meeting today..." opening in the e-mail tells the Proposal Teams immediately that they have not been approved. But as they read on, the message usually contains recommendations on other options to pursue if the FOAK Board truly believes the proposal has merit. Here are some examples:

- We believe the technical challenges are more complex than presented and [it is] far too early for a FOAK project with clients. We suggest that the team pursue working through one of the Brand Joint Programs to further develop the assets before pursuing a FOAK.
- We believe the assets have great promise, but they need packaging and commercialization support and not a FOAK project to move forward. Members of the FOAK Board have offered to help the Proposal Team establish the appropriate linkages with SWG and IBM's Research Business Development team to facilitate the process.
- The FOAK program has in the past sponsored projects in this technology area and therefore suggests that the proposal might be more suited to the Global Business Solutions Center (described in Chapter 6) for commercialization. Additionally, the Board strongly recommends that the team link with the Global Business Services Customer Relationship Management practice to ensure synergy and to validate the need and priority for the development, delivery, and support of the assets proposed.

Summary

Deliberations are never easy. As this chapter has made clear, FOAK Board members are a diverse group, and different values, perspectives, and experiences play into their questions, concerns, and opinions. The plan, the content, and the proposed IBM Project Team all figure into deciding how funding is allocated.

No magical formula leads to the right and fair answer. And although analysis plays an important role, so do the instincts and passions of the FOAK Board members. Proposals rise to the top based on specified criteria, a free exchange of ideas, and mutual respect.

Ultimately, practical concerns—money available, doability, strategic fit—dominate final considerations and lead to the choices that have become the basis for FOAK success. Chapter 6 looks at how the IBM project teams clarify the plans of the proposed projects.

6

The FOAK Process:
Phases II and III

Phase I of the FOAK process ended with submitting a proposal to the FOAK Board for review. We've looked at key elements of this phase in detail. At this point, the IBM Proposal Team gets good news. Their proposal has been approved! It is now a real project, and some (but not all) funding is available. The IBM Project Team must quickly take all the necessary steps to secure the best client partner, because if they don't do that fast enough, the project will be terminated.

Once they have a partner signed up, they need to perform the project, and the clock is ticking. They can mark the last day of the project on their calendars. It will not change. But that will not be the last day of work for the IBM Project Team, because their commitment is to get the assets adopted. In fact, Phase III, which deals with the transfer of the assets to the catcher, begins even before the project is completed.

Phase II

Once a project is approved, the lead researcher from the FOAK Proposal Team needs to assemble a working IBM Project Team and engage a client. Then the real work begins. Phase II, shown in Figure 6.1, consists of ten or eleven steps depending on when the joint publicity is created. This can take place during Phase II, upon contract signing, in Phase III, upon project completion, or really, at any point in the project, as negotiated by the partners. This step is captured as a footnote rather than a box to note this flexibility in the process. In addition, the Maintain Catcher Relationship step is noted as text and not a box because it is an ongoing activity throughout Phase II and Phase III.

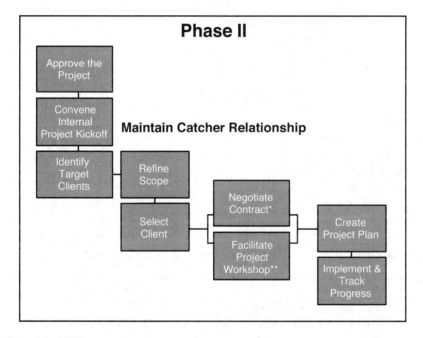

Figure 6.1   FOAK process, Phase II

*Publicity generated upon contract signing, during the project, or at project completion.

**Project workshops can be convened either before or immediately after contract negotiations.

The most critical enabler of Phase II is communications. Communications need to be effective internally, among team members and the catchers. They may be formal through workshops and status meetings, or informal via hallway conversations and cafeteria discussions. And there is also a critical need for good communications externally with the client during facilitated workshops or periodic checkpoints. Written project status reports are useful in ensuring that the expectations of both partnering organizations are being met.

Approve the Project

Approximately 70% of the FOAK proposals that are submitted to the FOAK Board are approved. This relatively high project approval rate proves the value of the project-filtering activities that the Industry Research Relationship Managers (RRMs), Industry Solution Boards, and FOAK Program Management Team (PMT) perform. Once a project is approved by the FOAK Board, the Proposal Team lead from IBM Research has a mandate to secure researchers for the IBM Project Team. Generally, FOAK projects have four or five researchers (or the headcount equivalent) associated with them, but some projects have included as many as eight. Relatively small IBM Project Teams are possible because these projects are not new development endeavors. In the FOAK model, FOAK participants are grabbing technologies that IBM Research already has invested in over the years. Thus, the project's duration and the required headcount are never as extensive as they would be for a new development initiative.

FOAK projects generally last one year. This is about as long as a sales channel can wait to see results, since they are driven by annual sales objectives to focus on near-term revenue. Multiyear projects are better suited to joint development arrangements, in which both the client and IBM invest equally in resources and funding to build something new.

> **LESSON: *Time a project's duration to meet the stakeholders' needs.***

Convene the Internal Project Kickoff

Once a project is approved, all members of the IBM Proposal Team and IBM Project Team and their supporters get together for an internal discussion of approaches, work products, tasks, resources, time lines, and roles and responsibilities. These sessions generally last half a day. The main objective is to chart the tasks for the next 90 days. Their most important task is describing the characteristics of the right client partner. Although many Proposal Teams have potential clients in mind as they build their proposals, pinpointing the best FOAK project partner takes additional thought and analysis. (This process is described in detail in Chapter 4, "Getting the Most out of Partnerships.")

At this point, the IBM Project Team can articulate the idea for the project and its value proposition for IBM and the marketplace.

Identify Target Clients

Within a given industry, generally several companies could benefit from a specific FOAK. The logic for increasing the pool of client candidates is clear when the process for qualifying candidates begins. Success is tied to the ability of IBM Project Teams to create a sustained, trusting relationship with aligned goals. It is possible to have a real need and be a valued client and still not meet the qualifications to be a FOAK partner. (Again, the attributes of a good FOAK partner are discussed in Chapter 4.)

As soon as they have specific candidates in mind, the IBM Project Team reviews and modifies the project's value proposition so that it better fits the target client. This is an essential exercise for the next step in the process. The IBM Project Team will devote time to crafting their messages—both for the presentations they'll give and the supporting documents they'll use.

Refine the Scope

Most FOAK projects are rich in possibilities, so it's not a surprise that, as partners get on board, the plans aren't simply fine-tuned. They get bigger, because the new participants add goals and activities. In addition, the facts and perspectives they supply may encourage the IBM Project Team to make additions.

As a result, projects can begin to expand their scope beyond what is possible, given the investments in time and resources. The IBM Project Team needs to take a hard look at how what others would like them to do compares to what they actually can do. While outsiders may play a role here, this work needs to be done by the IBM Project Team.

Successful innovation projects need engaged, passionate participants, and their dedication to the project can be put at risk unless the approach to limiting the project is fair and tactful. Things can fall apart at this stage, but this negotiation process has an upside. When it is handled well, it provides an opportunity to build relationships among team members, and these bonds can make a real difference as the work itself encounters the inevitable challenges.

The IBM Project Team, even after a proposal has been accepted, is open to the input of a range of committed partners. Aspects of the project's essential character may be modified to take advantage of new knowledge and perspectives. On the other hand, some good ideas cannot be accepted (although they may find a home later) due to funding and schedule constraints or fundamental differences on what the project is all about. Ultimately, a specific project is, by design, limited. And this constraint helps improve the likelihood of success and adoption.

Select the Client

Once a proposal is approved, the IBM Project Team has only *three funded months* to target, qualify, select, and gain a commitment from a client (with signed agreements). If, after three months, the IBM Project Team has not secured a client, the project is put on hold for three months without funding. Funding is withheld to ensure that the IBM Project Team stays focused on securing a client and ensures that enough funding is available to complete the project as soon as the actual client is engaged. During this time, the IBM Project Team must orient potential clients to the FOAK program and make clear to them the specifics of the project—the goal, how roles and tasks are roughly divided, and what their investment is. If a client still has not been secured after the three-month hold period (six months of total project time has now been expended), the project is terminated.

The clients also have work to do. They must identify the appropriate people and organizations that need to participate and gain their agreement and commitment to the project. In addition, real resources must be committed, in terms of both funding and personnel. Finally, legal and policy controls must be adhered to. This is nontrivial in any case, but it's particularly demanding when international partnerships are put into effect.

Given the range of requirements for engagement and the parties involved, it may seem unreasonable to have a hard deadline for securing final commitments. However, approximately 65% of the FOAK Proposal Teams with approved proposals can accomplish this. In fact, having a close-in deadline has been proven to help in many ways. It keeps the IBM Project and the Client Teams focused, it helps validate the true interest of the client and IBM partners, and it prevents projects—which are supposed to be forward-looking—from becoming obsolete before they start.

> *LESSON: Keep innovation teams focused by putting time limits on the steps from proposal approval to project kickoff.*

Except when the partners are already known (as with developers), typically sponsors, investors, or buyers are approached with an innovation only after the project can provide evidence of success. FOAK is committed to engaging its partners at an earlier stage, as it sets out on its journey toward success.

Negotiate the Contract

Most external candidates for a FOAK project already have signed IBM standard agreements in place at the enterprise level. But a FOAK project requires its own contracts to protect the intellectual property (IP) and minimize the risks associated with working with new technologies that are not yet proven in the marketplace.

Legal agreements can be an important obstacle. Surprisingly, it is neither the exploratory nature of the projects nor is it the technical work that creates the majority of the delays in the FOAK project schedules. Rather, it is the uniqueness of the terms and conditions (T&Cs). While FOAK projects generally work off a 12-month schedule, most of the work cannot be done without the client. After all, one of the cornerstone design points of FOAK projects is client collaboration. Therefore, a delay in the contract process can have serious consequences for the project's schedule. Standard FOAK contract templates and guidelines are published and reviewed with the IBM Project Teams during the internal project kickoff to highlight the nuances of the FOAK T&Cs and prepare the IBM Project Team to properly target clients and set client expectations.

Facilitate a Project Workshop

During the project workshops, the IBM Project Team and the Joint Project Team make decisions and set the stage for the project. Most notably, the participants zero in on a specific business process where the work is to be applied. Generally, the business unit has been identified prior to the workshop. This means that there is already buy-in on the project and an agreement for line-of-business resources to actively participate in the session. However, the specific business process needs to be identified, as do the resources and timeframes.

The project workshop can take place either before the contracts are negotiated, as a way to flesh out the Statement of Work (SOW), or just after the contracts are negotiated, as a means to kick off the project. The benefit of doing the workshop prior to the contract signing is that it gives both partners time to fully understand and get comfortable with the project scope and the responsibilities of each party. The downside is that, since formal agreements have not been signed, the sharing of information and ideas may be restricted, making it difficult to fully plan.

Additionally, if the workshop is facilitated with a client who does not become the actual FOAK partner, the researchers will have invested significant time in an activity that does not directly yield results. Worse, they will have consumed a portion of their project funding. When situations like these arise, the researchers need to restart the process with another potential partner.

In one instance, a FOAK project that set out to pilot a new approach to transforming core banking systems had invested in multiple workshops with a serious client partner, only to be blindsided by unforeseen merger and acquisition activities that precluded the client from moving forward with the FOAK project. Luckily, the Proposal Team was able to quickly identify another serious partner and secure signed agreements within the required timeframes. But, although some of the workshop materials were reused, the bulk of the work had to start all over.

Nonetheless, the best practice, based on FOAK experience, is to convene the workshop during contract negotiations with a qualified partner who is seriously committed to the project and is willing to invest the time of their IT and line-of-business people to participate in the workshop. The best indicator of this is a Client Sponsor who is passionate about the FOAK project and undaunted by the prospect of investing resources in it.

Create a Project Plan

One of the requirements of a FOAK project is that a professional project manager be hired from one of the IBM services units. Again, this work is less speculative and more directed than is typical of many other innovation programs. Results are expected, and the timetable is unmerciful.

You may never see a Gantt chart at a skunkworks, but it is hard to imagine FOAK without the discipline of milestones, assigned roles, reports, and conditions of satisfaction. Everyone knows what they are responsible for, and they are expected to be on task. This is not to say that the unexpected (both positive and negative) is not a part of FOAK projects. Every IBM Project Team experiences mid-course adjustments, learning, and even disappointments, but it's best to take these in stride and get on with it. Surprises don't equal excuses for nonperformance.

The project plan is developed using the milestones presented in the project proposal (Phase I) as a starting point. Additional project details are worked out during the contract negotiations process (Phase II) and are included in the SOW. The SOW serves as a guide in developing the detailed project plan and schedule. FOAK Joint Project Teams that have convened project workshops as part of the contract negotiations process may already have their project plans substantially done. These Joint Project Teams may move directly into implementation.

> *LESSON: Manage the execution of innovation projects as conscientiously as you would any other project.*

Implement the Project and Track the Progress

Once the clock has started, the IBM Project Team has just one year to complete a project, so adherence to schedules and milestones is mandatory. This is not easy when participants are from different business (and often national) cultures and time zones, but FOAK participants use familiar tools and standard project management approaches.

If executed well, all the targeting, selection, and filtering pay off when the Joint Project Team actually gets together to do the work, because the project ends up with aligned goals and expectations. In addition, many of the participants have had an opportunity to get to know and trust each other through participation in the workshops that are designed to flesh out the project's details. These come together to facilitate the project's implementation.

In addition, the project manager emphasizes clear communications. Roles, deadlines, and conditions of satisfaction are made explicit and confirmed regularly as part of the process. And the IBM Project Team gets an external review, tracking the progress against documented milestones and objectives, because of mandated quarterly checkpoint meetings with the FOAK PMT. Including the asset catchers in these meetings is a best practice since it subjects the IBM Project Team to a further reality check.

Maintain the Catcher Relationship

Nothing comes easy. To ensure that the assets from each project are successfully transferred, someone on the IBM Project Team must take responsibility for keeping the targeted catcher organization engaged so that they appropriately plan to invest in the assets.

The IBM Project Teams have had discussions with the targeted catcher organizations during the proposal stage (Phase I) to gain their support for the value of the work. These catchers have pledged their willingness to be the owner of the assets if proven successful. It doesn't matter. The job is not done. The IBM Project Team still needs to take steps to keep the asset catchers engaged throughout the entire project. This ensures that they stay informed, energized, and committed to owning the FOAK assets. Here are some techniques for doing so:

- Include the targeted catchers in quarterly status meetings and key client meetings.
- Identify a resource from the catching organization to be a full- or part-time member of the Joint Project Team (a best practice).
- Leverage the catcher as a consultant to the IBM Project Team, and include them in any internal and external publicity generated by the project. Instilling a sense of connectedness and ownership is the goal.

LESSON: The job of communications never ends for an innovator.

Create Joint Publicity

Since part of the value for IBM is the demonstration of thought leadership, publicity is an essential deliverable. This can mean a joint press announcement, direct client-to-client discussions, participation in analyst briefings and industry conferences, joint publications, and more. Usually, clients are eager to talk publicly about their leadership in partnering with IBM to innovate their businesses. And ideally, publicity is a high priority for all the partners. It is not unusual for IBM to hold a press conference as well.

The two companies negotiate the timing of when a project will be publicized externally. Some clients choose to make an announcement after signing the contract to get quick payback; this comes in the form of the luster of being an innovator in the marketplace. Others choose to wait until the project is completed to preserve their first market adopter advantage. Still others wait until the project has progressed far enough to give them the confidence and additional insights to make more pointed comments about the project and its impact on their business. The results can be a true win-win, with significant media coverage. And all the FOAK projects are *required* to deliver a working demonstration to the Industry Solutions Labs (ISLs) as a project milestone. (Chapter 9, "Telling the Story: IBM's Industry Solutions Labs," discusses in detail the ISLs and their contributions to FOAK).

Phase III

Moving from a lab prototype to a commercial product or service offering is one of the most difficult challenges for the IBM Project Teams. Phase III of the FOAK process, shown in Figure 6.2, includes the steps necessary to ensure successful commercialization of the FOAK assets that have been validated by the FOAK client.

Phase III

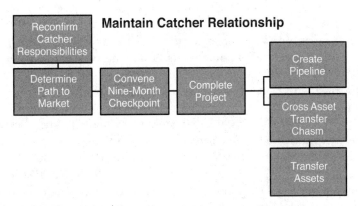

Figure 6.2   FOAK process, Phase III

Note: Press releases can be created and distributed either upon signing or upon completion.

Reconfirm Catcher Responsibilities

FOAK's asset catchers are responsible for enhancing, maintaining, and supporting the assets. It may seem at this point as if all of IBM's asset catchers suffer from attention deficit disorder. In reality, they just need standard contact management, the kind of hand-holding that businesspeople give their best clients. For the FOAK innovator, the catcher is the best and most critical client within IBM.

So, although sponsorship and support of the catcher are secured during Phase I, the job is still not done. A firm commitment needs to be worked on and negotiated throughout Phase II and Phase III to ensure a successful transfer within a reasonable time frame. Typically, it can take one to two years from completion of the FOAK project for a fully commercialized offering to become available. This does not mean that the assets cannot be made available on a limited basis to clients that are waiting for the fully commercialized assets to be available for broader market consumption. In fact, short-term licensing is often part of the negotiated FOAK agreements. (This is discussed further in the section "Cross the Asset Transfer Chasm.")

There are lots of potential commercialization options for FOAK assets. These include product brands, service engagements, business partner offerings, IP licensing arrangements, and venture capital agreements. Having so many options available provides a breadth of opportunities. However, exploring them all can be confusing and time-consuming, because each option needs to be tested in Phase I (when initially identifying the targeted catching organization), reinforced in Phase II (while performing the work and observing how the client is interacting with the assets), and confirmed here in Phase III (when reconfirming the catcher's responsibilities and schedules).

So which commercialization path is best? The traditional IBM product path is always available for commercialization of the FOAK assets, but it can take time. An alternative path, such as IBM Research Services—where IBM services include FOAK assets and their inventors on fee-based engagements—may be quicker to market, but it may not include the traditional level of support and maintenance that clients have come to expect from IBM. Every approach has trade-offs. For each project, the IBM Project Team must determine which organization will provide the greatest market exposure, future enhancements, maintenance, and support. Often, the final choice is driven by relationships.

As a project moves forward, the true state of the assets becomes clearer, and the level of customization and support becomes more evident. With more knowledge and experience, the IBM Project Teams can go back and reconfirm the asset catchers with greater substance.

Determine the Path to Market

Although we talk extensively about the role of the asset catcher, it is just as important to have people trained and ready to sell the assets. In most cases, after the IBM Project Team has identified the best asset-catching organization, they are naturally led to the path to market that is most often employed by that asset catcher organization. IBM has many paths to market available for its products and service offerings—including traditional IBM sales teams and services practices, business partners, systems integrators, distributors, and resellers. Each of these paths needs to be considered in parallel with choosing the ultimate commercialization organization. They go hand in glove. As such, most FOAK assets find their way to market through the traditional IBM sales teams and services practices, where the FOAK program has a bit more control over the various pieces of the go-to-market puzzle.

However, the other paths are not excluded. Having early insight into what the assets are, the level of customization required (is this a product or service?), and the skills needed to work with the assets helps the IBM Project Teams winnow the options and home in on the best path.

Convene a Nine-Month Checkpoint

The Nine Month Checkpoint is specifically targeted for a discussion on asset transfer. During this discussion, the IBM Project Team shares with the FOAK PMT where they are in their asset transfer discussions with their catchers. The meeting is scheduled to be thirty minutes longer than other quarterly checkpoint meetings to allow for discussion. Catchers of the assets are included in the meeting. Actual plans, resource requirements, timing, entry into the asset database, and the business model (such as how a client will buy this asset) are discussed in detail. It is not surprising that in some instances, after working with the client and truly understanding how the assets will be used, the IBM Project Team may realize that their original targeted asset catcher is really not optimal and that another option needs to be considered.

For example, while proposing the Smart Surveillance for Intelligent Oil Fields project, which provided data analytics software for intelligent well data analysis, the Proposal Team believed that the Global Business Services organization would be the targeted catcher. A services organization made sense as a partner, given the thrust of the *proposal*. However, as the *project* proceeded, they began to realize that, although there was a significant level of customization services, there was also an analytics engine that was too code-intensive for a services practice to maintain and support. Thus, the IBM Project Team needed to work with IBM's Software Group to commercialize the asset. This is all part of the FOAK program's value proposition: to validate the requirements, test the market readiness, find the right commercialization organization, and validate the path to market.

Complete the Project

Next, a final project completion meeting is convened, where next steps and lessons learned are discussed with the client. For some clients, next steps include continuing to test the innovation in their environments. For others, it means negotiating a follow-on contract to further enhance and extend the assets. And for some, it equates to reapplying the IP to other areas of the business. Still others might opt to wait for a more fully commercialized offering before proceeding with full deployment.

When the FOAK IBM Project Team successfully completes the project, this does not mean that the participants have fulfilled all their commitments. While the tasks and deliverables of the SOW may have been met, the IBM Project Team still is expected to help build a pipeline of additional client opportunities and work with the catcher to transfer the new assets to a delivery organization within 12 months.

Of course, in some cases, completion may mean moving on to other things and not deploying the FOAK content at all. FOAK's exploratory nature implies that some ideas won't deliver on the promise of their value propositions. This is expected and accepted. In fact, while no one wants failure that results from bad execution, an innovation program with no failures is, arguably, not testing the limits.

Create a Pipeline

At every stage of the game, innovations are in competition for time, money, acceptance, and priority. At the proposal stage, they are in competition with other innovations, but once the project has delivered, the innovation is in competition with established products and services, both internal and external.

So it should be no surprise that one of the key requirements for commercializing assets is to have a credible pipeline of new sales opportunities that will directly drive revenue for the commercialization organization. A healthy pipeline will motivate the catcher to accelerate the commercialization process. While others may contribute, the IBMers on the IBM Project Team are encouraged to work to create opportunities for sales tied to their asset. A number of activities can help them do this: generating early publicity, showcasing the results of the projects at the ISLs, creating internal awareness through presentations to key communities and postings on IBM's intranet site, training the sales and delivery organizations, and developing materials that will help the sales teams sell the assets. These are the components that can help take FOAK projects from the first client to the second and third clients, and so on.

FOAK innovators have a powerful card to play—the ISLs. Not only do the ISLs provide broad exposure to projects, but their visitors provide insights into other applications for the FOAK assets, both within and across industries.

Cross the Asset Transfer Chasm

At this point, the IBM Project Teams have successfully passed the Industry RRM, Industry Team, and FOAK Board approval processes. They also have navigated the client selection process, tackled contract negotiations, wrestled with all sorts of technical challenges, and proven the merits of their inventions. Yet now, just when they have valuable IP that they need to get to market, their targeted catcher might not be ready to receive their assets.

This may be true for a number of reasons. Funds may get cut, priorities may get shifted, people might change jobs, the catcher might be less than an ideal match to the deliverables, and, yes, the catcher may just overlook including the FOAK assets in their plans.

A continuing challenge for FOAK is that the program makes its investment decisions on a quarterly basis, yet most of the IBM Corporation makes investment decisions annually. If a FOAK project is fortunate enough to sync up with the annual planning cycle, they have the opportunity to get their assets included in the catcher's fall plans for commercialization funding. However, if the project is finished at some other point in the year, the IBM Project Teams must wait for the next plan cycle. Or they must hope that the catching organization has remembered to include a placeholder for funding the commercialization of the FOAK assets somewhere in its plans.

On the other hand, as with the Smart Surveillance for Intelligent Oil Fields example described earlier in this chapter, the IBM Project Team may have discovered while working with the FOAK client that the targeted catcher is not optimal and that they need to take the assets to a different catching organization. That new catching organization might know nothing about the technology or the FOAK project, meaning that the IBM Project Team would need to reinitiate their process of securing catcher support.

> **LESSON:** *Since surprises are inevitable with innovation projects, always have a "plan B."*

The list of reasons for having difficulties here can go on and on, but these IBM Project Teams now need to keep their assets alive while they rework their commercialization plans. Figure 6.3 shows the FOAK asset transfer chasm and the many different programs available within IBM that can be leveraged to keep the assets fresh while securing a final commitment from an appropriate commercializing organization.

Let's explore three of the programs available in IBM leveraged by the FOAK program to help FOAK IBM Project Teams cross the asset transfer chasm when kinks arise in their commercialization plans.

Figure 6.3 Crossing the asset transfer chasm

IBM Research Services

IBM Research Services is a partnership between IBM Research and IBM's services business units. It is intended to bring the right mix of business and technical expertise to a client via fee-based consulting and systems integration engagements. IBM Research Services can help a client think differently about their challenges and opportunities, develop breakthrough approaches to their business challenges, find new opportunities in their existing marketplaces, or develop game-changing ways to move them ahead of their competition. In a nutshell, IBM Research Services enables IBM to deliver IBM Research resources to clients for a fee.

For the FOAK program, clients that want to continue their relationship with IBM Research beyond the FOAK project can do so through an IBM Research Services engagement. Likewise, a new client interested in adapting the results of a prior FOAK project to their environment may do so through IBM Research Services. Thus, IBM Research Services becomes an accelerated path to market for FOAK projects.

A good example of IBM Research Services engagements that had their origins in the FOAK program are the Model-Driven Business Transformation (MDBT) projects. For executives and line-of-business operations managers, MDBT answers this question: How do I rapidly implement and deploy newly transformed business processes across the enterprise? MDBT has been successfully put to work in IBM Research Services engagements for the retail, banking, and insurance industries and government.

Faced with the chasm, the researchers from the initial MDBT FOAK projects were made available to additional clients on IBM Research Services engagements. Adoption of MDBT became their mission. And each time the researchers reused the assets on client engagements, the assets were further enhanced, and more and more services professionals became aware of the value of the innovation and how MDBT could be leveraged more broadly on service client engagements. Those engagements, along with a series of ongoing discussions with IBM services executives, led to the inclusion of components of MDBT in a tool kit used by services practitioners today without the help of the researchers.

Global Business Solution Center

IBM's Global Business Solution Centers (GBSCs) are located in India and China. They provide clients worldwide with a broad range of high-value business solutions. The GBSCs have cadres of IT professionals who harvest and harden (add extensions, documentation, quality testing, and so on to make them easily reusable) assets from client engagements for reuse on services engagements. The GBSCs create and enhance a portfolio of replicable industry solutions that are developed by combining the strengths of IBM's business consulting, research, software, systems, engineering, and emerging technologies.

One of the reasons why gaining the sponsorship of the Industry Solution Boards for FOAK projects is so critical is that the GBSC's portfolio of investments is managed by the Industry Solution Boards. These Industry Solution Boards prioritize the work of the GBSC resources. If a particular Industry Solution Board believes the FOAK project presents an opportunity for them to enhance and extend their portfolio of offerings on the back end of the FOAK project, they are more likely to invest the GBSC resources. Such an investment will take the FOAK assets and commercialize them into offerings that the worldwide services practices can include in services engagements in every regional market.

The asset transfer of the On-Demand Maturity Modeling (ODMM) FOAK was made possible because the original proposal was sponsored by the Automotive Industry Solution Board. From early on, the sponsors were prepared on the back end to allocate the resources in the India GBSC to commercialize the assets. ODMM allows automotive manufacturers to make real-time decisions to optimize resources across concurrent complex development processes based on the design's real-time status. To make it fit, the India GBSC packaged Java tooling and methods into a service offering. The researchers from the FOAK project provided the India GBSC with the assets and documentation they created. When it was accepted for development, the researchers performed skills transfer to the India GBSC through a combination of conference calls, webcasts, and face-to-face meetings (when possible). The researchers remained accessible to the India GBSC as needed to answer questions and help resolve problems.

IBM Systems & Technology Group Lab Services

IBM Systems & Technology Group (STG) Lab Services consists of a worldwide team of systems engineers, programmers, IT architects, and skills development professionals located in 35 labs worldwide. STG Lab Services professionals work directly with clients to help them implement systems solutions and optimize their IT resources. They apply intellectual know-how and technology innovations from IBM's development laboratories to enable clients to get the most out of IBM systems and storage products.

The FOAK program has leveraged STG Lab Services as a way to cross the asset transfer chasm. Most recently, the Multilingual Automatic Speech-to-Speech Translator (MASTOR), briefly mentioned in Chapter 1, "A Program That Works," was transferred to STG Lab Services. MASTOR allows users to converse naturally, producing audible and text translations of the spoken words that can run on a variety of devices, such as Personal Digital Assistants, tablet PCs, and laptop computers.

Originally slated to be transferred to IBM's Engineering and Technology Solutions business unit, the MASTOR IBM Project Team found themselves without a catcher for the assets when the business unit went away during a restructuring. With a persistent FOAK IBM Project Team and a marketplace still very interested in the technology, STG Lab Services stepped into the void.

The Advanced Speech and Translation Technologies team in STG Lab Services has the skills to work with MASTOR. They follow a rigorous development methodology and have extensive practical experience in speech and natural language processing, software engineering, product development, and speech and software consulting. This made the STG Lab Services organization a particularly good fit for MASTOR.

Transfer the Assets

Once the catchers commit to taking the assets forward into the marketplace, the researchers work with them to formally transfer the assets. This usually includes multiple levels of design reviews, training sessions, and the creation of documentation. The researchers are engaged either full time or part time, depending on the assets' size, complexity, and maturity. This not only facilitates the transfer but also shortens the learning curve of the catching organization's people.

In a few instances, IBM Research has transferred not only the assets, but also the researchers to the commercialization organization. This is because, for the transfer to be truly successful, a critical mass of skills was needed. This is much like the venture capital model in which the assets, IP rights, and people are spun off into an entirely new business unit or company. The MedSpeak example described in Chapter 1 and the SSS FOAK discussed in Chapter 2, "The FOAK Process: Phase I," are two examples of this approach to commercialization.

Summary

A FOAK proposal enters Phase II and becomes a FOAK project as soon as the Board approves it. The work begins to turn a well-thought-out design into an actionable plan, and the biggest order of business is getting the right partner on board, with all the appropriate legal papers in place.

With the researchers selected for the IBM Project Team and a client engaged, the FOAK Joint Project Team can come together to work out a detailed plan. Through a process of negotiation and assignment, the work is divided up and the team members jump into their tasks. The project now is structured, managed, and executed with interim deliverables, meetings, and milestones. Flexibility can be exercised in how the work is done, but the deliverables and finish date are locked in.

Phase III begins while the work is still in progress. The IBM Project Team needs to take on the tricky job of engaging in more specific terms with the catcher. They need to clarify what the path to market will be and prepare for the detailed review of the Nine-Month Checkpoint.

When the last project deliverable is packaged up and team members go back to their regular jobs, the IBM Project Team still has a lot of work in front of it. They need to find buyers, work through the specifics of crossing the asset transfer chasm and play a hands-on role in the actual work of transferring the assets to the catching organization.

This chapter has provided an overview of these phases of the process. The following chapters delve into the details.

7

Clarifying Project Plans

However a FOAK innovation originates, it must traverse the path from gleam in the eye to realized commercial asset. Creating the proposal is only part of the process because, even with guidance, discussion, and the engagement of stakeholders, no proposal is complete and actionable. The real world intrudes in the form of deadlines, availability of people, or melting away of opportunities. Objectives and roles that seemed clear and desirable suddenly lack detail and may look less appealing in the face of commitments and needed deliverables.

The plan must be built with attention to practical concerns and contingencies. The best contributions should be drawn from each organization and from each individual. Finally, the plan must be built with sensitivity to the participants. Is the division of labor fair? Are the processes reasonable? Are people being listened to?

How a Proposal Differs from a Plan

In essence, FOAK proposals are sales documents. It's true that, because of the pragmatism of the FOAK Board, projects do not get funded unless they have many elements of a good plan: well-defined deliverables, head count and the specifics on which IBM organizations are participating, assets used, identification of the industry that the work is relevant to (and candidate partners), costs (including client funding), and milestones. And, of course, the time frame for all projects is defined as one year. Much of this goes directly into the plan, but omissions can modify and even eliminate some elements of the proposal as it is translated into the ultimate plan.

For example, on one FOAK project, the IBM Project Team needed sales data. But it wasn't until they received the first batch of files from the client that they realized that the data could not meet their analysis requirements. Suddenly, the IBM Project Team had a new objective: find ways to clean up and consolidate the data. Fortunately, the IBM Project Team had the flexibility and talent to do just that.

Perhaps the most significant (and intentional) omission of most proposals is the identification of a specific client to partner with on the project. As stated earlier, keeping options open helps to generalize proposals and hedge against placing a bet on a single client. But the Client Team coming on board, after a proposal is accepted, may have information the FOAK Proposal Team didn't have access to or missed. The client may also have a different perspective and different priorities. All this needs to be resolved via frank and specific conversations. In addition, the client's culture and measurement system may materially alter elements of the proposal. And there may even be interorganizational agreements and local laws to consider.

On one FOAK project in India, after months of negotiating with the targeted client, the IBM Project Team learned that the client had a tough requirement tied to security concerns: None of the essential data could, in any instance, leave the client premises. Such a condition was unprecedented for the IBM Project Team, and it took considerable thought and effort for them to find a workaround. Placing transcribers on site to work with the data fulfilled both the needs of the IBM Project Team and the client's obligations.

However, it's never possible to anticipate every obstacle, and sometimes a FOAK IBM Project Team meets one that cannot be overcome. In the end, this same IBM Project Team had to abandon the project because the client was unable to purchase the call recording system required and originally agreed to in the FOAK contract.

When the IBM Project and Client Teams come together for their project workshop as a Joint Project Team, the proposals also lack many details of who does what and when. Real work always relies on skills and experiences. It includes both "good" work and "unattractive" work. Individuals need to commit to deliverables that meet both conditions of satisfaction and deadlines. Sorting out the work requires effective foresight, reasonable estimates, and not a little diplomacy. Before a plan is finished, the Gantt charts need to come out, and the project manager needs to sharpen his or her pencil. But the process itself needs to be carried out in such a way that the relationships are protected and trust is built.

In fact, a hidden process under clarifying goals is team building. FOAK is not an exception to Tuckman's model of "forming, norming, storming, and performing." In fact, since people come from different organizations, they have the additional burden of "reforming" the relationships between IBMers and clients. Ultimately, there must be one strong Joint Project Team, not two teams that are casually associated. One IBM researcher, working out of the Zurich lab, specifically credited the strength and membership of his Joint Project Team for making their achievements possible.

"The team structure has certainly been one of the most important factors that drove the success of this project. The team consisted of researchers, a team of IBM executives (who have very good relationships with and knowledge of the client), and a team of marketing practitioners from the client who were strongly dedicated to the project. The team managed to work together with great synergy and with great visibility, as it had strong client and IBM exec sponsorship," he said.

LESSON: The process of clarifying plans is also a team-building process, so from the start, creating good relationships needs to be one of the objectives.

Key Questions to Get Started

The first question for any innovation team project workshop (as mentioned in Chapter 6, "The FOAK Process: Phases II and III") is "Who are we?" Straightforward sharing of resumes and introductions may suffice, but there are distinct advantages to looking at the participants beyond their formal skill sets. When a face-to-face meeting occurs, a casual dinner beforehand or asking less-direct questions that reveal more than what is on the resume can help the team begin to build social capital. Since trust is so important, finding personal connections is a good starting point for success.

Many practical questions about how to do the work need to be answered as well:

- What are the overall ground rules?
- How are we constrained by law, custom, or contract?
- What are the lines of authority?
- What processes are used to gain access to decision-makers, talent, data, and resources?
- How will decisions be made? How might they be appealed?
- What platforms, tools, and applications will be used?
- How will activities be tracked and reported? What forms will be used?
- How will individual and team contributions be measured?
- Where will work take place?

While it is generally desirable for individuals on an innovation team to have input into the answers to operational questions, it may be more efficient to have many of these worked out beforehand, at least in a draft form. But even if all the answers are set in stone, they should be presented personally to the participants so that they can voice concerns and ask questions.

Getting onto the Same Page

Language is full of ambiguities, inferences, and hidden meanings. Clarity, even for those operating within one culture and one firm, is difficult to achieve consistently.

The Joint Project Team comes together for the first time at a project workshop. Here they take the first step toward consensus on what the FOAK project is all about, and that step is simple: present the proposal. This is essential, since many of the people who will be doing the work on the project were not part of the original FOAK discussions where project goals, objectives, and scope were initially conceived and agreed upon. Under normal circumstances, just hearing the proposal expressed generates questions, new ideas, and elaborations. At times, agreement and mutual understanding may be simple, especially if the FOAK project relies on highly specific technical achievements. For example, on a FOAK project to develop a method of detecting and characterizing faults on electrical grids, the IBM Project Team just had to talk to the client's engineers, who spelled out exactly what types of faults were most important and what types of sensors they had available to the project. Clarification amounted to the exchange of a few sentences.

But where variations are possible, some participants will have definite ideas about how they see the FOAK project, and these can get in the way of moving to consensus. Often, a dominant voice shuts out new ideas and perspectives, and some participants may even become disaffected. It is good to remind those who are most engaged with the proposal that getting to know the project through new eyes is a *good* thing.

Whoever is facilitating needs to make sure that everyone's opinion is heard and respected. Smart people with all the answers have a tendency not to listen and even to cut off others in the middle of a sentence. Without allowing the project workshop to become derailed, it's usually helpful to leave plenty of room—more than may seem necessary—for comment and discussion.

Besides going over the basic material, it is useful to provide concrete descriptions. What does success look like? Who will use the innovation, and what benefit will it provide? How does the innovation compare to today's approach or other approaches in development?

Descriptions should be on the project level, but they also should be on the level of milestones, deliverables, and, if possible, individual contributions (although the last may come later in the process).

LESSON: Get people to discuss the project's details, even those they can't change, so that they become owners.

Exploring Options and Concerns

Approved FOAK project proposals tend to be intriguing. They spur the imagination (which is why they get chosen for funding). Therefore, the usual problem when the Joint Project Team first comes together is managing all the good ideas, critiques, and answers that participants come up with. Conversation rarely lags. (If it does, turn to the enthusiasts. If you don't have any for an *innovation* project, walk away—quickly.)

Generally, the facilitator or project manager has the problem of keeping the project workshop focused without losing the great ideas. For FOAK, focus can be maintained by referring directly to the promises made in the proposal. These commitments are what the Joint Project Team needs to deliver on if all else fails. A FOAK project can go in many different directions, and the objectives can be achieved in many ways, but a FOAK project that accomplishes much without achieving the stated project objectives cannot be considered a success. So good ideas need to be recorded and considered, but those that do not support the achievement of the stated objectives cannot be given priority.

For example, on the Contact Agent Buddies (CABs) project described in Chapter 2, "The FOAK Process: Phase I," the original FOAK proposal had no notion of creating a tool to support decision-making. When the FOAK IBM Project Team performed their diagnostics on the client's call center data, they discovered that there was a big problem with first call resolution. Customers were not getting what they needed. To help the client manage the situation, the IBM Project Team built the proof of concept of what came to be known as the Decision-Making Tool. The client liked the tool so much that, in a follow-on engagement, they asked the researchers to create a pilot version. Currently it is planned for production deployment at that client site.

Even those who love a FOAK project may arrive at the project workshop with a laundry list of things that won't work. Looking at the challenges, both real and imagined, is not for the faint of heart. But this is part of the exploration. People can't believe in the FOAK project unless they believe it can succeed. Putting their concerns into perspective, ranking them (often by both likelihood and impact), and, eventually, getting people to suggest solutions to the problems improves both the odds of success and the attitude across the Joint Project Team. Some of these problems will disappear and be forgotten in short order. Inevitably, the Joint Project Team will miss some real challenges. For the latter, the can-do approach taken at this early stage will carry on as unexpected difficulties arise.

Distinguishing Between Good and Bad Answers

Oddly enough, it may be the Joint Project Team member's answers, more than his or her concerns, that get in the way of a FOAK project's full success. Smart people quickly figure out how to achieve goals and meet challenges. And a good number of people will want to do things in ways that have succeeded before, even if those approaches are inappropriate. There may even be people on the Joint Project Team who have hidden agendas.

No matter what their source, many of the answers people come through the door with need to be considered, not just accepted. Every choice that is made at this stage reduces the Joint Project Team's options. So keeping things open, dynamic, and undecided for a while can pay off as people with different perspectives assemble the pieces.

One approach is simply to collect the answers in an organized manner and keep them in front of the Joint Project Team. The more answers that are available on whiteboards, screens, or Post-It notes, the less power each member has individually. And making them all visible allows Joint Project Team members to make connections that are not obvious when each answer is considered in isolation.

The exploration may come in the form of probing questions, shared experiences, hopes, and analogies. However the Joint Project Team chooses to explore the proposal and its possibilities, it is important that the process be open, both to identify opportunities and to build the relationships between Joint Project Team members. As one researcher noted, "If the relationship is flawed, every bump will lead to a disaster."

Keeping a Project in Scope

The usual result of open discussions is a lot of surprising and attractive approaches and ideas. These enrich the FOAK project and build commitment and enthusiasm. But they can't all be done. First and foremost, the proposal's promises must be fulfilled. And the Statement of Work (SOW) is the starting point for setting boundaries. This means that wonderful ideas that are not relevant to the FOAK proposal must be put aside. This can be challenging for IBM researchers who respond willingly to client remarks such as "Wow, that's great. Can you make it do this...?"

KEY QUESTIONS TO PROMOTE CONSTRUCTIVE CONVERSATIONS

On occasion, the discussion doesn't occur spontaneously. In these cases, it is worthwhile to engage and provoke the participants. Scenarios, which can provide intellectual prototypes, can be useful here, but if they are too well drawn, they can become models in and of themselves. An easier approach is usually a good set of questions:

- What is new about the proposal?
- What technology or approach would compete with a fully realized deliverable?
- What are the critical success factors?
- Who are we creating this for?
- How will success here change the world?

The answers to some questions will be obvious. Some that seem obvious, when posed to a diverse team, won't be.

Rather than dictating what is in scope and out of scope, it is useful to have the objectives and real-world boundaries clearly stated, and then have the Joint Project Team decide what is in scope and out of scope. Sometimes this is arrived at simply by prioritizing the activities, approaches, and deliverables. When everyone participates and they are allowed to look at and get used to what is critical and what is not, relationships can be built rather than broken.

As one researcher put it, "People have different perspectives and needs. This was solved right from the beginning as we defined and agreed on a very clear mutual understanding of project objectives, scope, resources, and deliverables. And because we adopted a professional project management approach to running the project. There were a few issues, due mostly to changes in priorities of the tasks to be performed, but, because of the strong communication and tight working relationship, these bumps were easily smoothed out."

LESSON: Always keep the innovation project's promises front and center.

Choosing Approaches

How things are done can become another area for tough decisions. Often, there are a number of valid approaches. What is best for one Joint Project Team member may not be what is best for another. The people involved, their interests, and their skills need to be weighed against the FOAK proposal's promises. The Joint Project Team may need to make tough choices when practical concerns are balanced against opportunities to do something innovative. Because FOAK is results-oriented, the bias is toward delivering on commitments rather than learning something new. However, sometimes it is possible to have it both ways. Making the choices is more an art than science, but a difference in approach can make all the difference in the quality of the output.

Establishing Real-World Limits

All FOAK projects have tight limits on the time and resources available. No deadline extensions are possible, and no supplementary funds are available from the FOAK Board. In addition, organizations, nations, contracts, and the laws of physics put limits on what the Joint Project Team can do and how they do it.

So, sooner or later, the plans and ideas that the Joint Project Team comes up with need to be checked against the real world. In practice, this tends to happen along the way. In fact, keeping every idea surfaced from being surrounded and consumed by the restrictions people battle with every day is one of the key challenges of an effective project workshop. Many of these, as mentioned, can be creatively overcome or dodged. Others cannot.

Working effectively within these limits is part of the job of the Joint Project Team. Paradoxically, the clearly stated limits help the Joint Project Team design the plan in detail. Timing, sequence, and investment often are dictated by availability of resources, budget cycle, and executive calendars. Approaches may make sense only in terms of the infrastructure that *must* be used. As one researcher noted, "Getting strong client involvement, good communication, and project management practices in place are key factors of success, especially in these kinds of risky projects, from which business sponsors tend to disengage quickly if they don't see a sustained potential value."

The most important aspect of examining FOAK project constraints is to do the job thoroughly. This reduces surprises that can seriously decrease the potential of a FOAK project. Such surprises can also damage the relationships between the IBM Project Team and Client Team members if they could have been reasonably anticipated.

After the Joint Project Team has examined the constraints and determined the minimum for the project's implementation, some of the options that go beyond the proposal may be added back in.

Building in Flexibility

Of course, every innovative project has surprises, both good and bad. A plan with no contingencies or one that programs every hour and dollar is apt to run into problems. During the FOAK project workshop, the Joint Project Team needs to actively review plans to ensure that they have not painted themselves into a corner.

The effort to build in flexibility may be started by identifying the elements of the plan that are most uncertain and most important. One advantage of a diverse team, with different perspectives, experience, and knowledge, is the ability to think around the issues. (The value of diversity can be realized only if all participants believe they will be heard and respected. This is one reason why the process for earlier steps in clarifying goals needs to be open.)

Aspects of the plan need to be examined in terms of assumptions, which may at times be hidden. They also need to be looked at in terms of changes to the economy, power structures, technology, organizational structures, and the availability of people, data, and equipment. The IBM Project Team also needs to look at the plan *in toto* in terms of the uncertainties, since smaller uncertainties may combine to create bigger uncertainties or have follow-on effects.

The Joint Project Team should prioritize identified uncertainties. The Team then can take on the task of coming up with options around those that would be expected to have the most impact on the project's success. (Where it is prudent to do so, the Joint Project Team members may also find ways to reduce uncertainty.) In addition to creating specific options, the Joint Project Team may increase flexibility by reserving enough time and money to handle worst-case scenarios.

One Joint Project Team during the very early stages of a Risk and Compliance FOAK project realized that they would be challenged by their need to secure data from the client. This was not due to the lack of responsiveness from the client. It was because the undertaking to capture the data was such a big job that the client wanted to take extra time to be thoughtful and ensure that they captured all the data needed the first time. So the project manager asked the FOAK PMT to delay some of the funding. This modification to the plan reserved enough funding to take the project through anticipated delays.

Assigning Roles and Responsibilities

Once the timelines, tasks, and milestones are clear, the Joint Project Team must make decisions about the roles and responsibilities. And hands go up quickly when the work is interesting and the people have the skills. Many of the efforts clearly belong to one group or another. But a number of areas have potential for conflict or apathy: routine and administrative work, conditions of satisfaction, who owes what to whom, and areas for further study.

Many innovators abhor doing familiar activities and satisfying bureaucratic requirements. Unfortunately, FOAK does not provide a paradise that is exempt from quotidian concerns. FOAK Joint Project Teams need to work methodically. They need to file reports. They need to attend meetings. And although some of these tasks can be put onto the project manager's shoulders, others can't.

The routine work, especially when the objective is to create a real-world prototype, needs to be executed well. This means it must be divided in a way that ensures quality output. It also must be divided in a way that is transparent and does not overburden participants. Finally, the expectations for record-keeping and meetings need to be communicated by the effort's project manager. Often this means that forms and tools need to be explained and examples need to be given to participants. And, of course, this is a good time to put deadlines and commitments on calendars.

In addition to making clear the requirements for acceptable output from routine and administrative work, the Joint Project Team needs to take on the conditions of satisfaction for the rest of the essential deliverables. Since some of these may have novel characteristics, it may not be possible to describe them completely. Nevertheless, they must be expressed in enough detail to guide the efforts.

Description of work products naturally leads to who owes what to whom. In many cases, a work product may have different levels of completeness. For instance, as code is developed, it may be equally reasonable for a group handing off the code or for a group receiving it to perform certain tests. Do I owe you a rough form or a polished form?

Why? Will a polished work product actually be more difficult for the receiving team to work with?

Finally, many cases will have "known unknowns." The project workshop aimed at clarifying goals will identify these, and the Joint Project Team members will need to perform research, experimentation, interviews, and studies to refine the plan. Some elements of the plan also might need to be reviewed and validated by key stakeholders, such as sponsors.

FOAK Joint Project Teams often want to run every issue to ground during the project workshop, but it is usually impossible to spec out everything in detail. After all, this is an innovative project, and new work is being done. Many elements will remain vague at this point, and many will need to be revisited as the FOAK project goes forward.

Working Within Defined Parameters

Many agreements have been reached and decisions made before the Joint Project Team comes together for the project workshop. Legal documents have been created, reviewed, revised, and put in place by staff, lawyers, and executives. These agreements are not reopened at this point. They are part of the environment in which the Joint Project Team must operate.

However, as discussed, many approaches, assignments, and deliverables must be worked out among Joint Project Team members. In reality, this is not a discussion among equals. Managers have responsibilities and powers. Contracts provide rights to different parties. Knowledge and ownership of resources (including access to executives) is not the same among Joint Project Team members. As the members sort out roles and responsibilities, some members have the power (and even the duty) to dictate terms.

However, usually things can be worked out to the satisfaction of both the client and IBM. Because relationships are so important, the project manager will have a bias toward negotiation and discussion during the project workshop. Naturally, the negotiation should proceed via best practices—creating a good climate for give and take; being frank about strengths, weaknesses, and needs; generating lots of options; keeping discussions honest and aboveboard. The goal isn't scoring points; it's taking advantage of what Joint Project Team members have to offer so that the best efforts of each can be obtained.

Maintaining Good Relationships

Anyone who has experienced a labor dispute where "work-to-rule" has been a tactic knows the folly of expecting that clear plans and agreements will allow for efficient and effective teamwork. (Even worse is "malicious compliance," in which disgruntled participants can plunge a project into a Dilbert world of dysfunction and dispute.) While clarity is certainly a prerequisite, the interest, focus, and good intentions of the participants are really the drivers of success on an innovation project.

FOAK is no exception, which is why so much attention is given to maintaining good relationships at each step of the way. Clarifying goals necessarily turns lofty dreams into personal to-do lists. Items on these to-do lists will include jobs that provide little intrinsic reward to individuals, as vital as they may be to the value of the overall project. As such, there is a danger of the reality, or at least the perception, of bias in how assignments are made.

The first step toward fairness, of course, is transparency. Making it clear to everyone in advance what the ground rules are and the bases of decisions can go a long way toward keeping participants from feeling that assignments are made in an unfair or arbitrary manner. (And if the processes and rules are mutually agreed to, even better.)

Some people may challenge the fairness of the leadership and the process in real time. Without taking the whole project workshop off the rails, these challenges need to be dealt with through listening and discussion. Depending on the nature of the concerns, they may need to be put aside for one-on-one conversations. If so, they need to be attended to as soon as possible.

> *LESSON: When team members come from different cultures and organizations, it becomes more critical to make the process of decision-making and work assignments transparent.*

When agreement is reached while working within the group, there may be a temptation to consider the matter settled. Unfortunately, some people may agree only because they feel pressure from the group to "sit down and shut up" (even if the phrasing is diplomatic). The leader of the group needs to check back later, either directly or indirectly, to see if the individual with the concern is satisfied with the outcome. Similarly, some people may have unvoiced objections, so, after a project workshop, one-on-one conversations with all members should be held.

Overall, the goal is to make sure that trust between Joint Project Team members grows rather than declines. Innovation is a dangerous business. In some cases, it feels as if you are climbing Mount Everest. Who do you want with you? People who have the skills to help you reach your destination. People who will not leave you in the snow and ice when the going gets tough. So, for innovation activities, trust is about working with people who are competent and who have the project's best interests in mind.

Summary

Clarity is one of the classic pillars upon which effective leadership is built. As the Joint Project Team members get together for the first time during the project workshop, many ambiguities of intent must be clarified, and the big questions of "how" must be resolved. In addition, the members of the Joint Project Team must work through the operational concerns of deadlines and conditions of satisfaction.

However, since FOAK projects are steps into the unknown, not everything can or should be completely described during the project workshop. Some options need to be reserved, and the FOAK Joint Project Team must build in a level of flexibility. Overall, attention must be paid to the promises made in the proposal. While many possibilities for approaching the project's execution may emerge, it is essential that the IBM Project Team stay focused on its commitments.

Finally, it is natural for Joint Project Team members to disagree as they move to clarify goals, and not everyone will be happy with the assignments they draw. This means that the process for discussion and the move toward roles and commitments must be fair and transparent. Trust is critical for any successful innovation project, and the project workshop is an opportunity to begin building the effort on a foundation of mutual respect and confidence.

Now that everyone knows who is who and why they are together, how do they actually do the work of the project? How do they effectively collaborate and reach their goals? That is the subject of Chapter 8, "Ensuring the Work Gets Done."

8

Ensuring the Work Gets Done

Researchers, developers, and others dedicated to the creative side of innovation tend to be fluid in their views of what is possible and what is impossible, the reality of business frameworks, and the role of authority. They have spent much of their lives finding holes in arguments that usually go unchallenged. They color outside the lines.

And while some are ambidextrous, working easily in the world of imagination and the world of processes and forms, many are not. This creates natural tension on any FOAK project, and this conflict must be managed. The project manager and the leadership of any innovation project need to balance between imposing too much structure (with the resulting loss of creativity and breakdown of relationships) and allowing curiosity to lead team members into side trips that make achieving the goals impossible.

FOAK has a level of complexity in getting the work done that may be more than that for most innovation programs. The project manager has overall responsibility for ensuring that the work gets done, but responsibility for leading the project is not solely in his or her hands. Many leaders are embedded within FOAK Joint Project Teams. Generally, these include someone from IBM Research, someone from IBM services, and someone from the FOAK client. The leaders on the Joint Project Team may also consist of folks representing industry or sales, the catcher, sponsors, and more. Knowing what each leader has to offer, ensuring that their skills are put to good use, and understanding their roles is important to avoid confusion and drive efficiency.

The efforts of these leaders are put into effect by a variety of activities: defining (and refocusing) the goals, allocating resources, tracking achievements, and developing member capabilities. In addition, with FOAK, part of the job is always to look beyond the final day of the project to the eventual reuse of any deliverables.

Achieving the Goals

While every effort is made to avoid too much structure in FOAK projects, the commitments are firm and specific. The final day of activity is fixed. Sponsors expect results. And the array of obligations goes beyond, say, delivering an application on time. That deliverable must not be a one-off. It must meet standards. It must be documented and constructed in such a way that it can be productized. Essential skills must be effectively transferred. It must have begun a socialization process that will encourage its adoption in the real world.

This means that, as the FOAK project proceeds, the FOAK Joint Project Team must constantly assess itself. Are we on task? Are we moving quickly enough? Are changes valid? Are we engaged and aligned with our organizations, end users, clients, and sponsors? More than anything else, the structure and controls need to be put in place to ensure that the goals of the FOAK program and the specific contractual commitments are met.

Of all the goals, the most difficult is socializing the innovation. For many innovation programs, this is not considered to be part of the job. The work itself is the focus, and the participants consider the people part secondary. Many expect the concept and benefits to be compelling and to sell themselves.

With FOAK, socializing the innovation is an explicit part of every project. As was seen in Chapter 4, "Getting the Most out of Partnerships," a substantial effort is made to partner and build relationships, even before the project gets under way. As the FOAK project proceeds, the stakeholders (sponsors, clients, catching organizations) continue to be updated, asked for their opinions, engaged, and persuaded. As discoveries are made, the stakeholders are given the news. When tough choices must be considered, they are often consulted.

An IBM Project Team recently found an interested and ready-to-work client candidate for a new project aimed at speeding drug development. However, the client does not have IBM's Solution for Compliance in a Regulated Environment (SCORE) installed. Since achieving the purpose of this FOAK is tied to enhancing IBM's SCORE solution, the IBM Project Team consulted the catcher, the SCORE product manager. The result: As long as the IBM Project Team works with the SCORE product development team to ensure that the interfaces they deliver are compatible in future installations, they should go ahead, because there is still tremendous value in doing the project with this client. This case illustrates a circumstance in which consulting with a stakeholder actually led to a less restrictive view and allowed a project to move forward.

A further responsibility of the IBM Project Team is to keep abreast of organizational changes and shifts in marketplace perspectives. For instance, the Anonymous Biometrics Matching FOAK project saw its catcher retire midway through the project. The project's objective was to implement a biometrics matching system whereby an individual's true biometrics are never stored or matched. Instead, they are transformed into a similar representational form that cannot be reverse-transformed to reveal the original biometric. Currently, the IBM Project Team is taking the initiative to work with the new catcher's chief architect to see how the FOAK assets might fit into his product plans.

This kind of communication and engagement—continual, targeted, and creative—is one of the keys to FOAK's success. Participants aren't just encouraged to build their technical capabilities; they're encouraged to strengthen relationships and learn more about the players, their businesses, and even the politics. Understanding what the elements of success are for stakeholders enables them to build anticipation for the assets and ease their introduction.

> *LESSON: The social/political side of innovation is at least as important as the technical side. Care must be taken not to push goals at the expense of relationships.*

Dealing with Constraints

For any complex project, scope is continually challenged. Given the uncertainties of an innovation project, problems and opportunities continually crop up. Each of these causes of change forces choices (and, for FOAK, the choices usually go across the different organizations). Each is an opportunity for distraction and disagreement. Each is a challenge to the available resources, attention, and project's schedule.

Because these are newly formed collaborations and some members may not be used to working within bounds, the leaders of the FOAK Joint Project Team may need to provide guidance to people who take initiative. It's true that rules were put in place during the project workshop, but participants may not follow them as closely as they need to. After all, the culture of innovation generally is "Ask forgiveness, not permission." So what's a little cheating between friends? Some of the participants may interpret rules broadly. Rules that have been only stated and not experienced may not seem real to the Joint Project Team members. Finally, some members or subteams may be used to acting with a large degree of autonomy.

To maintain awareness of and compliance with the rules, Joint Project Teams generally have weekly meetings. These meetings help the Joint Project Team members understand new requirements, refine scope, schedule work, and get specific, assigned tasks. The meetings also (as with the initial project workshop) lead to the creation of a number of subteams. These subteams work in parallel to improve the overall efficiency and productivity of the total FOAK work effort. However, the introduction of subteams does create more work for the project manager, who must ensure that all the moving parts are aligned and focused on a common end goal.

When the structure becomes too loose, deadlines are missed, budgets are overspent, and goals are not met. FOAK can't afford any of this, so variances need to be detected and diplomatically corrected. Those leading the FOAK Project Team must confirm in specific instances the acceptable scope for individual decisions and the occasions when approvals are needed. These weekly meetings help keep everyone in line and on task.

In addition, paperwork, reports, adherence to standards, and timeliness must be enforced. With each experience, the correct approach and the real limits must be reemphasized. How people are trained to the system and

made attentive to the unforgiving constraints determines the spirit and dedication of the Joint Project Team as the work moves forward.

Few people like constraints, so this may be a real test for the project's
leaders. Standing firm while listening, disputing, empathizing, and
sometimes enduring complaints is difficult for some. In fact, a leader
might be tempted to avoid looking for variances and ignore or excuse
those that become evident. While this might be tolerable in other innovation programs, FOAK works within limits that can't be disregarded.
The result is that those who lead FOAK projects often develop conflict-
management skills, patience, and decisiveness that serve them well in
other innovation efforts and add new dimensions to their careers.

One researcher went so far as to say that the FOAK program is the
"one program in Research that I think we cannot, must not, live
without—ever." This researcher asserts that the time spent with the
FOAK client on-site challenged him to demonstrate leadership in two ways:

- By managing the research-client relationship, including helping the
  client embrace innovation as an opportunity for growth
- By driving a research agenda beneficial to IBM's strategy

This leadership did not go unnoticed, and the researcher found him-
self on an accelerated career path. For the researcher, the FOAK engagement "significantly shaped my view on how to instill innovation with
clients in consumable portions." Currently, the researcher is leading a
highly visible project with several million dollars of internal funding
entrusted to him to drive innovation. The sponsoring VP told him that
he would have a hard time trusting the agenda and approach if it weren't
for the researcher's experiences working with external clients.

Managing Procurement

As with any project of this size, the Joint Project Team must follow
applicable procurement processes. In the case of FOAK, this may mean
understanding and following a process that is unfamiliar to some members. By contract, one process from one participating organization will
take precedence, so education and tracking will be required as everyone
learns to follow that process correctly.

People naturally compete for resources, and this can create extra difficulties for an innovation project. With a traditional project, available

resources are usually specified, and their allocation is mandated from the beginning. With an innovation project, the money, time, and personnel may be in place at the beginning, but every unexpected obstacle or newly discovered opportunity creates the possibility of conflict over resources.

FOAK has an additional twist. Clients always need to buy IBM services as part of the FOAK agreement. The FOAK Program Management Team (PMT) requires a certified IBM project manager as a minimum for each FOAK project. Additionally, clients may need to buy IBM (or other equipment provider) hardware and software to enable their environment for the FOAK. The procurement of the hardware, software and services becomes an explicit part of the agreement for the FOAK. Failing to make the appropriate purchases can set a project back or even lead to its termination (as in the example Chapter 7, "Clarifying Project Plans").

Again, good relationships are essential to making this work. This is why so much time and energy are dedicated to finding the right partners and IBM Project Team members. It is also why the best FOAK leaders track and actively manage the relationships among the Joint Project Team's members and subgroups.

LESSON: With innovation collaborations, differences in team members' assumptions about processes, knowledge, measurements, and tools must be detected and resolved.

Although FOAK projects may work from more detailed plans than other approaches to innovation, they also work within strict boundaries that other innovation teams might not face. In addition, a natural rivalry exists between organizations as choices are made. Each subteam could do a little more if you gave them a little more, and each organization could take back a bit more to peers at the end if one decision were made over another. The weekly Joint Project Team meetings, described earlier, help surface opportunities for subteams to drive greater value.

Tracking Progress

Since FOAK projects include project managers, normal controls and tracking systems are put in place. The Gantt charts, meetings, audits, and version controls on software and documents do not vary from what

WHAT RESOURCES DO YOU HAVE?

Resources are money, people, time, and materials, but for an innovation project, they also can be explanations and influence. This list can be used to do an inventory, with optimization in mind:

- **People/talent:** Who do you have to work on this (including people beyond the team), and what can they do?
- **Track record/reputation:** How much confidence and commitment can you create?
- **Knowledge/extraction methods:** What do you know, and how can you find out more?
- **Perspectives:** Can you engage with people who have different points of view that provide new ways of framing the innovation?
- **Funding:** Do you have money? Can you get more?
- **Sponsor/power:** Can someone marshal resources and mandate action for you?
- **Value proposition:** Is there a compelling reason why this needs to happen now?
- **Communications:** Do you have both the ability and the channels to tell the story of the innovation and move people to action?
- **Sizzle/buzz/coolness:** Is the innovation naturally attractive and image-enhancing?
- **Rights:** Do you own or have free access to relevant intellectual property?
- **Customer, receiver:** Is there a demand among customers or those who would take the innovation forward?
- **Supporting data:** Can you convince people of the viability of the innovation with demonstrations and facts?
- **Plan:** Have you specified the steps, requirements, people, and resources necessary to move the innovation to the next level or even to the marketplace?
- **Urgency:** Is there a deadline? Is this innovation required for survival?

- **Access:** Can you get to the talent, market, and decision makers required for success?
- **Passion:** Are you and your colleagues driven to make this happen despite sacrifice and disappointment?

It is rare that you will start out with every resource you need to realize an innovation. An objective assessment of what you have and what you don't have can be your best tool in crafting a pathway with a higher probability of success. And don't be discouraged if the list of assets is short. Really good ideas tend to attract more people and more resources over time. As the French writer Victor Hugo said, "Nothing is so powerful as an idea whose time has come."

you would see on any professionally managed project. The only interesting spin on this is differences between organizations. In some cases, this simply means choosing an approach and making sure that everyone has the knowledge to comply with it. On occasion, records must be kept in ways that satisfy the supervisors, auditors, and organizational controls of both IBM and the client partner. (And, of course, everyone needs to be trained in these circumstances.)

Since this is an innovation project, identifying and documenting variances (where we are versus where we should be) becomes more important. As one researcher described it, change makes it "a very tough job to keep everyone enthusiastic and understanding why and how the interim goals are moving. Changing the goals incrementally requires a lot of trust between all the members—on both the client side and the IBM side." And for FOAK, documentation is not routine; it is an essential part of demonstrating and enabling the feasibility of follow-on projects and keeping everyone on the same page.

Typically, a project manager tests a project for viability, with "not viable" being a possible outcome and discontinuing the project being an option. Although this is acceptable for other innovation projects, it is unacceptable for FOAK. In this sense, FOAK is peculiar. Certainly, a project manager must do ongoing risk analysis, based on a sober and unsentimental view of performance, achievement, and the likelihood of reaching goals. But while the ability of the assets to be transferred and commercialized is never a sure thing, a FOAK project cannot accept a situation where the assets are not delivered on time.

Ensuring Quality

Often, an innovation project has the creation of a prototype as its final goal, or at least an important milestone. While this is sometimes true for FOAK, more often a prototype is complete before the project begins. The work of the study is adapting and testing assets in a real environment. This puts the focus squarely on what is "good enough," and much of the endeavor is tied to making sure that whatever is produced delivers on the value that has been promised.

With an established offering, it is easy to see whether a deliverable meets the required standards. Quality assurance is trickier in the realm of innovation. The original vision may be unrealistic. Worse, it might be incomplete. Some things always turn out to be more difficult than imagined. And, along the way, fixes and patches are used to deal with problems.

For example, on the Reliable, Responsive, Real-Time Messaging FOAK, some of the technology the IBM Project Team was planning to use from an IBM product lab was not ready in time to meet the project schedule. The project aims to create a reliable, responsive, real-time messaging backbone across new and legacy systems to enable real-world-aware, event-driven applications. Think of any environment where it would be helpful to sense what is actually happening in real time and to be able to act on that information. The IBM Project Team had worked with the product lab, and even though the researchers made their requirements and deadlines well known, the product lab could not deliver. The IBM Project Team eventually worked out an agreement with the product lab to use a fallback plan, using a different code base.

The IBM Project Team did agree to reconsider moving back to the original planned code base, but in the end they stayed the course with the fallback plan. The decision was easy to make, because the IBM Project Team had hard deadlines and open communications with the product lab. They also had jointly identified the fallback with the product lab (which, by the way, was their catcher). Ultimately, perfection is impossible. To paraphrase the French poet Paul Valery, a project is never finished, only abandoned. Quality is not a Six Sigma ideal for the FOAK program; it is tied more to creating deliverables that meet the agreed-to objectives.

> *LESSON: Rather than use arbitrary measures of quality, the innovation team needs to clarify the precise needs of stakeholders and put in mechanisms to ensure that they are met.*

Agreed-to objectives that can be renegotiated in the face of change can become a trap. Under normal circumstances, the project has visibility to stakeholders, including executives and end users. They may have their own opinions, requests, and requirements. And although some are enormously helpful, in other cases, the project manager needs to run interference to allow the participants to do their jobs.

And while the project manager works to keep things moving without pushing things to the point where they are distorted or frustration becomes animosity, the IBM Project Team is not alone. For IBM Project Teams, the project checkpoint meetings with the FOAK PMT are as certain as death and taxes. These meetings, described in the next section, provide an outside view. However, the PMT is well aware of the project's commitments and the FOAK program goals. This group is invested in making the project a success. They bring their experience and cool heads to the IBM Project Teams and, like a good board of directors, can help them detect and correct any real problems. They can also provide encouragement, which is always appreciated by those who venture into unknown territory.

Project Checkpoint Meetings

One of the FOAK PMT's primary responsibilities is to convene quarterly checkpoint meetings with each of the IBM Project Teams. Each meeting lasts approximately 60 minutes. The exception is the third-quarter checkpoint, which is scheduled for 90 minutes to allow sufficient time for detailed discussions about the asset transfer and business model. The following is a summary of the guidance that is given to the IBM Project Teams to prepare for the checkpoint meetings:

- First-quarter meeting:
  - Measure progress against the milestones recorded in the funding letter.
  - Put the meeting focus primarily on the status of the client negotiations.

- Second-quarter meeting:
  - Measure progress against the milestones recorded in the funding letter.
  - Put the primary focus of the meeting on work with the client and refining the deliverables.
  - Initiate a discussion on how to create an Industry Solutions Lab demonstration (see Chapter 9, "Telling the Story: IBM's Industry Solutions Labs").

- Third-quarter meeting:
  - Measure progress against the milestones recorded in the funding letter.
  - Review the work with the client.
  - Discuss the asset transfer plan.
  - Review the plan to log the asset in an asset database for broader reuse.
  - Discuss the business model for delivery of the asset to other clients.

- Fourth-quarter meeting:
  - Measure progress against the milestones recorded in the funding letter.
  - Review the asset transfer status.
  - Review the business model.
  - Discuss lessons learned.
  - Check the status of the client reference.
  - Identify issues and next steps.

Managing the Project as a Whole

Ultimately, the pieces need to fit together. Above the subteam level are oversight responsibilities that are essential to the project's success. The project manager is responsible for the stuff in between—the linking of subteam deliverables, the integration of assets into the larger context, and determining that work is aligned with regard to timing and quality. He or she also needs to monitor efforts by the subteam to integrate their work products, from the perspectives of seeing that function is delivered and determining that the relationships between the subteams remain positive and constructive.

The characteristics of individual team members can become a factor in the project's success. As one IBM research FOAK leader stated, "Highly productive people typically can have difficult personalities. Outsiders who are not influenced by social pressure are a real problem. Sometimes it is better to do without them or divide the project so they have an isolated piece and are not part of the overall project's social fabric. They just soak up an enormous amount of management time."

As with any project, the project manager is responsible for making sure that controls are put in place and adhered to. Are changes in scope detected and reviewed? Is there a process for introducing changes? How and when is quality checked? Who is permitted to spend money, and how is the budget tracked?

The project manager needs to actively explore dependencies between groups, anticipating what each subteam needs and when. This becomes a moving target as changes are made or drifts in scope or goals occurs in subteams. Anytime a corrective action is needed, it is up to the project manager to make sure things get back on track. The scope of the Reliable, Responsive, Real-Time Messaging FOAK project, discussed earlier, was modified and refined multiple times over the project's lifetime (requiring lots of flexibility and focus on the part of the project manager). The IBM Project Team tried their best to accommodate the client's requirements, while also making sure that the changes could be supported by the resources available and that the research and the solution had enough innovative elements.

> **LESSON:** *The interactions between subgroups need to be actively managed with an eye toward doing what is best for the overall project.*

So there is a social aspect as well. The overall spirit of the Joint Project Team needs to be monitored. Conflicts between subteams need to be detected and resolved. And, since FOAK goes beyond the execution of the project to real-world adoption, the Joint Project Team, as a whole, needs to build a good reputation and even create excitement and anticipation beyond itself. Some Joint Project Teams also speak at conferences and write papers about their FOAK experiences. Making sure that the Joint Project Team members actively promote the FOAK project outside of the immediate team, maintaining communications and even seeking out opportunities to gain more recognition for the program, is part of the job for those leading the FOAK Project.

Developing Joint Project Team Members

FOAK projects provide learning opportunities for all involved. While the innovation itself introduces people to new concepts as they are explored, team members can develop career-changing skills and perspectives. The FOAK Board and PMT take this seriously—and not just because the experience of working side-by-side with IBM researchers is one of the program's selling points.

Those leading the FOAK projects may be responsible for specific transfer of technical skills. But they also are encouraged to create workshops, meetings, and one-on-one sessions to share points of view on innovation, work within specific organizations, socialize new ideas, and interact with executives. Those leading the FOAK projects will mentor and support other Joint Project Team members as they mentor each other.

This support is not limited to the IBM Project Team members. On one FOAK project at a large retailer, one of the researchers spent weeks teaching the FOAK client's staff things like Services-Oriented Architecture, process-driven modeling, and business analysis. He hosted weekly seminars and was even fondly referred to as "the professor" by the client's staff.

The environment must have a bias toward transparency if the FOAK Joint Project Team members are to get a clear view of how different disciplines approach problems, tackle organizational constraints, and deal with different values and cultures. Almost without exception, people on a FOAK Joint Project Team are faced with views that take them out of their comfort zones. The leaders of the Joint Project Team need to show the way by listening to other perspectives and tolerating, or even celebrating, the team's diversity.

No one comes to a FOAK project without development needs; ideally, no one leaves without growing professionally. Capabilities, mentoring, skills transfer, specifying roles, transparency, patience, teaching, next steps, and documentation all need to be mastered. FOAK is full of teachable moments. The proof that these are put to use for development of the participants is proven by how often FOAK participants take on related challenges.

Dealing with Setbacks and Obstacles

What happens if things go wrong? More correctly, what happens *when* things go wrong? As with any endeavor, new challenges must be made visible quickly. Problems that simmer usually don't go away; they get worse.

Although the FOAK PMT works to create a collaborative environment where frankness is encouraged, realistically, a FOAK IBM Project Team is always dealing with people who work in different organizational cultures. As one researcher noted, "The only thing that works when the problems are tough and you are depending on individuals who cannot be replaced is to get their buy-in. Make sure they feel it is their problem, and that they ... see how their contribution influences the results."

Getting such buy-in may take some creativity. The FOAK Joint Project Team often works across different national and ethnic cultures. Some of those who lead the Joint Project Teams prepare to deal with adversity by telling stories of past experiences. This is a powerful way to get people to talk and to promote the idea that it is okay to bring problems to light. However, behavioral examples are more powerful. How the first challenge, ugly surprise, or mistake is handled will determine in large part the willingness of participants to bring their problems forward.

LESSON: Because innovation collaborations involve different (business/national) cultures, leaders' responses to problems and mistakes need to be deliberate so that difficulties don't go unreported.

Operationally, any corrective action, as mentioned, must be documented and aligned to the overall goals. More subtly, the process of choosing the right action needs to be apparent to avoid damaging relationships between members of a Joint Project Team or its subteams.

There is another challenge. Since deadlines and resources are fixed, FOAK projects can be high-pressure. Setbacks, as they hit schedules, disrupt coordinated efforts, and absorb funds, can be a real blow to a Joint Project Team that is bent on realizing an idea they believe in. Passionate people can become deeply discouraged and even turn to blaming each other. The leaders of a Joint Project Team need to be the cool heads when things go wrong.

One FOAK IBM Project Team leader said that he needed to support the people doing work and portray a sense of optimism and a willingness to take his fair share of the blame—or, better yet, more than his fair share—but not too much, because that would undermine the importance of the people on the team. "Team members will generally chip in and deal with pressure if they feel they need to in order to be part of a well functioning team."

Deliverables

Each FOAK project has its own set of tangible deliverables. A broad description of these is specified in the contract, including roles and responsibilities. But more detailed descriptions, schedules, and contingencies are developed during the FOAK kickoff meeting (IBM internal) and the project workshop (the client and IBM).

Along the way, many of these deliverables are inevitably transformed, and responsibility for delivery may shift. As noted, any changes need to be well-documented. But IBM leaders of FOAK Joint Project Teams have the added responsibility of reaching out beyond the Joint Project Team to the catchers, sponsors, and others whose continued support will be needed if the assets created are to have a life beyond the project. Even subtle changes to a deliverable could make it unattractive or unusable.

For instance, code may have many contingencies, based on its requirement to run on certain systems, to accept data from various sources, and to deliver reports and other output. If the output doesn't make sense to those who are receiving (or catching) it, the asset may be valuable only after training, raising the cost of its adoption, and creating resistance among the end users. And if the code can't get along with the infrastructure that is in place, or if it is too difficult to maintain, it may be rejected out of hand. This was the risk that the FOAK team faced with the SCORE example described earlier. The IBM Project Team mitigated that risk by checking with the catcher before moving forward in a client environment that was not exactly aligned with the SCORE infrastructure.

Part of the FOAK delivery is closing down the project. Assets may not be simply handed off. Usually, they must be put into a form where they can wait for the next step and can be picked up easily. Open items must be handled. And because some members will be absorbed by what the work leads to, new research or development efforts suggested by the project's insights may need to be put on hold or redirected to work that goes beyond the FOAK project.

All contracts and commitments need to be reviewed to ascertain that the agreements have been met, and met to the satisfaction of all parties. Finally, leaders must gently remind Joint Project Team members of continuing responsibilities even as they are gracefully saying good-bye.

Beyond Deliverables

Completing the project is not the same as completing the FOAK commitment. FOAK assets need to be moved into the mainstream. As opposed to most innovation endeavors, if there is no reuse, even a project that delights the client and demonstrates its value cannot be counted as a success in FOAK. It becomes a one-of-a-kind that is not commercially viable.

Most members of the IBM Project Team probably will go back to their normal jobs—with the provision of acting as information resources to development teams. However, the leaders of the IBM Project Team need to reach out to the catchers, who have been oriented, cajoled, nurtured, and inspired along the way. They need to maintain their involvement—answering questions, providing code and documentation, presenting reports, and making the case for further investment in and commitment to commercialization of assets.

The IBM Research lead in the Joint Project Team for the Smart Surveillance Solution (SSS) FOAK, discussed in Chapter 2, "The FOAK Process: Phase I," was transferred into the asset commercialization organization for a period of time. He spent countless hours continuing to push the importance of SSS and the need for commercialization. Without his personal commitment, SSS never would have grown into a full-blown IBM services offering.

From a practical standpoint, the leaders of the IBM Project Team need to get onto stakeholder calendars and sync up with the budget cycle. They need to handle the when, how, and where of transferring assets. The trickiest part of this, which most FOAK projects face, is making sure nothing is lost during the hiatus between the end of the project and the beginning of commercialization. This may involve safely storing prototypes, putting code onto new systems, testing it to confirm it is working properly, and putting documentation into a form that will be clear and accessible to the commercialization team.

Obviously, a clean transfer of technical know-how also needs to occur. Ideally, this is well under way as part of the project. In some cases, the IBM Project Team members have moved right into the commercialization team (as was the case with the MedSpeak, SSS, and High-Performance Stream Processing FOAKs, mentioned earlier in the book), making transfer unnecessary. In most cases, however, the leaders of the IBM Project Team need to reach out to manage the process of getting informational materials into the hands of technical people who are receiving the FOAK assets. They need to introduce them to the overall project and identify a process for training. This effort may include bringing in the technical people from the IBM Project Team to answer questions, monitor work, and help iron out any remaining inconsistencies between the assets created and the development environment.

Since thought leadership is part of the design of FOAK, work must be done on promotions, especially the press release and an ISL demonstration (discussed in detail in Chapter 9). For the press release, the IBM Project Team as a whole may be engaged to validate copy, provide quotes, and make themselves available for interviews. Perhaps the most important duty here is to look closely at the project's story and make sure that it is told accurately and completely. The real benefits and achievements need to be clearly explained, and any distortions or exaggerations need to be challenged and eliminated.

> **LESSON:** *Telling the innovation story is essential to maintaining a program, but the innovators must be involved in how these stories are told so that misrepresentations are avoided.*

Figure 8.1 shows a FOAK press release. IBM wrote it with the University of Ontario Institute of Technology (UOIT) for a FOAK project that aims to help doctors detect subtle changes in the condition of critically ill premature babies.

First-of-a-Kind Technology to Help Doctors Care for Premature Babies

IBM and University of Ontario Institute of Technology Collaborate With Canadian Hospital to Help Protect Changes in Infants' Condition

ARMONK, NY and TORONTO – 23 Jul 2008: IBM (NYSE:IBM) and the University of Ontario Institute of Technology (UOIT) announced today a first-of-a-kind research project to help doctors detect subtle changes in the condition of critically ill premature babies.

The project will see a group of internationally recognized researchers, led by Dr. Carolyn McGregor, a UOIT associate professor and Canada Research Chair in Health Informatics, use advanced stream computing software developed by IBM Research to work toward greatly enhancing the decision-making capabilities of doctors. The software ingests a constant stream of biomedical data, such as heart rate and respiration, along with environmental data gathered from advanced sensors and more traditional monitoring equipment on and around the babies.

The researchers will also use the software to apply findings from Dr. McGregor's body of research to help make "sense" of the data and, in near-real-time, feed back the resulting analysis to health-care professionals so they can predict potential changes in an infant's condition with greater accuracy and intervene more quickly.

Physicians in neonatal intensive care units (NICU) at Toronto's Hospital for Sick Children and two international hospitals are participating in the study.

Monitoring "preemies" as a patient group is especially important as certain life-threatening conditions such as infection can be detected up to 24 hours in advance by observing changes in physiological data streams.

The type of information that will come out of the research project is not available today. Currently, physicians monitoring preemies rely on a paper-based process that involves manually looking at the reading from various monitors and getting feedback from the nurses providing care.

"This research has the potential to really impact neonatal care through reduced mortality and morbidity rates and overall health-care costs," said Dr. McGregor. "By merging our research and technology, we are able to get advanced early warning of emerging patterns that could predict a medical event."

When fully developed, IBM's software will be capable of processing the 512 readings per second generated by some of these medical devices, and UOIT researchers will further test and develop its ability to analyze these vast quantities of data in real time.

Initially researchers will use NICU medical devices in UOIT's state-of-the-art Health Informatics Laboratory to test IBM's software using simulated patient mirroring data. Then the software will be tested using de-identified actual patient data. The de-identified data is recorded in a way that enables researchers to alter some variables, play it back, and run simulations for further study.

IBM awarded Dr. McGregor access to the prototype software patented by researchers at its T.J. Watson research facility in New York under its First-of-a-Kind program, which is designed to accelerate the delivery of innovative technologies to the market and link IBM's research work to real world problems.

"Right now, there is an enormous amount of critical data produced by machines monitoring patients," said Don Aldridge, business executive for IBM research and life science. "That creates a challenge. The ability to quickly analyze that data and make informed decisions will help improve the overall quality of health care."

About UOIT

For more information on UOIT, visit www.uoit.ca.

Figure 8.1   Sample FOAK press release

Finally, those leading the FOAK Project Team must find ways to influence all the parties relevant to asset transfer. This involves facing all the typical challenges of change management. As they move into the real-world environment, with all its competing demands and even active opposition, the IBM Project Team must remind stakeholders of what the project is and why it is worth continued investment and focus. They need to provide demonstrations and clearly state the value propositions, keyed to specific audiences. They need to validate commitment from the essential individuals. They need to make sure that people see the path for adoption or adaptation of the assets, and that all parties have what they need to play their roles.

The Mobile Measurement Tool (MMT) FOAK project was originally targeted for commercialization by IBM's Global Technology Services organization. The project developed a tool to diagnose where, how, and when power is being used in datacenters. Using a rolling cart with sensors to determine hot spots, air leakage, and other inefficiencies in datacenters, MMT has enabled multiple clients (including IBM) to realize, on average, energy savings of approximately 10%. But for the catching organization, priorities shifted. The MMT FOAK temporarily became a lower priority in their commercialization plan, and the FOAK IBM Project Team suddenly found themselves looking for a new catcher.

Working together, the IBM Project Team identified and pitched to another group in IBM that provides selected services based on hardware platforms and datacenter management. They became immediately interested in MMT and began offering it as one of their services. Later, the original catcher was able to prioritize MMT as a solution. Currently, both organizations provide MMT as a service offering.

The process of convincing others, getting commitments, and making sure that the value of the FOAK assets is realized can take many forms. But it usually involves researching organizations (and getting up-to-date news on financial concerns, product plans, success criteria, and the organization's vision), learning more about the decision makers, and creating and executing a plan for asset adoption. In addition, the IBM Project Team needs to hold one-on-one meetings and create collateral, such as chart talks, to clearly and persuasively tell the story of the assets and how they must be accepted, supported, and maintained.

Summary

The project manager takes the lead in making sure a project proceeds to completion, but FOAK uses a coordinated approach that involves a number of people acting as leaders on a FOAK Joint Project Team. Clarifying and refocusing goals takes on a different character when catchers are engaged. Taking advantage of the experience of the IBM PMT and scheduled meetings may help the Joint Project Team keep the broader view from eroding and the scope from growing.

There is almost no flexibility in budget or deadlines, and, because of commitments to the client, the usual option of shutting down a project in trouble is unavailable. At the same time, quality cannot be compromised (although it is not quality that aims for perfection).

Within all the work, time and effort must be taken to develop Joint Project Team members professionally, explicitly building their capabilities and skills. This is as much a deliverable of the FOAK program as lines of code or business architectures. And, of course, the commitments don't end when the project ends.

Once the FOAK project is completed and asset commercialization plans are being finalized, the IBM Project Team needs to share the results of the project more broadly to generate demand for the assets. Chapter 9 explores one mechanism (the Industry Solutions Labs) that IBM Project Teams use to tell their FOAK innovation stories to the masses.

9

Telling the Story: IBM's Industry Solutions Labs

At the conclusion of each FOAK project, the FOAK Joint Project Team has an important accomplishment: They've created a solution to a real business problem or new market opportunity, and it has been proven with a single client. But the job isn't done. The IBM Project Team still needs to work on gaining broader marketplace awareness of the results of its project so that the work can generate market demand and attract the attention of the catching organization(s). A healthy pipeline of new opportunities will motivate the catching organization(s) to accelerate their efforts in commercializing the assets.

The IBM Industry Solutions Labs (ISLs) help do this for FOAK. In a sense, they are often the program's alpha and omega. It is not unusual for a FOAK idea to originate at an ISL, and *all* FOAK projects are required to provide the ISLs with demos. These demos are automatically queued to be presented at one of the ISLs. More broadly, the ISLs provide an example of an approach to taking complex, technical, and unfamiliar stories and making them both relevant and appealing to a variety of audiences.

The ISLs are executive-level briefing centers. They enable the FOAK program to take the results from a single project with one client and share them with thousands of other clients and partners. This featuring of projects allows IBM to continue exploring new uses for the FOAK innovations.

Demonstrating Innovation

There are currently four ISL locations: Hawthorne, New York; Zurich, Switzerland; Beijing, China; and Delhi, India. The mission of the ISLs is "to inspire clients and IBM's business partners to choose IBM as their long-term solutions and services partner by providing an innovative environment where they can experience the depth and breadth of IBM's flagship technology, industry expertise, and thought leadership." Each of the ISLs is colocated with an IBM Research lab, which provides a rich source of researchers who have hands-on knowledge and deep expertise. These researchers, along with subject matter experts from across the IBM Corporation, meet with clients and business partners visiting the ISLs to share market, solution, and emerging-technology insights.

The ISLs have boardroom-quality meeting space for briefings, discussions, and workshops, but the heart of an ISL is the exhibit floor. Here, hundreds of demonstrations, artifacts, and prototypes are showcased, with written explanations that span a selected range of innovative industry solutions, product offerings, and research prototypes. They present solutions available today from IBM, as well as the research innovations of what is to come tomorrow, including the results of FOAK projects. But the exhibits aren't merely a glimpse of technology for technology's sake. They are true examples of how technology was applied in collaboration with a client or business partner to solve a business problem. They offer ISL visitors a chance to stretch their thinking and explore technology from a totally new perspective. Guests, usually C-level executives, may wander the floor during breaks and literally read the writing on the walls.

Hardly your typical briefing centers, the ISLs offer agendas focused entirely on bringing together clients, business partners, and IBM's top industry experts and researchers from around the globe. The agendas can be focused on an immediate business opportunity or problem, or they can be more broadly crafted to explore an array of emerging technologies. These gatherings result in a rich exchange on the implications of industry and technology trends. At the ISLs, visitors can imagine how a particular technology might move their business forward—or allow their business to be outflanked, if they fail to adopt the technology before the competition.

The ISLs host over 8,000 external visitors each year. Figure 9.1 provides a snapshot of the groups that visited the ISLs in 2008 by sector. Each sector represents a group of industries, including the following:

- **Communications:** Telecommunications, Energy & Utilities, Media & Entertainment
- **Financial services:** Banking, Financial Markets, Insurance
- **Distribution:** Consumer Products, Wholesale Distribution & Services, Retail, Travel & Transportation

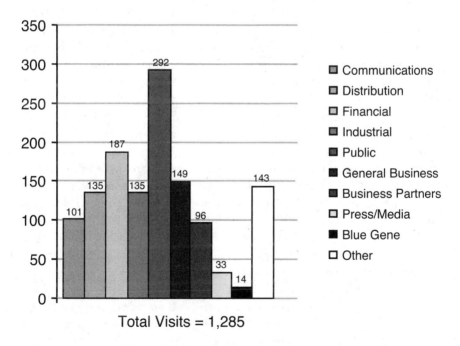

Figure 9.1   2008 worldwide Industry Solutions Lab visits

- **Public:** Government, Healthcare & Life Sciences, Education
- **Industrial:** Automotive, Electronics, Chemical & Petroleum, Aerospace & Defense

In the past, the financial services sector accounted for the largest number of visits to the ISLs, but with the emergence of the life sciences market and the increase in government spending worldwide in areas such as defense and security, the public sector has taken the lead in generating the most visits (from 2005 to 2008).

The ISL client programs generally are one or two days in duration. They begin with the client discussing their vision, challenges, and opportunities with an audience of IBM industry thought leaders, research scientists, and technology experts. Each IBM participant then positions his or her messages within the context of that specific client, fueling more compelling discussions. These mutual exchanges provide both parties with new approaches to business and technology challenges or, better yet, the spark that ignites a whole new business by applying technology in ways never before considered. Recall the High-Performance Stream Processing Platform FOAK discussed in Chapter 3, "How Ideas Take Shape." The original FOAK idea surfaced when the client visited the ISL. The discussions during that visit led the way to the FOAK project, which in turn led to the announcement of a new offering from IBM Software Group: InfoSphere Streams.

The ISLs' extensive demonstration floors are intended to bring together the best of IBM innovation and leadership into one consolidated showcase. Thus, they are also an appropriate venue for press and media events. Each year more than 30 such events are hosted at the ISLs, increasing IBM's mindshare. The events can be as simple as a photo shoot or as complicated as a live TV broadcast to multiple sites around the world.

Although the floor is effective in stand-alone mode, it really comes alive when the Content Managers (the ISL employees responsible for the exhibits and presentation) and IBM subject matter experts use the exhibits to explain new solutions and technologies, talk about client business value, listen to client comments, and answer questions. Often, ideas from one industry are shared with clients in another industry to broaden their perspectives on ways to innovate.

Turning a FOAK Project into a Prototype Demonstration

The development of a compelling FOAK demonstration is all about asking questions, making suggestions, tweaking, and reframing. The documentation from the FOAK project is the foundation for development, and the Content Manager absorbs, analyzes, and reinterprets it. The Content Manager then acts as a consultant to the IBM FOAK Project Team, helping them build a demonstration that highlights not only the technology innovation, but also its business value. The Content Managers spend hundreds of hours doing demonstrations, so they have tremendous knowledge of what works and what doesn't. They know what they need in a demonstration to make it communicate across many audiences.

After the researchers build the demonstration and install it at one of the ISLs, the researchers are invited in to discuss the project with the ISL Content Managers. This is not a presentation. It is an informal explanation to Content Managers by someone who knows the project intimately. The Content Managers may interrupt and ask questions. The whole session is taped.

Now the Content Manager is transformed from demonstration consultant to developer of the presentation. He or she must extract the salient points from the researcher's talk and organize them into a narration that takes full advantage of any pictures, words, artifacts, and simulations that are at hand. The narration must get the messages across in business terms and make them memorable. The researcher, who has been working with the Content Manager all along, picks at any errors or misleading shadings of the narration.

Interestingly enough from a FOAK perspective, the content that gets showcased at the ISLs doesn't necessarily need to be from a "successfully" completed project. The ISLs do showcase prototypes from FOAK projects that were terminated for lack of securing a client or projects that finished successfully yet did not make it to the marketplace as a commercialized offering. Why would the ISLs do this? Because the prototypes are still proof points of innovation. They can stimulate interesting discussions with clients about why IBM couldn't secure a client, the challenges the IBM Project Team experienced trying to commercialize the assets, and the lessons that were learned.

In fact, in some instances showcasing "unsuccessful" prototypes at the ISLs has actually generated a renewed interest in the innovation. One case in point is Veggie Vision (shown in the background of Figure 9.5). It captures the color, texture, shape, and size of an item to automatically deduce what it is. That way, retailers can truly compare apples and oranges. The result is fewer errors and faster checkout lines. Veggie Vision was an exploratory IBM Research project back in 1994. It gained renewed interest in 2000 when clients visiting one of the ISLs decided that they wanted to have the prototype installed at one of their model stores of the future. That client bought multiple licenses for deployment of the solution in their stores in Europe.

Going from Demonstration to Exhibit

Literally hundreds of demonstrations of IBM products, solutions, and prototypes are hidden within the nooks and crannies of the IBM labs, sales offices, and even on the laptops of thousands of mobile workers worldwide. It is not realistic, or even necessary, to have every demonstration that exists in IBM installed at the ISLs. But what *is* important is to have in place content that is relevant to the audience and comprehensive enough to tell an end-to-end story without overwhelming or, worse, boring the audience.

The ISLs have Content Managers who are responsible for combing through IBM for proof points that will help the ISL tell a story about a particular industry, solution area, or hot new technology space. The Content Managers need to ensure a balance of content that has broad appeal—technical versus business, today versus tomorrow, global versus local. When determining what to showcase, a number of factors need to be considered. Who is the primary audience, and what is their comfort level with technology? What level of funding is available—not just for the initial procurement and installation, but also for the ongoing maintenance and support? What knowledge is required to do a quality job in demonstrating the solutions and prototypes? What is the anticipated shelf life of the content, and how much space will it consume? All of these factors, along with the local market requirements and the specific research lab's areas of expertise, are considered when determining what content goes into each of the ISLs.

> *LESSON: There is so much to say about an innovation that it is essential to develop consistent, clear, results-focused messages before any exhibits or other mass communications are created.*

According to John Mackay, a Content Manager at the Hawthorne ISL, even before a FOAK project is completed, he and his colleagues are busy learning about the technologies, their applications, and their potential for presentation to clients and business partners. The messages have to be conveyed in a short amount of time, and IBM wants the clients and business partners to learn something new that is relevant or interesting to them and that helps improve their image of IBM. It is also important that clients remember the messages after they leave, and even tell someone later about the interesting things they learned during their ISL visit.

When a Content Manager forwards presentation slides on a laptop during a mobile computing presentation using a working Linux watch with Bluetooth, this not only instills a level of credibility, but it is also entertaining and can inject a different level of energy into the discussion.

One frequent presenter would come to the ISL with his pockets filled with all sorts of gadgets. He was like a magician performing a show, drawing his audience further and further into the future of mobile computing.

Having a concrete sample of a concept or innovation makes it more real. Most people can imagine things in an abstract sense, but your imagination really kicks in when you can see, touch, and interact with something. That is why the ISLs invest significantly in their solution and technology showcases. These exhibits reinforce the IBM brand messaging, help generate credibility, and fuel interesting conversations.

John points out that, from the early days of exhibit development, he keeps three things in mind as he works with the FOAK IBM Project Teams:

- What are the messages?
- How can the narration be simplified?
- What are the possibilities for visuals?

The messages IBM wants to deliver to specific audiences may not simply be a translation of the FOAK project goals. In fact, the "sweet spot" for messages may even be in a different industry from that of the FOAK project. A message could have a larger impact on or more appeal to the guests who visit the ISL if positioned within a different industry. Or the messages might also be integrated into a Big Story—a complex of eight or even more demos that can provide a high-impact experience for an executive.

Once the Content Manager has determined what story and which exhibits are needed, he or she needs to decide how to tell the story. Is an exhibit needed to provide some level of background and education? Perhaps a historical perspective on where this technology, solution, or industry came from would help the audience appreciate the full value of the innovations. Is a full-blown, live system required, or will a more lightweight format (such as an automated video) suffice? Will this be a 5-minute FYI or a 30-minute deep-dive discussion?

Simplification may also be required, because researchers bring along too many specifics. And the reasons why they are interested in the FOAK project tend to differ from the reasons why an ISL guest would be interested. Deciding what to leave out and what to include can involve numerous conversations and, in some cases, negotiations. Faulkner's advice to writers was "Kill all your darlings." Something similar is required here, but it is not easily carried out. The Content Managers have the ultimate rebuttal to a frustrated researcher: "I know the audience."

> **LESSON:** *To paraphrase Einstein, communications around technologies should be made as simple as possible, but no simpler.*

Because Content Managers *do* know the audience—distracted executives with to-do lists in their heads and BlackBerries in their hands—they are always looking for movement, color, and composition. Catch the eye, and you catch the brain. The visual possibilities of a project may stand out at times, but often they need to be invented.

A tremendous amount of thinking goes into not only the content, but also how the content needs to be presented. The process starts with an initial discussion with members of the ISL staff to collect ideas. But the Content Managers of the ISL don't stand alone. Designers are contracted with to act as sounding boards and work through the options with the Content Managers.

CREATING EXHIBITS FOR COMPELLING DEMONSTRATIONS

A presenter can choose from a host of different types of exhibits when trying to get people excited about innovation. Some are more complicated and harder to maintain. Some have a short shelf life, and yet others seem to live on forever. Let's explore just three of the many different options:

- **Props:** Having a mock-up of a futuristic newspaper when discussing the future of digital media, a blood pressure cuff when describing the future of healthcare, or a laminated chip when talking about the miniaturization of technology can help the audience join the presenter on a journey into the future.

- **Live systems:** Live systems run real code on full-blown systems. They can be local or networked into larger infrastructures. Live system exhibits generally require a higher level of investment, more time and resources to upgrade and maintain, and higher levels of skills to demonstrate and support. Also, they generally are more difficult to manage. But they are the real McCoy and bring a tremendous amount of credibility. If they are networked, they demonstrate interoperability and enable the sharing of scarce resources, which in many cases is the deciding factor.

- **Simulated systems:** Simulated systems look like live systems, but they are not truly operational. They are built using tools such as Flash, HTML/XML, PowerPoint, and Camtasia. They can be designed to be multipath or single-path. Multipath simulated systems allow the operator of the demonstration to interact with multiple threads, whereas single-path simulated systems limit the operator to only one path that can be traversed.

These exhibits give the audience a good sense of what the environment would look like at a very high level. They whet the appetite and many times generate an action item for a deeper dive.

Having a design firm that truly understands your brand and mission, and that is easy to collaborate with, is essential. A design firm can help the Content Managers create exhibits that are useful, yet interesting and engaging to broad audiences. The attractiveness is especially important, because some guests may not be escorted by a trained IBMer as they view the exhibits.

Generally, the ISLs look for a combination of past, present, and future messaging to tell the story of a particular technology or solution area. For example, the Grid & Autonomic Computing exhibit takes the audience through the evolution of Web standards, a deep dive into the underlying infrastructure of New York City, and then a demonstration of the power of grid computing, using advanced systems and scheduling algorithms.

In all instances, the ISLs try to craft exhibits in a way that allows an exhibit to be refreshed or totally transformed to keep up with the pace of innovation while preserving the base infrastructure for reuse. These exhibits take time and resources to design and are costly to fabricate. Being able to reuse components is important and facilitates the process of introducing new content. The Content Managers currently are transitioning the Grid & Autonomic exhibit at the Hawthorne ISL into a cloud computing exhibit. They anticipate being able to reuse many of the original components.

Together, the Content Manager and the designer outline the exhibit's goals and share preliminary ideas. Then a series of back-and-forth discussions take place between the ISL team and the design firm. Eventually, a rough schematic emerges that includes shapes, layouts, and dimensions. The schematic is shared within the ISL and with other IBM organizations responsible for IBM's messaging in the specific solution or technology area being developed. When a level of confidence with the design has been achieved, a miniature to-scale prototype of the exhibit is created, as shown in Figure 9.2.

With the prototype established, individual components of the exhibits begin to emerge, each with its own mock-up. The office of the Content Manager leading the development of an exhibit becomes a mini studio for the exhibit, as shown in Figure 9.3, where mock components of the exhibit are displayed on the walls. People within and outside of the ISL are invited in to review and contribute to the evolving exhibit. Not incidentally, designers become a rich source of naïve questions. If you can explain it to a designer, you probably can explain it to an executive. The tougher audience is more likely to be an IBM client executive with an interest in the topic. These executives, with a deep understanding of clients and industries, will look over every aspect of the exhibit and presentation before they go live with a real audience. Where necessary, signs are reworded, models are rebuilt, and narrations are rephrased until they are ready to go.

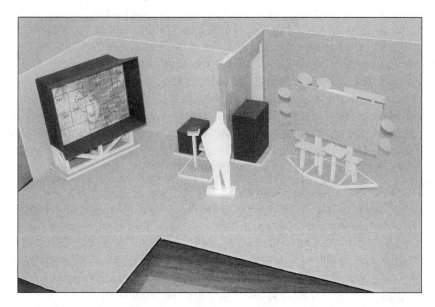

Figure 9.2 Industry Solutions Lab exhibit prototype

Figure 9.3 ISL exhibit prototype development in Content Manager John Mackay's office

DEVELOPING MEANINGFUL EXHIBITS

At the ISLs, IBM uses a mix of demonstrations, videos, props, and presentations to tell a broad end-to-end story about a specific solution or technology area. An exhibit is a kaleidoscope of education and historical retrospective, with a glance into the future. If properly designed, an exhibit should give a Content Manager or subject matter expert the flexibility to talk to a client anywhere from five minutes to one hour. One IBM consultant commented upon seeing the Component Business Model to Service-Oriented Architecture exhibit shown in Figure 9.4, "I can deliver my entire presentation right here!"

Since these exhibits are costly to design, lots of energy is invested in the upfront design to ensure longevity, versatility, and future repurposing, if needed. For example, the technology innovation wall at the Hawthorne, New York ISL was designed and installed in 1997 when the ISL was first opened. As new IBM Research milestones were achieved, they needed to be added to the exhibit. Since the exhibit was designed with modularity in mind, it has been relatively easy to make additions over the

Figure 9.4   Hawthorne ISL exhibit designed in collaboration with Puches Design, Inc.

years. This exhibit is at the entrance to the Hawthorne ISL. It continues to draw interest and spark discussions on where technology comes from and where it is headed.

For a business intelligence exhibit, the original concept was to use a ball of string to represent the complexities or "spaghetti"-like nature of information, with its intricate relationships inside and outside an organization. The Content Managers decided that if they ever wanted to repurpose the exhibit, a ball of string would be limiting. The ISL team opted for a more flexible set of three fiber-optic illuminated grids to illustrate the collection, storage, and management of volumes of information; the analysis of the information; and the insights that are gained from providing the right information to the right people at the right time—the holy grail of information management. Currently the sign above the exhibit is being updated to align it with IBM's new Business Analytics and Optimization service line campaign. Because the exhibit was designed with flexibility in mind, the alignment is easy.

For each component of the exhibit, decisions need to be made about the materials, colors, lighting, text, and fonts. Although these seem like simple decisions to make, anyone who has had the experience of building or remodeling a home knows they are not. Trying to visualize what the full-scale exhibit will look like with the components in various materials is difficult. As the exhibit moves toward completion and components are finished, it becomes necessary for the design firm to create a true-to-scale mock-up of the exhibit.

This is done in the design firm's studio. Field trips to the studio become a part of the process at this point, so when a design firm is chosen, the location of its studio is a consideration. As each component of the exhibit is completed, the components of the life-sized prototype begin to be replaced by the actual components of the exhibit until the completed exhibit is standing in the design firm's studio. After final review, the exhibit is dismantled and reinstalled in the ISL. This process, although long (typically 6 to 12 months), ensures that no misunderstandings occur about what the exhibit will look like and how it will fit into the ISL's infrastructure.

Effective Demos Require Skilled Communicators

Not everyone is suited to be an ISL presenter. The Content Managers and subject matter experts who perform on the demo floor must be highly skilled and credible. They need to be equipped with not only technical skills, but, more importantly, soft skills that make them easy to approach and enter into discussions with.

The best of them have a presence that attracts people and keeps their attention. They are skilled at using body language and tone of voice to underline their points. They stay "on message" in the midst of side discussions, and they avoid the temptation to make quotable but unprofessional remarks.

Above all, good ISL presenters have several characteristics:

- They are lively and entertaining while remaining focused on their message.

- They are good at customizing presentations so that they match the audience's interests.

- They are genuinely curious about and interested in what they are talking about; they have internalized their narrations.

- They know the details of the subject and how it links to key aspects of client industries.

- They know how to articulate key points and how to express the essence of the discussion.

- They listen actively.

- They are credible.

The best presenters have broad industry knowledge and deep technical skills in an emerging technology or solution area. They need to be able to talk at the strategy level and yet dive deeply into the technical aspects of their field without overwhelming the audience. They need mature networks to draw on to secure new content, training, and ongoing support. They need to be savvy enough to pick up on the body language of their audience and know when to move on, when to dive in more deeply, and when to abandon a topic. But perhaps the most important aspects are good communication and passion. Audiences cannot help listening to good speakers, and, when they are passionate, the audience has no choice but to get emotionally involved.

In effect, the Content Managers, as both developers and presenters, are translators who take on the challenge of bringing valuable insights from one world—the world of technology—into another world—the world of business or government. They orient, explain, and persuade in as little as 15 minutes. And while they may not be able to go as deeply into the topics as the researchers and other subject matter experts, they provide enticing information that engages executives so that relationships are deepened and follow-on activities, such as workshops, are scheduled.

Beyond the Exhibit: Big Stories and the Customer Experience Center

Like all the Content Managers, John Mackay is always on the lookout for the Big Story. As time goes on, natural selection takes place on the ISL floor, with the exhibits that resonate with clients and that catch the zeitgeist, making themselves evident. To subjective observations, he adds the quantitative data of which exhibits are chosen most often for client visits. And, through monthly discussions with peers at the other ISLs, he finds out about new exhibits in development at those ISLs, as well as what his colleagues are hearing with regard to what IBM clients are focused on worldwide.

In some cases, this may just mean that a specific exhibit gets enhanced. But occasionally a Big Story emerges, such as High-Performance Computing. Big Stories tend to have an anchor exhibit: one demonstration that makes the point well, clearly, attractively, and broadly. Anchor exhibits will have already shown that their narrations are popular, resilient, and rich in possibilities.

To the anchor, a Content Manager adds other narrations from elsewhere on the ISL exhibit floor or from reference materials, such as newspaper articles or histories. The goal is to build a more compelling basis for a presentation, with options that allow both subject matter experts and Content Managers to generate deep, involving conversations on-the-fly. These conversations can be customized to make the case for a far-reaching and significant theme, or they can lead to an exploration of a real and immediate solution.

In parallel with Big Stories, the ISLs are creating scenario-based exhibits called Customer Experience Centers, as shown in Figure 9.5. These are industry- rather than solution- or technology-centered, and they provide another way to generate rich and productive conversations. Essentially, these exhibits leverage all the different approaches just discussed and physically place the audience in that environment (a store, a warehouse, a bank, a hospital). This is perhaps the most compelling way to present innovation. However, it should be noted that Customer Experience Centers are expensive to install and maintain, require the most real estate, and require superior subject matter expertise to credibly operate and position all the different aspects at both a business and technical level.

Figure 9.5   A Customer Experience Center at the Hawthorne ISL

Using Scenarios to Promote Discussion

IBM's intention in building the ISLs was to create circumstances for meaningful, productive conversations with key clients and business partners. Scenarios are used because stories are engaging and tend to provoke more discussion than alternatives, such as presentations on technologies and industry trends. Their unfinished and somewhat speculative nature provides openings that lead to questions and the imagining of new possibilities. Because they deal with actual uses of technology in a business context (and not just bare function), they invite the participation of people from a range of disciplines who can discuss opportunities on a level playing field.

For scenarios to work, the participants (both IBMers and clients) need to be forward-looking people. They must know what a scenario is and how it can be used. They must be comfortable with stories put to work for business purposes (that they're not a waste of time) and with unpolished presentations. They must be willing to be interactive. They must be comfortable enough (tested by early conversations) to use the chosen scenario as a tool for imagination.

If any of these criteria are not met, a scenario may not be appropriate. As attractive as they are, it is good to keep in mind that scenarios are not the only way to achieve rich conversations.

Scenario scripts draw from many sources, including IBM Research's Global Technology Outlook. This is a comprehensive analysis that looks five to ten years into the future, and considers the cultural and business contexts in which new technology will be used and the impact it will have on IBM and the world. They may also come from the IBM Global Innovation Outlook (www.ibm.com/ibm/gio/). This is IBM's annual technology and business forecasting process. Finally, they can be drawn from market intelligence and research from the IBM's Institute for Business Value (briefly described in Chapter 5, "Choosing the Best Projects"). Subject matter experts review scenario drafts for industry relevance, technical accuracy, messaging, and usability. The last step in developing a scenario is the customization done by the ISL teams, including the presenters.

Scenarios must be created with a target audience in mind:

- Right industry
- Right role
- Right interest points
- Right vocabulary
- Right pacing

The success of scenarios and stories depends on their focus on purpose, understanding of audience, execution, and context. Scenarios and stories have tremendous power, but they are effective only if their designs are aligned with their purpose. Correct execution of the scenario is all about having the right person tell the story with the right presentation skills and the right support.

For scenarios to be executed well:

- The format must be appropriate in terms of use of audiovisual material, pacing, and openings for conversation.
- The storyteller must listen as well as talk and be able to adjust in real time.
- Supporting people and collateral must be available.
- Ideas and commitments must be recorded and prepared for follow-up.

The storyteller must buy into the scenario (it can be out of his or her comfort zone, but he or she can't just be following orders), be able to listen, and have some ability to improvise. Questions are prepared in advance, and other IBMers must know their roles.

Storytellers need to be able to clearly present the chosen scenario. They need to highlight messages and the enabling technologies, to answer questions about technologies (or offer to follow up on these), and to contribute to the discussion. If the scenario is not connecting for some reason, the storyteller may need to shift to a variation, and he or she needs to be prepared to do so. Since the purpose of the experience is to engage in discussion, it's possible that the conversation will move beyond the scenario. This is a good thing; storytellers shouldn't feel obliged to complete the scenario.

LESSON: *A major part of telling the story of an innovation is listening to the audience.*

The story's context—room, timing, state of the audience, audiovisual material, distractions, even the dress code—also can have a major impact on success. The room must support the experience, theme, and purpose.

Where the scenario is placed on the agenda and the time committed are important. The audience needs energy and focus. Audiovisual materials need to fit the audience and environment. Distractions of noise, interesting sights outside the windows, laptops, and phones can kill the impact. Scenarios cannot be multitasked.

Finally, results must be the focus. For instance, if the scenario is intended to create follow-on sales opportunities, members of the sales team need to be present and to assume the responsibility of following up on the opportunity.

Managing the Content of the Exhibits

Content management at the ISLs is a continuous process. IBM is a big company with lots of new commercialized products and services being introduced each day, along with a steady stream of new inventions emerging from its eight research labs. Staying on top of all this new content is a challenge, and the ISLs struggle with balancing time, money, space, and skills. Let's look at some of the key tasks that need to be completed to bring new content into an ISL:

- **Content identification:** Just scouting IBM on a regular basis to understand what is available is not workable, because it is so time-consuming. A better approach for the ISLs was to establish a network of subject matter experts for a specific industry solution or technology area and to reach out to them periodically to gather suggestions for new content. Over time, many of these subject matter experts have started to actively contact the ISLs, alerting them of new content that they think would have a place in the ISLs.

- **Content tracking:** All the information about a particular exhibit or demonstration is maintained in a database. This includes the following:

  - Owner of the content
  - Subject matter experts who can help demonstrate and answer questions
  - Configurations with start-up and shut-down procedures
  - Scripts and training videos
  - Intellectual property law (IPL) clearance forms
  - The specific location of the installed exhibits and demonstrations

Multiple views of the data are offered so that the ISL can see at a glance what is installed, planned, or retired. With hundreds of demonstrations in flight, a central repository is essential.

- **Space allocation:** The ISLs can never contain all that IBM has to offer. Understanding space requirements helps determine what actually makes it into each individual ISL. Some exhibits and demonstrations are just too big. The task of allocating space involves not just finding the room, but ensuring that the exhibit is in an area of the floor that makes sense.

When moving visitors from one exhibit to the next, you want to do so in a logical flow. Bouncing back and forth from alternate points on the exhibit floor is disruptive to the conversations and consumes time.

- **Intellectual property law:** Any research content that is installed at the ISLs needs to go through an IPL clearance check. It is the responsibility of the Content Manager to make sure the researcher gets this done. This clearance basically ensures that all the proper patents have been filed and that the naming used by the IBM Research team has been cleared for public use. This step often prevents a new demonstration from being showcased. It is one of those processes that annoys the researchers but is necessary.

- **Installation:** For each exhibit and demonstration, equipment needs to be configured and ordered, and the base systems need to be installed. Once the base system is ready, the owner of the content can install his or her components in their lab or in staging areas outside the public ISL exhibit space. With the IPL clearance in place, the content can then be moved onto the ISL floor.

- **Documentation:** One of the most important yet least attractive tasks for a Content Manager is creating supporting documentation. It is necessary to have each exhibit and demonstration well-documented so that anyone on the ISL staff can work with it. Documenting the start-up and shut-down procedures, along with scripts and key talking points, is essential.

- **Training:** As stated, after the exhibit or demonstration is installed, the owner of the content is invited to the ISL to do onsite training of the staff. The training is recorded as a reference and to train new staff members.

Maintaining all the ISL exhibits, demonstrations, and equipment can be unwieldy. So it's crucial to document and exercise the tasks just described as part of a standard process.

But the real enabler of content management at the ISLs is effective communications. It takes time and energy to ensure that everyone who has a hand in the development, installation, maintenance, and use of the content is aware of its status and location and that they have access to the documentation.

Keeping It Fresh

Innovation has a short shelf life. Daily interaction with clients, business partners, and the host of IBMers who visit the ISLs each day helps drive awareness of what interests people most. Listening to the ISL visitors while understanding IBM's portfolio of current offerings and having insight into what is going on in IBM Research enables the ISLs to identify a continuous stream of new and engaging exhibits, demonstrations, and topics.

It is absolutely a team effort—an effort that spans not only the ISLs, but the entire IBM Corporation. IBMers visiting the ISLs make suggestions on new content and take extra steps to help make the connections. By word of mouth, IBMers refer other innovators to the ISLs as a forum for their inventions to gain more market exposure. But without the proper level of funding and a cadre of skilled Content Managers, there is virtually no way to keep up with the rapid rate of change in innovation.

Summary

Innovation is an important topic for enterprises, but many enterprises don't know where the best opportunities are. A showcase of innovation can help companies understand the art of the possible. To hear clients discuss among themselves how a piece of technology, a methodology, or a use case can be leveraged in their enterprises to solve a business problem or help them capture a new opportunity is invigorating. Innovation forums such as the ISLs give clients and business partners the landscape to begin building a plan for the future of their businesses.

Not incidentally, the demonstrations in the ISLs help build support for the FOAK program and create connections that ultimately lead to new projects. This is one way in which FOAK is renewed on a regular basis.

But with opportunities for FOAK coming in from the ISLs and other sources, a systematic effort must be made to make sure that these opportunities add up to a balanced portfolio that is market-focused and looking toward the future. How the FOAK Board and Program Management Team (PMT) manage this balance is the subject of Chapter 10, "Portfolio Management."

10

Portfolio Management

The FOAK program is fortunate in the number of promising proposals it attracts, but its resources are not unlimited. Earlier chapters detailed the project selection criteria and the role of the FOAK Board in making the initial investment decisions to approve 20 to 25 projects annually. This chapter looks at how the program as a whole is managed. In particular, it looks at the work involved in maintaining the program in a way that makes it vibrant, diverse, and valuable to its stakeholders.

We'll also look in detail at the FOAK Program Management Team (PMT), how funding is secured, how projects are tracked and monitored, and the metrics that are used to evaluate the program's overall impact. This chapter concludes with a discussion of why some FOAK projects fail to engage partners.

FOAK Program Management Team

The FOAK PMT is a small group that supports the FOAK Board by monitoring and managing all operational aspects of the FOAK program, including the following:

- Performing portfolio management support activities such as securing funds and monitoring and tracking each project's progress via quarterly project reviews
- Creating standard templates for FOAK proposals
- Maintaining a database of all past and present FOAK-related materials
- Managing and facilitating FOAK Board meetings and agendas
- Coordinating a communications plan that exploits project successes
- Guiding and tracking IBM Project Teams through the FOAK asset commercialization process

Currently, the FOAK PMT is staffed by three people who spend half their time managing the FOAK program and the other half performing non-FOAK tasks for IBM. So, essentially the equivalent of 1.5 full-time people manage the FOAK program globally. Although the low overhead enables the program to optimize the number of client projects it funds each year, it does, at times, result in program constraints. For example, sometimes the PMT struggles to find sufficient time to broadly communicate and market the results of each project to all the promising internal and external communities of interest, and this can lead to missed opportunities for FOAK investments.

To compensate for its limited resources, the FOAK PMT has become resourceful in leveraging other organizations within IBM for support services. For example, the PMT notifies the IBM industry marketing and communications teams when new FOAK contracts are signed or when projects have successfully completed. The PMT hopes to draw their interest in working with the IBM Project Team and the clients to create press releases, case studies, mini-documentaries, and so on.

The New Venture Group (NVG), discussed in detail in Chapter 11, "Contracts and Intellectual Property," provides the FOAK program with contracts and legal support. The NVG is engaged continuously throughout the year, beginning with a planning discussion each January to share information about budgets, resources, anticipated volumes of projects, and process changes. Additionally, monthly calls are held to discuss the status of all contracts and negotiations across the entire portfolio.

IBM Research Business Development is responsible for generating income for IBM Research. They do periodic reviews of the FOAK portfolio to identify opportunities to license FOAK assets externally. At times, IBM Research Business Development is engaged upon project completion if the IBM Project Team sees signs that their IBM asset catcher is backpedaling on its commitment to commercialize the project's assets. Without these kinds of external support organizations, the FOAK PMT would be unable to execute the FOAK program.

> **LESSON:** *Leverage existing support staffs to optimize your innovation program resources and processes.*

Funding

No matter what you are trying to do, without funding you usually can't do much. FOAK is no different. And funding gets more complicated when you are dealing with collaborative innovation. Business justification is hard because short-term results cannot be guaranteed, return on investment (ROI) business cases are difficult if not impossible to create, and financial planners have virtually no patience for emerging solution and technology programs when short-term expense pressures are being applied. The FOAK PMT invests a tremendous amount of energy in securing and managing funding, at both the program and project level to optimize the program's impact and ensure sufficient annual program funding.

Program Funding

On a regular basis, the FOAK PMT members invite FOAK funding stakeholders and influencers to tour one of the Industry Solutions Labs (ISLs), where they can see the actual results of FOAK projects. They also make a point of periodically publishing highlight reports and circulating new press articles from FOAK projects to ensure that the program's influential stakeholders and funders are continuously reminded of the program's value and impact.

Why do they do this? Because it is the PMT that is responsible for managing FOAK's funding process. During annual planning, they need to build a business case to take forward to the Sales and Distribution (S&D) executive team that highlights the program's successes and business impact (both quantitative and qualitative). The business case must include funding required to fulfill the existing client commitments to FOAK projects that are already in process (since most projects are a year in duration and many will traverse two calendar years), along with the funding needed to generate a projected number of new projects. This becomes the base investment plan for the FOAK program.

As stated in Chapter 6, "The FOAK Process: Phases II and III," funding for the IBM Corporation is done on an *annual* basis yet the FOAK program invests on a *quarterly* basis. This can cause problems for the FOAK program, because reviews and approvals of FOAK projects occur on a quarterly basis. This means that a fairly significant portion of the annual FOAK budget is already committed to client projects in the prior year. So, each year right out of the gate, the funding that the FOAK PMT has available for initiating new projects is significantly less than the total budget it receives. Thus, the FOAK PMT needs to explain this disparity in funding to the finance and S&D senior executives each year. This ensures that proper funding is made available and strikes a balance between fulfilling client commitments and seeding new projects.

And since the FOAK program is based on the matching of S&D funds by IBM Research, it is critical that IBM Research agrees with the funding being requested. They need to match that funding in available resources (such as head count).

Project Funding

Over the years, the FOAK Board has tested various project funding models to optimize FOAK's investments and improve the success rate of its projects. Each of these variations in funding models attempted to either fix some aspect of the program or optimize the program's investments. Some models ended up creating more problems than they fixed, while others just created more problems and fixed nothing. FOAK is exploratory, and the FOAK Board will continue to explore new models as it continues to transform to meet the needs of its clients, its business, and the world. A review of a few of these approaches will reveal some of the limits and complexity of providing resources for collaborative innovation.

Funding Non-Researchers

In the very early days of the FOAK program, FOAK funding was not limited to the funding of researchers. IBM Project Teams, if they chose, could use a portion of their FOAK funding to fund other resources—including project managers, consultants, and IT specialists—to perform non-research-related tasks that were needed on the projects. This impacted the program in two ways. First, from a funding perspective, every dollar that was spent on a non-research resource was not matched. The match was available only from IBM Research for research labor. So, in essence, funding these resources actually decreased the amount of resources available. Ceasing to fund non-researchers effectively increased the pool of funding for FOAK.

Second, the non-research people engaged this way did not always demonstrate a commitment to the projects. They seemed to view their funding as nothing more than an internal transfer of funds. It is not surprising in retrospect that many of these people took the funding but did not fulfill their full commitments to the FOAK project. Today, these people are funded by the client partner, and their work products are described in detail in a Statement of Work (SOW) that is part of the FOAK contracts and negotiations process. When it is a client that is investing in the non-researchers, it gets the attention of the non-researchers' organizations and encourages commitment beyond the tasks performed.

Seed Funding

With seed funding, the FOAK Board gave candidate FOAK projects three months of resources to better tease out the project concepts, requirements, scope of effort, and target clients/markets before making a final funding decision. This was tested as a way to build better projects, because the ongoing discussions with potential FOAK clients injected newer thinking into the proposed project scope.

The FOAK Board cautioned the Proposal Teams that their projects were not fully approved or funded and that they should refrain from making any type of client commitments. These Proposal Teams were asked to return to the FOAK Board after three months to present an updated proposal based on their learnings. If upon return to the FOAK Board the project was approved for full funding, there were few or no issues. Unfortunately, if the project was not approved, it caused lots of pain for the researchers, who felt they had wasted three months, and for the clients, who felt IBM had enticed them into a deal only to renege on the agreement.

Mega FOAKs

Mega FOAKs sought to mirror the traditional IBM Research Joint Programs described in Chapter 1, "A Program That Works." Here a collection of smaller projects were rolled into one big FOAK project. The objective was to build more-comprehensive solutions. This model was piloted in cross-industry segments, such as Product Lifecycle Management, Customer Relationship Management, and Business to Business in the 2000 to 2002 time frame.

But the model proved difficult for the FOAK PMT to manage. It was hard to gain clarity on the scope of each of the subprojects, and measuring their impact was difficult. Currently, this model is being considered again for a series of mobility projects across multiple industries with multiple clients. However, this time the FOAK Board has funded an overall IBM project manager who is responsible for clearly defining the scope, resources, tasks, contingencies, and deliverables of each project. Additionally, the project manager will report back to the FOAK Board at each quarterly Board meeting. The FOAK Board is exploring this model again because it believes that the progress in the marketplace toward open innovation and the need for businesses to drive value across their ecosystems has made this model more viable.

Waiting List

In an attempt to better optimize funds, one year the FOAK Board kept a waiting list of FOAK proposals that it had reviewed and liked but could not fund because it had an outpouring of solid proposals throughout the year that consumed all the available funding. The idea was to not let a good idea die for lack of funding, but rather confirm that it was a good idea. Then the Proposal Team would be told that the FOAK Board wanted to invest in their project and that they would be contacted once funding became available.

This became a game of waiting for funded projects to terminate. For both the FOAK PMT and the researchers (those whose projects were about to be terminated *and* those seeking the funding), this whole approach was disheartening. In the end, the FOAK Board decided that the waiting-list approach actually diminished one of the program's great design points: the rapid release of funding to enable FOAK IBM Project Teams to begin work immediately.

LESSON: Innovation programs need to be innovative about approaches to funding and then learn from failures as well as successes.

Setting Priorities

Over the years, a systematic approach to priorities has brought focus to industries such as banking, geographies such as China, solutions such as Model-Driven Systems Engineering, technologies such as grid, pain points such as risk and compliance, and trends such as green initiatives. The FOAK PMT gathers input on setting those priorities from senior S&D executives, Industry Solution Boards, industry and global market trends, corporate initiatives, and brand focus areas. During the first FOAK Board meeting of each year, these various viewpoints on priorities, as well as those of the FOAK Board members, are shared and discussed. This discussion provides the basis for decisions throughout the year.

Essentially, this process of prioritization allows the FOAK Board to reenergize and rebalance the portfolio on a regular basis. The FOAK Board reviews proposals that are in development and projects that are under way in terms of the new priorities. It looks to see how the prior year's investments align with the new priorities.

However, because of its commitment to the FOAK partner, the FOAK PMT will not terminate a project just because of a shift in program priorities. Rather, the FOAK PMT will try to rebalance the portfolio through the next project approval cycle. And just as an individual's financial investment portfolio may be out of balance because of shifting market values, the FOAK investment may need to adjust because of changing priorities.

So it is out with the old, in with the new, and clear identification of needs that should be filled as ideas, proposals, and projects make their way through the year. Not surprisingly, in most years, little investment adjustment has been necessary, because the FOAK program lives and operates in the marketplace and therefore naturally reflects its needs and trends.

Balancing Investments

Although the FOAK Board does not aim to evenly allocate its investments in projects so that all stakeholders get an equal share, any good investment management strategy looks to balance its investments across multiple dimensions. The FOAK program is no different. Dimensions that the FOAK Board uses to manage its portfolio include industry, geography, technology, solution, IBM Research initiative, and S&D focus areas.

Many exploratory programs also manage their investments by time horizon (near-term and long-term) or level of risk. Here, the FOAK program is different. By design, the FOAK Board does not view its investments across these dimensions. This is because the program lives in the sales channel, which has a very short time-to-market outlook. Longer-term investment decisions belong in IBM Research and the IBM brand Joint Programs. Likewise, high-risk projects have no place in a clients' business environments. They are much better suited to the research or development labs until they are ready to be introduced to client environments via the FOAK program. (It is important to note again that FOAK is only one instance in the spectrum of IBM investments in innovation. Other investments in IBM Research and the product development labs have portfolios measured on time and risk.)

Periodically, the FOAK Board also looks at the FOAK portfolio from an industry track record point of view. At times, this has prompted the FOAK Board to counsel a particular Industry Solution Board with lack-luster performance (for example number of project terminations or lack of successful asset transfers) to focus its energy on making its existing FOAK investments successful rather than developing new proposals for FOAK projects. These views also give the FOAK Board input on the credibility and track record of the Industry Solution Boards.

Any innovation portfolio is tied to the goals and constraints of the organization. FOAK's viewpoint is based on a considered perspective on what success means for the *FOAK* program, not on traditional approaches to balancing the portfolio. Rather than cloning the FOAK viewpoint, it is useful to consider what stakeholders need and the options available.

Here are some questions to ask:

- Do we have the right geographic coverage?
- Are we too invested in today's solutions, products, and service offerings?
- Will we miss the next new solution, product, or service offering?
- Are we investing enough in growth markets?
- How much are we investing in mature markets?
- What is our brand coverage from a commercialization perspective?
- Are we being too conservative, or are we really reaching beyond today's capabilities?

Measuring Success

At the heart of any portfolio management system is a set of metrics that prove the portfolio's value. As mentioned, the FOAK Board chooses to invest virtually all its funding in client projects and not in program overhead. As such, few resources are available to aggressively track metrics. Thus, a simple set of metrics is employed to manage the program. The FOAK program metrics revolve around status, revenue, assets transferred, and references.

> *LESSON: Measurements help innovation programs find and maintain funding, so they must prove the value of the program in terms that are simple and relevant to sponsors.*

Status

One of the simplest metrics that the FOAK PMT tracks is whether the FOAK project completed successfully. For FOAK, this boils down to projects that can secure a client. Understanding why a particular FOAK project has difficulty securing a client is something that the FOAK PMT is keenly interested in. This has been one of the sources of the guidance on how to choose a good FOAK partner, which is the essence of Chapter 4, "Getting the Most out of Partnerships." Historically, 70 to 75% of FOAK projects successfully engage partners and are completed.

Revenue

This is revenue generated both directly and indirectly from a FOAK project. Direct revenue includes revenue IBM gains from the initial FOAK partner, including any follow-on sales related to the reuse of the FOAK assets. Direct revenue also includes revenue from other clients that reuse the FOAK assets.

Indirect revenue is based on using the FOAK project as a way to differentiate IBM. This is revenue that is generated thanks to FOAK-related conversations. An example of indirect or influenced revenue is closing a deal with an Energy & Utilities client by using IBM's experiences with FOAK projects in the area of intelligent utility networks to establish credibility and open discussions into other areas of opportunity. The deal may or may not have anything to do with an intelligent utility network itself, but the conversation about the FOAK will establish credibility and uncover other opportunities.

It's worth noting that both direct and indirect revenue are difficult to measure and probably are underestimated. In practice, this FOAK revenue is tracked by sending an e-mail to the members of the FOAK IBM Project Teams, asking them for any known revenue resulting from follow-on engagements, asset reuse, or differentiation. The data is spotty at times (some IBM Project Teams are more responsive than others), and it is only tracked for up to two years after completion of the project due to limited FOAK PMT staffing.

Also, the FOAK PMT does not track the revenue after the assets are transferred into a commercialization organization. It is just too difficult to determine what portion of an IBM commercialized offering is really attributable to the FOAK assets versus the offering itself.

Currently, the direct FOAK revenue is estimated at more than $440 million over the 2002 to 2007 period. Indirect or influenced FOAK revenue is estimated at approximately $4.2 billion over the same time period.

Assets Transferred

As stated, the FOAK PMT keeps track of the state of the assets from FOAK projects by periodically reaching out to the IBM Project Teams and inquiring about their progress. All FOAK assets are required to be registered and stored in a common database so that they are easily accessible to other organizations for reuse. This helps facilitate the transfer process. The FOAK PMT captures the names of the assets, a short description of them, the targeted catcher of the assets, the date of the transfer, and any noteworthy comments about their progress. The PMT also leverages the Industry Research Relationship Managers (RRMs) to help identify projects that seem to be struggling to transfer their assets to see if the PMT or a FOAK Board member might be able to help. These asset transfer reviews take place with the Industry RRMs periodically throughout the year to ensure continued focus. Approximately 65 to 70% of the projects that engage a partner and successfully complete transfer their assets to an organization for commercialization.

References

As mentioned, client references are incredibly valuable to both IBM and the client partner. The FOAK PMT keeps a record of the specifics of the reference agreements. Some are more confining than others, and in all instances the FOAK PMT does not want to compromise the contractual agreements. Chapter 4 describes some of the types of references negotiated. Virtually 100% of the FOAK projects deliver references.

The FOAK Scorecard

With this core set of metrics, the FOAK PMT can confirm the program's value and maintain its credibility. A quick snapshot of these metrics, along with some other key pieces of information about the projects, are maintained in a FOAK Scorecard, as shown in Figure 10.1. It reflects the portfolio's status at a glance. Although not visible in this grayscale figure, it uses the classic red, green, yellow approach by metric to give senior executives a snapshot of the portfolio's performance against the established metrics.

FOAK Scorecard

Project	Status	Reference	Catcher	Transfer	Asset DB	24 Month Results
Project A	12/02	XXX	SWG ABC Brand	12/03	Yes	
Project B	06/02	XXX	SWG XYZ Brand	08/03	Yes	
Project C	06/02	XXX			Yes	$65K+
Project D	06/03	XXX	GBS CBO	01/06	Yes	
Project E	03/02	XXX	STG XYZ Brand	05/04	Yes	$40M HW Deals
Project F	03/03	XXX	SWG XXX Brand		No	1.2B XYZ Deal Differentiator
Project G	12/01	XXX	Alphaworks	01/03	Yes	
Project H	12/01	XXX			Yes	$215K
Project I	12/01	XXX	XYZ Business Partner	01/03	No	$215K
Totals	XX		XX%			XX%

Figure 10.1   Sample FOAK scorecard

Why Projects Fail to Secure Client Partners

In all cases, the FOAK projects terminated are good ideas, based on sound proposals, yet the IBM Project Team's inability to secure a client precludes them from testing their idea in the marketplace. Over the years, hindsight has given the FOAK PMT insights into the reasons why some of the projects are unable to secure clients. Some examples are described in the following sections.

Too Early

At times, FOAK projects have been shelved because the market just wasn't ready to test them, even with the FOAK investment model as an incentive. Later, these technologies and ideas may resurface in a different form, attacking a different problem or opportunity. The Advanced Software for Distributed Data Collection and Control Systems in Networked Sensor Environments FOAK project of 2001 was never able to secure a client. However, years later, the key assets from that project (although not completed) became the core components of the new Intelligent Utility Network offerings for IBM.

Market Shifts

Depending on how rapidly the technology is advancing and the market is adopting the technology, it may turn out that what was an innovative idea at the start of the FOAK proposal process isn't anymore. It may actually have become a necessity in the marketplace and may no longer be considered exploratory.

A good example is the Auto ID Infrastructure for On-Demand Supply Chain FOAK project back in 2003. The project set out to build an architecture that conformed to the emerging RFID (Radio Frequency Identification—using a device sensitive to radio waves to track and identify an entity such as a product) standards of the time. It also generated key infrastructure specifications and components that would enable privacy, scalability, and distribution. While discussing the FOAK opportunity with multiple potential FOAK partners, the Proposal Team gained valuable insights into market requirements that became input into the IBM product line. However, the Proposal Team was unable to convince any of the targeted FOAK partners to do a pilot of the FOAK technologies.

The clients viewed the RFID space as ripe for solutions of the day and were not interested in exploratory partnerships. All agreed that the components of the FOAK project were critical to enabling their RFID solutions, but they did not want to experiment; they wanted solutions right then and there. Although the FOAK was terminated for lack of a client, the Proposal Team was able to take the insights from these FOAK discussions with clients and build a prototype solution. This prototype was used to work with multiple clients, IBM brands, and services practices, enabling faster development and delivery of new RFID solutions to the marketplace.

Wrong Segment

Since the raw technology can serve multiple markets, sometimes, even with careful market planning, the industry and application selected are not optimal, preventing the FOAK program from engaging a client. The 2003 Audio-visual Speech Recognition for Trading Floors FOAK project is an excellent example of this. It was an innovative solution to dealing with the problem of high-noise environments (multispeaker environments, trading floors, automobiles) interfering with speech-recognition technologies. It involved using visual speech information (lip-reading using a camera) simultaneously with audio information to dramatically improve speech recognition accuracy and performance in high-noise environments.

Originally, this project was proposed and accepted as a FOAK for the financial services sector to enable voice-activated transactions on noisy trading floors. A serious financial services client was extremely interested, and contract negotiations were well under way. However, a merger reset the client's priorities, and the FOAK IBM Project Team found themselves back at square one.

Not having a backup client, the IBM Project Team eventually ran out of time, and the FOAK project was terminated. However, the technology was still viable and was later redirected toward the automotive industry. There, speech recognition in the noisy vehicle environment was begging for a solution that could be easily mounted to the driver's visor to enable hands-free communication with the vehicle and its applications.

Interesting Idea, But...

Sometimes a FOAK project is interesting to our clients, but none of them, when approached, is interested in doing the project due to resource constraints or priorities. The 2008 Business Service Management for Business of IT Dashboard FOAK is a good example.

The FOAK project aimed to develop an IT lifecycle management solution with a template-based means of acquiring, maintaining, and enacting business policies for evaluating business criticality and urgency of IT incidents in an automated manner. Although most of the clients approached agreed that solving this business problem would be valuable, and multiple clients expressed an interest in being the FOAK partner, no single client emerged as a serious or timely partner for the FOAK project. The project was subsequently terminated.

When this happens, those involved need to be reassured. They do not need to reassess their approaches or their view of the world; they just need to try again.

Identifying Emerging Business Opportunities

After missing out on a number of emerging market opportunities in the 1990s, IBM instituted a program at the corporate level to specifically focus on new, high-growth markets for the long term. Called the Emerging Business Opportunity (EBO) program, it is aimed at growing new businesses outside of IBM's traditional short-term, results-oriented management system. It encourages each individual business unit to look beyond its current markets and existing portfolio of offerings to identify new growth opportunities for the company.

Over the years, the FOAK program has provided headlights into many of these emerging markets and has delivered a base of market-tested intellectual property (IP) for these new businesses to leverage.

For example, in the mid- to late '90s, the FOAK program began investing in projects that led to a series of assets that became the base of IP for IBM's Life Sciences EBO. When the Life Sciences EBO was announced in 2000, it had a base of client-tested IP from the FOAK program to build upon. Here are some of the prior FOAK projects that contributed to the Life Sciences space:

- **Data Integrator (1995)** developed a proof-of-concept multimedia system that provided the ability to interrelate data across multiple environments with a broad range of querying capabilities into a single, cross-source query. This made large collections of data stored on diverse systems more accessible and usable.

- **Information in Context (1997)** created an integrated information management system to provide unified access to disparate data sources and applications. It used context modeling to reduce the time spent finding, accessing, preparing, filtering, and reformatting data. This allowed professionals to focus on interpreting and extracting knowledge for planning and decision making.

- **Teiresias and SPLASH (1999)** applied IBM pattern discovery software and algorithms to identify key relationships in DNA and protein data. It did so in a totally unsupervised manner with no prior assumptions embedded in the analysis (no data model). This helped experts rapidly identify the causes of disease and reveal new paths toward treating diseases.

Having a base of market-tested assets and early client experiences from the FOAK program helped the Life Sciences EBO quickly build its new offerings and accelerated its entry into the marketplace.

Today, the FOAK PMT continuously mines the FOAK portfolio, looking for trends to highlight to IBM Corporate Strategy and the IBM brands. Additionally, Corporate Strategy and the IBM brands periodically review the FOAK portfolio, seeking out new areas of opportunity and linkages to their strategies and plans.

Summary

Innovation portfolios are not off-the-shelf, but are a result of a deep understanding of the needs served by the program, along with its constraints. The FOAK portfolio management process begins with the initial discussions between the business unit and the Industry Research Relationship Manager and passes through filters until the FOAK Board applies the final filter.

Portfolios need to be renewed and rebalanced as changing times take the program in new directions and project cancellations distort the allocation of the funding. Portfolio management emerges from restatement of priorities, specific checkpoints on approved projects, attention to measurement, and a disciplined understanding of project termination. It is the responsibility of the FOAK Board and the FOAK PMT to look at the program from a higher perspective and to continuously prune the portfolio and redirect funding to drive impact and seed new ideas.

Of course, those ideas are realized only if IBM and its partners have a good relationship. Person-to-person relationships need to be strong, but that is insufficient. For any innovation collaboration, questions of shared responsibilities and ownership of IP need to be clarified. This is where the lawyers come in with contracts and various written agreements, and that is the subject of Chapter 11.

11

Contracts and Intellectual Property

When we discuss partnering and collaborating for innovation with clients, business people, and researchers, two questions always come up: How are the contracts structured, and who owns the intellectual property (IP)? This area has real potential for conflict and even legal action. What rights come with our agreement? Who is the real inventor—me, you, or us? Can I keep using your software after the project is disbanded? Can I share what I've learned with your competitors? Did I just give away my competitive advantage?

On the one hand, organizations want to be open and collaborative, but on the other hand, each partner needs to protect their IP and preserve their right to freedom of action. In this chapter, we discuss the FOAK terms and conditions (T&Cs) at a high level and share some lessons learned from negotiating literally hundreds of contracts over the years.

Preserving Confidentiality

Before any collaboration can begin, each partner needs to feel that they can talk freely, sharing ideas and information. Ultimately, this is a practical concern, not just a way to keep things friendly. If members of the Joint Project Team on both the client and IBM side have to worry about revealing information, this strains the interaction and precludes the Joint Project Team from truly collaborating. In actuality, neither party is interested in sharing the other party's sensitive information beyond the FOAK collaboration. However, agreements need to be put in place to ensure that everyone is aware of their responsibilities when sharing sensitive information. Plus, it keeps the lawyers happy.

IBM has a good starting point—its standard confidentially agreement called the Agreement for Exchange of Confidential Information (AECI). All FOAK projects require that both parties sign this agreement. In many cases, the confidentially agreement is already in place between the two companies. It outlines the following:

- How information will be disclosed (in writing, verbally, through access to databases)

- Each party's obligations when handling disclosed information (use only for the intended purposes; avoid disclosure, publication, or dissemination outside the intended parties; who in the organizations will have access to the information)

- Length of the confidentiality period and any exceptions to the obligations (information already in possession, publicly available, received via another party, or retained within the memories of those who had access to the information)

- Disclaimers regarding warrantees, liabilities, and rights to licenses

- General terms (no assignment or transfer of rights to other parties without written consent, compliance with import and export regulations)

Without a signed confidentiality agreement in place, the conversations that can take place are of limited value and do not really go beyond simple, initial discussions regarding the proposal.

Terms and Conditions

The standard terms and conditions of a FOAK contract are simple and fairly straightforward. This is driven by a need to reach contract signature as quickly as possible in order to move forward with the project while the technology is fresh, resources are available, and the researchers are energized. The T&Cs are posted on the internal FOAK website, are included in a sample client presentation, and are reviewed with the IBM Project Team during the internal kickoff meeting.

> *LESSON: Where T&Cs and other legal documents are nonstandard, get them in front of partners as early as is reasonable to avoid surprises.*

The FOAK T&Cs have evolved over the years and are reviewed annually. They include the following:

- IBM maintains ownership of all IP related to the work product described in the contract. (After all, IBM has invested in the FOAK assets and many have patents already filed. IBM may share or defer to the other party in other partnerships, but FOAK keeps things simple by having this in place.)

- In general, the client receives a license to the assets for one to two years from the contract signing date. (This is usually enough to reward their participation with a reasonable lead on their competitors.)

- No exclusive rights are granted. (If they were, the work would become a one-off.)

- IBM may use ideas, concepts, and know-how obtained from the FOAK engagement related to IBM's business activities. (This provides freedom of action, as well as the potential for follow-on offerings.)

- Neither party is precluded from assigning its employees in any way it may choose or from providing similar products and services to others. (This gives each partner the flexibility to manage their skilled resources and reallocate them if needed.)

- Either party may terminate the project, without any obligations or commitments. (With high-risk projects, there is comfort in knowing that you have a parachute if things don't go as planned.)
- The work product is provided "as-is," without any warranties or indemnification. (This is important and needs to be explicit, because IBM provides extensive support for its regular offerings. There can be no confusion here.)
- IBM does not promise that the work product will be made commercially available. (IBM would like every FOAK to lead to commercial work products, of course, but it is the nature of leading-edge innovation that some do not. And sometimes, the technology behind the work product migrates to too many different products and services, so that the commercial usage varies significantly from what was demonstrated on the FOAK Project.)
- The FOAK partner agrees to be a reference. (This is so that both parties can get the benefit of building their reputations as innovators.)
- The FOAK partner agrees to contribute financially, funding the hardware, software, and services required to perform the FOAK project.
- IBM agrees to fund the costs of the IBM Research labor. (This is a substantial, appealing, and differentiating contribution from IBM.)

On the surface, these terms look fairly reasonable in the context of enabling innovative partnerships. But once the lawyers begin analyzing the detailed text and general terms of the contract, a series of redlined document volleys takes place. Some of this back-and-forth negotiation is driven by a lack of understanding of the FOAK program and the essence of what it is trying to achieve, and some is the result of lawyers just being lawyers.

If prior IBM agreements are already in place, the lawyers generally are familiar with IBM standard terms and are surprised by the nonstandard terms in the FOAK contracts with regard to the deliverables, licensing, and support. Because of this, the FOAK contract negotiations often need to start with an education about what a FOAK project is and proceed from there.

There have been plenty of situations in FOAK history where neither party was able to accept the other's redlined agreements, and a negotiated agreement was never reached. In one instance, after months of grueling negotiations, the IBM client-facing team insisted on not giving up. They believed that getting a successful FOAK contract in place was necessary to establish a base for doing more collaborative projects with the client in the future. The team did eventually get the FOAK contract successfully negotiated and signed. The client-facing team believed it was worth the effort, and they now have a model in place to draw upon for future collaborative innovation projects.

FOAK Intellectual Property Ownership

As mentioned in the preceding section, IBM maintains the ownership rights to all IP related to the FOAK work products as described in the contract for the project. This is because, in the FOAK model, IBM applies innovations that it has solely invested in and developed over the years. The purpose of the FOAK project is to validate the features and functions of the assets and test the market's readiness to accept them. While client participants put their efforts into other areas of the project, virtually all the work being performed on the assets—before, during, and after the FOAK project—is performed by the IBM researchers and not the client.

During the FOAK project, the client is working on their internal systems, piloting the FOAK assets, and providing feedback on how the asset might be applied or tweaked and tuned to add greater value in their environment. FOAK is not codevelopment. In a codevelopment project, the IP terms would give IP ownership rights to each party based on each party's level of investment. In fact, FOAK IBM Project Teams will already have filed all the patents associated with their inventions prior to the start of the FOAK project to ensure protection of the IP.

If a new innovation or invention were to surface during the FOAK project that was jointly developed, it would be jointly owned. Sole inventions made by a single party are owned by the conceiving party but are broadly licensed to the other. This prevents potential conflicts over whether one or both parties first conceived an invention. It is notable that to date, there has not been a single instance of this in the FOAK program. However, lots of time has been expended talking through the what-ifs with lawyers and procurement officers.

Likewise, IP ownership of any IP brought to the table by the FOAK client partner resides with the client partner. In most cases, IBM would not be granted a license outside of the FOAK project and related demonstrations. Usually, this is of no consequence. This is because, in most instances, the client's IP is so unique to their environment that there is little need or value in IBM's receiving a license to it. In most instances, the client's IP concerns are not about rights, but about getting more of an assurance that IBM will not take the client's data and reuse it on other client engagements. However, FOAK IBM Project Teams are warned early in the client selection process that if a client is insisting on rights to the IBM IP, they should quickly move on to another client. Essentially, the issue is dealt with before it needs to be fixed.

In one situation, the contract negotiations were going smoothly until the client's procurement organization got involved. They insisted on rights to the IBM-developed IP and the right to commercialize the IP on their own if IBM chose not to commercialize the assets. They also wanted to provide no financial investment. After lots of education, explanations, and discussions, an agreement was finally reached.

It should be reiterated that, outside the FOAK program, IBM does have partnerships with clients wherein shared IP exists. For example, a team of IBM, Sony Group, and Toshiba engineers collaborated on development of the Cell microprocessor (the chip that's at the heart of most video gaming systems) at a joint design center established in Austin, Texas in March 2001. That design center delivered a multicore architecture with ultra-high-speed communications capabilities to deliver greatly improved, real-time response for entertainment and rich media applications.[1]

In another partnership, a joint development agreement with Taiwan's Industrial Technology Research Institute (ITRI) aimed to explore an entirely new approach to solid-state memory called "Racetrack Memory." It was conceived by an IBM Fellow, Dr. Stuart Parkin, at IBM's Almaden Research Center in San Jose, California.[2]

As one more example, Linden Labs and IBM entered into a joint development agreement to create virtual-world interoperability by teleporting avatars between virtual-world server platforms. Both companies plan to offer the extensions developed as open-source to facilitate and promote interoperability and the advancement of the industry to an interconnected model.[3]

Contracts, Agreements, and the People Key to Their Success

Successfully negotiating FOAK contracts takes the concerted effort of multiple committed players. Each needs to work their part of the contract process and leverage relationships both old and new to get the job done. Coming to agreement on collaborative innovation is never easy. With FOAK, where sales documents, patents, and other legal instruments come into play, the process is especially complex. The FOAK IBM Project Team is helped by having many past experiences in coming to agreement with clients. When the client is a veteran of the FOAK program, that can help, too. Above all, having a good relationship and trust between the parties facilitates getting the legal aspects taken care of quickly and effectively.

Although a variety of approaches to framing collaborative innovation agreements are possible, the starting point is the relationship between the individual lawyers or the legal teams. It is important for them to be friendly as well as professional. Starting out with notes full of warnings and claims can be off-putting (even for people who write warnings and claims). A FOAK best practice is to have all parties meet face-to-face to discuss the unique nature of FOAK partnerships. The most difficult negotiations arise when the client's legal department is inaccessible by phone or in person during initial FOAK contract discussions, or when the contract is passed from one attorney to another, requiring reeducation.

Ideally, the client legal team should be briefed on the FOAK program. A successful negotiation usually begins with the lawyers and the FOAK IBM Project Team discussing the project's business and technology benefits before delving into contract terms. This overview helps take FOAK out of the discussion space of a typical contract with IBM and begins to set the expectations.

> *LESSON: Innovation programs need to tell their stories and rationale for existing to lawyers and other people involved in controls before they begin discussions on the exceptions they need.*

For some client legal teams, the FOAK approach is a complete surprise. It is not unusual for many questions to follow, both during the meeting and after the client legal team goes back and meets with interested colleagues at their firm.

Relevant documents need to be shared early in the process. These include current contracts between the parties (or, more likely, references to them), contracts with third parties that might be limiting, copies of relevant IP that has been claimed, and sections from any laws that may apply. (On this last point, an example is government, health, and privacy laws, which may be more comprehensive in parts of Europe than they are in the U.S.)

Recently, the IBM New Venture Group (NVG), a team within the legal department that is described in the next section, developed a FOAK Grant Announcement letter. It outlines the potential benefits to the client and their responsibilities—the award selection criteria, which is in essence a summary of the T&Cs, and a checklist of the agreements and terms of the FOAK contract. This helps get the client-facing teams and researchers onto the same page and aids in setting client expectations appropriately and consistently across the board. It is like a cheat sheet for IBM to use with the FOAK client.

It is also useful at this point for the NVG team to give the IBM Project Team the standard FOAK contract template and even an example of a contract from a previous FOAK project. They also include a note outlining the elements that differ from other agreements and an explanation of why these are present. This enables the IBM Project Team and client-facing team to begin asking for clarification of points. They also can outline concerns, restrictions, and requirements that they believe may be an issue for the potential FOAK client. After an agreed-upon internal draft contract has been created, it is sent to the potential client. The agreement begins to take shape.

Within IBM, the challenge of putting together collaboration agreements around innovation is now recognized to be significant and different from other legal work. This has meant reorganizing the legal team that drafts, negotiates, and amends contracts and Statements of Work (SOWs) for the FOAK program. But it also has meant that the IBM Project Team and others who are integral to establishing partnerships have had to learn how to deal with the expectations, needs, and approaches of other stakeholders, including procurement organizations, IBM's client-facing teams, and, of course, the clients themselves.

New Venture Group

The legal aspects are not simply handed off to the lawyers. As just mentioned, IBM has a special legal team called the New Venture Group (NVG). The NVG's mission is to handle mergers and acquisitions as well as IBM "Special Relationships," including alliances (such as joint marketing, joint development, and special licensing) and FOAK agreements. The NVG team is critical to successfully negotiating FOAK contracts.

The IBM NVG team takes the lead to develop and negotiate the contract, but the IBM Project Team remains involved to clarify the deliverables, IP, and roles and responsibilities. As stated, the contract is built using a contract template that contains all the FOAK T&Cs. The template is used to maintain consistency, facilitate the process, and drive efficiency. During the IBM internal FOAK kickoff meeting, the assigned NVG professional is introduced to the IBM Project Team. The contract terms are reviewed, along with the sample documents that are available to help the client-facing teams and researchers successfully negotiate the contract.

IBM's NVG includes skilled lawyers with a myriad of FOAK contract negotiations under their belts. They are invaluable to the IBM Project Teams and, at times, may work for months on a single FOAK contract. The IBM Project Team is directed to engage their assigned NVG contact early—definitely before talking to any potential clients. In fact, the funding letter tells the IBM Project Team who their NVG contact is, and the NVG contact is sent a copy of the letter.

These NVG professionals work with the potential FOAK client's equivalent organization, sending redlined contracts back and forth, talking on the phone, and guiding their respective teams.

The FOAK Contract

In addition to the confidentiality agreement described earlier, either one or two other documents need to be negotiated and signed before work can begin.

The FOAK PMT prefers to have two separate contracts or SOWs signed. The first is for the FOAK, which is fully funded by IBM. The second is for the supporting services (and, if appropriate, hardware and software). These are essential to the project's success and are funded by the FOAK client. These two contracts have language embedded in them that refers to the other contract. This is done to ensure that the IBM Project Team does not end up with a FOAK agreement without the hardware, software, and services required to do the project.

Generally, both parties prefer to have separate contacts. If the FOAK client requests a single contract to make it easier to get through their processes, the two contracts may be combined.

> *LESSON: Fine-tune legal processes and documents to make it easier for people to work with them to make the right decisions for your innovation program.*

Client Procurement

Warning bells go off when a communication is received from the client's procurement organization. Surprisingly, FOAK contracts are almost always easier to negotiate with the client's attorney than with its procurement arm. Usually a client's attorney has the insight to understand the project's uniqueness and its benefits to his or her company, as well as the comfort level and authority to agree with special terms that are part of a FOAK. But the FOAK project's emphasis on technology and collaboration does not fit within procurement's neatly defined box of vendor concessions and cost savings.

As part of their orientation, the IBM Project Teams are cautioned that once they find themselves negotiating with a procurement organization, they need to reach out to their Client Sponsor for help. FOAK projects don't fit the standard templates used to measure value by procurement organizations. And although IBM provides the bulk of the financial investment on these FOAK projects, procurement organizations are always seeking a better deal. By definition, FOAK projects start from a point of negotiation that leaves little room for IBM to back down from the FOAK terms. An effective Client Sponsor will intervene and work with procurement to handle FOAK as an exception to their standard process, or steer the contract to a client attorney or executive who has the authority to make decisions on behalf of the client.

One failed FOAK attempt was aimed at securing a client for an Image and Context Analysis for Claims Triage Solution. This FOAK project would have captured auto accident damage with digital photographs and used context analysis to assess the damage and determine the next steps in the claims process. However, the IBM Project Team found themselves bogged down in procurement, debating licenses, IP ownership, and financial commitments. At one point, one of the procurement officers, in a discussion with the IBM client-facing team, NVG, and FOAK PMT, went so far as to say, "IBM should be paying us for doing this [FOAK] project."

Needless to say, the deal was off. And the FOAK project was canceled. The real issue for this client was not the terms they cited. It was that they were looking for a solution for today, not an innovation for tomorrow. As they continued to try and make it fit in their procurement templates, the people negotiating the agreement became frustrated, and the dialog became strained. If the FOAK IBM Project Team had had a strong Client Sponsor to personally hand-carry the FOAK contracts through the procurement process, the project might have survived.

IBM Client-Facing Team

The IBM client-facing team is crucial to putting agreements in place. Within IBM, they own the relationship with the client. They want to be sure to protect that relationship and deliver value to their client.

Sometimes, the IBM client-facing team can be so protective of their clients and the relationship they have nurtured that they do not want to even propose a FOAK project, with its potential risks to their client. Other times, the client-facing team is so focused on client satisfaction and fulfilling their client's wishes that when they do propose the FOAK to their client, they move into a position that is not necessarily in the best interests of either the client or IBM.

In one instance, the IBM client-facing team put tremendous energy into to trying to get one of the IBM product brands to agree to insert some text into the FOAK contract. This text would make his client more comfortable with what would happen to the assets at the end of the proposed FOAK project. It is one thing to soften the terms in the contract; it is another thing to make them potentially instill false hope for the outcome. Much discussion occurred with the targeted IBM product brand catcher, along with reviews of sample text authored by the creative client-facing team. The catcher helped the client-facing team understand that inserting such text in a contract could harm the client relationship by leading them down a path that had not yet been paved. And, from the IBM side, it would force IBM to commit to a product that did not yet have a proven market.

Ultimately, the lawyers working on each side were able to come up with text that made both parties comfortable. The FOAK project is currently under way, with this stipulation: Upon completion of the project, if both sides agree to continue working with the FOAK assets, both parties will negotiate a new agreement in good faith at that time.

Client Sponsor

The contributions of the Client Sponsor enable the IBM Project Team to build a value proposition that resonates well with their company. The Client Sponsor assigns a person from his or her organization to work with the IBM Project Team.

Together, they open doors for the IBM Project Team that help sell their FOAK concept. They work the back channel to ensure that expectations are appropriately set while ensuring the greatest value to their company. They work the contracts and become FOAK evangelists and true partners. They educate lawyers and work up the reporting chains to bring problems to higher levels in the organization and get them resolved. They keep a watchful eye on the contracts and negotiations process and demand frequent updates. If they sense delays due to contract terms or procurement roadblocks, they jump in and run interference.

In a nutshell, the optimal Client Team needs to worry about the FOAK project going to another client. They need to be committed to ensuring that their company gets the FOAK. That kind of personal commitment to the project motivates them to stay on top of the contracts process and demand resolution of outstanding issues, while still preserving their company's interests. One FOAK IBM Project Team in India attributed their smooth contracting process to the CIO. He was so convinced about the value of the proposal that he pushed to move as quickly as possible on the project.

Making Exceptions

Rules are made to be broken, especially given the vagaries of innovation. While guidelines are put in place as an attempt to reel in the mavericks, innovation attracts creative people. And creativity mixed with contracts and negotiations can sometimes lead to improperly set expectations. When expectations are incorrectly set, exception requests surface.

One of the more delicate aspects of administering the FOAK program is managing the exceptions prudently to maintain the program's integrity and fairness. Some exceptions are reasonable. An example is minimizing the financial commitment for the PHIAD project mentioned in Chapter 5, "Choosing the Best Projects." The FOAK PMT believed that getting Israel, Jordan, and the Palestinian Authority to collaborate was significant enough to merit working through the financial constraints of the Middle East Consortium on Infectious Disease Surveillance (MECIDS) to make the contract close.

Given the potential benefits of the FOAK projects that are in play, it is tempting to cut corners. But once an exception is made for one FOAK project, you can be sure that similar requests will follow. So the FOAK PMT carefully considers each request and responds favorably to only those that are truly unique. Over the last three years, less than 10% of the projects were granted exceptions by the FOAK PMT. The majority of these exceptions were related to the length of the license granted, and this drove the FOAK PMT to extend the standard license from one year to two years.

> *LESSON: An innovation program needs to maintain a reputation for fairness and integrity, so exception requests need to be evaluated and tracked closely.*

Summary

Agreements are about creating clarity between parties. This is difficult for any innovation project because of the inherent uncertainties, of both process and outcomes. FOAK faces the additional challenge of stepping into established relationships, especially when dealing with the expectations created by the support IBM provides with its traditional offerings. Orienting people on the client side, especially the legal team, is essential to facilitating the contracting process.

For FOAK, a further complication is the need for agreements around any purchase of the IBM hardware, software, and services that are essential to the project's success. These need to be put into context, and the commitments need to be in place before the FOAK project begins.

Inevitably, exceptions occur. These need the close attention of the FOAK PMT, because bad exceptions put the program at risk, and good exceptions (such as extending licensing) can help it prosper.

In the contract and negotiations process, many people are involved on both sides. Ultimately, the relationships and trust built between the organizations and individuals make the difference between coming to a good agreement or reaching no agreement and abandoning the project.

The potential of the FOAK program as a whole can be realized only in a climate of fairness and responsibility.

The lessons here are familiar—identify all the players, learn how they work and what they need, orient them to the program, get them on board, and develop and use champions. Most people we talk to about collaborative innovation see contracts and IP as a barrier (often an insurmountable one). It can be tough. But these tasks are part of the job. And it is also a mechanism for building trust and clear communications—which are both of value for any kind of collaboration.

FOAK has provided many lessons like these, as well as object examples. They are described in each chapter of this book, but ultimately their practical application involves bringing them together into a plan. While we can't create your plan for you, we can provide a sequence of activities, questions, considerations, and lessons in one place. That is the objective of Chapter 12, "A Guide for Creating Innovative Programs."

Endnotes

1 IBM press release: "IBM, ITRI Collaborate to Advance New Solid-State Memory," September 17, 2008.

2 IBM press release: "IBM, Sony, Sony Computer Entertainment Inc. and Toshiba Disclose Key Details of the Cell Chip," February 7, 2005.

3 IBM press release: "Linden Lab and IBM Achieve Major Virtual World Interoperability Milestone," July 8, 2008.

12

A Guide for Creating Innovative Programs

Throughout this book, we've provided examples taken from the experiences of the FOAK program. If you're already involved in specific innovation programs, we hope that some of these will confirm best practices, some will suggest improvements, and some will provide clues as to why things aren't working as well as they should.

This chapter is intended to help you if you need to put together an innovation program from scratch or if you want to see the ideas abstracted as a series of activities, almost in the form of a checklist. It probably is impossible to create a universal guide, given the differences in goals, resources, and limits. However, this chapter provides one quick view that we hope will give you a good starting point.

Developing a Program Step by Step

People within an organization, even people within the same group, often have different views on what innovation is and what needs to be accomplished. So obviously, the first step in creating a viable program aimed at innovation is making sure that the main stakeholders have reasonably good agreement about what they're trying to accomplish.

Workshops, questionnaires, and open-ended discussions are just some of the approaches that might be used to make sure that everyone is on the same page.

Formulate the Purpose and Goals

Why are you creating the program? Is it for competitive advantage? Is it for cost savings? Is it to make sure that other people don't get ahead of you? Or is it just to have sizzle? Many valid reasons exist. In fact, more than one reason may be acceptable. For FOAK, deepening relationships with clients, demonstrating leadership, and revitalizing IBM's offerings all contribute to justifying the investment.

It may be that at the goal-setting stage, complete value propositions are developed and written for each of the main stakeholders. Or, these value propositions may be written later for one or all of the stakeholders. What's needed at this point is to create language—perhaps in the form of a vision statement or goal statement—that brings together the innovation team around a common objective. And that objective must be articulated in more detail than simply "innovation."

Define Critical Success Factors

The next essential step is to determine the critical success factors. What is needed so that the program will achieve its objectives? How much money? How much time? How many people? Which executives need to be on board? What promotional material and collateral need to be in place? What organizational needs (lines of authority, budgeting, legal qualifications) must be fulfilled?

It's also useful, when looking at the critical success factors, to take a hard look at how things might go wrong. How might the program's vision, title, or goals be misread or hijacked by a key person in the organization? Who competes for funding? What is the general environment like, in terms of both financial stability and culture?

Determine how a program, even one that seems unique, might fit in or be adapted or adopted by the organization. In general, it is much easier to gain acceptance for a modified program than it is to gain acceptance for something that's brand-new. However, an important caution must be noted here. One of the mantras of larger organizations is "We already do that." Many a genuinely new idea has been crushed as entrenched interests have claimed it on the basis of territory. If they don't or won't "get it," the program needs to be isolated organizationally, with its own funding and political protection.

At the same time, don't create a "me-too" program. FOAK's approach was to bring together partners who hadn't really worked together before and to narrowly define an innovation program that was distinct from several existing innovation programs at IBM. And since programs are always being proposed, any program that wants to continue to exist must maintain its distinct identity in the face of a continuing line of people who discover or reinvent their concept year after year.

Determine the Right Level of Governance

Governance is an important factor in success. Certainly, authority must be clear and well understood. In fact, it may be that for some areas, such as budgeting and hiring, the organization needs to meet legal requirements. Besides managers and those with executive responsibilities, other roles, such as safety and quality control officers, may need to be made explicit. Finally, taking the time to create defined processes for routine operations can save participants time and resources.

But against the value of putting governance and processes in place in the early stages is the danger of straitjacketing the team or making them prey to the bureaucrats. This can stifle creativity and drive away the most imaginative people. With FOAK, the effort to keep governance and processes light has helped keep the burdens low and the costs down. Keeping things simple takes a conscious effort, because stakeholders and participants often have a bias toward reducing the messiness and chaos of innovation. And, of course, when something goes wrong, it's tempting to add rules and processes so that it "never happens again." This is natural, logical, and deadly to innovation.

The FOAK leadership constantly has to remind itself to keep things light, not to overreact to failures, and, above all, to trust people to get it right. When changes are made, they are always tentative. All of them will be challenged after they have had time to prove (or disprove) themselves. Many of the rules that were put in place were terminated when they didn't help or made things worse.

Get Your People Engaged

Determine who really needs to be on the program team. What are the criteria for program team membership? Certainly, as was seen in the FOAK program, people must have expertise and a genuine interest in what innovation promises. It is also important (and this is often missed) to bring in people who can help with all the steps of socialization that are required to meet the program objectives. With FOAK, a wide range of people were involved, stretching from those responsible for IBM Research assets, through those responsible for project deliverables, all the way to those responsible for the ultimate adoption of assets as part of an offering. If at this point no value propositions have been created, it's time to begin developing them. More people need to be engaged, and they will need to know why they should bother doing so.

Of course, program team members, especially at the beginning, need to be deeply committed to the program's success. And as time goes on, there should be mechanisms for determining that program team members are doing more than assuming a title—that they're making real contributions.

It's helpful for the program team itself to have some sort of mandate, preferably written down and agreed to by the participants as well as the sponsor. The essence of this should be that the team is responsible for overseeing the proposal process, engaging with potential participants, maintaining an effective process for selecting proposals, tracking and reporting on progress, and maintaining relationships that justify the program's existence and ensure that its resources are doing their part to support the program's success.

Naturally, not every team member takes on all the work of fulfilling the mandate. Different people on the program team assume different roles. These may evolve naturally, or they may be designated in more formal ways. This depends on the organizational culture.

Develop Sources of Great Ideas

FOAK had the good fortune of being born in an environment teeming with good ideas—IBM Research. In the early days, many ideas were "shovel-ready." But over time, the balance shifted toward market needs. The questions—Can we fix this? Can we make this better? Is there a new possibility here?—have become at least as important as the new capabilities being generated by researchers. Just as everyone has an opinion, most everyone seems to have an idea. But even if you have an ample supply of ideas, it is important to both solicit ideas from the marketplace and to feed your creative people with the facts, questions, and stories that will help them focus their imaginations on areas that have the promise of delivering value.

Your idea people also need to be oriented toward your innovation program:

- What are its goals?
- What are its limits of time and budget?
- How do they get on the calendar?
- Who do they need to contact?
- What is the secret to getting funding?

It is helpful to provide stories, examples, and forms. The whole process should be delineated and explained. From FOAK experience, redundancy is also important. The drift from the facts of the program to rumors and hopes is inexorable—especially with a successful program. Everyone associated with FOAK is encouraged to orient stakeholders, tell them the story, and then orient them again.

Make it easy to submit ideas, but not too easy. More ideas is better than fewer, but the ideas that have the most value are those that are underlined by passion. At one time, the Industry Research Relationship Managers (RRMs) were encouraged by IBM Research management to submit as many proposals as they could. The result was a plethora of low-quality proposals that wasted the FOAK Board's time. Just as suggestion boxes (especially those that offer rewards) pick up a lot of ideas that seem to have "What the heck?" written all over them, idea programs that don't have direction and standards can attract ideas that not even the originators believe in. You want people who are dedicated to their ideas, so raise the bar high enough to test the commitment from the start.

One way to raise the bar is to make sure that more than a few people support the idea. With FOAK proposals, a Proposal Team presents the ideas, and they need to include the endorsements of people who will help realize the value. While not every innovation program will have the same kind of supporters, it's a good idea to provide guidance on whose support *is* appropriate—and then to insist that the Proposal Team get their backing. Another approach employed by the FOAK program is to force the Industry Teams and Industry RRMs to prioritize their proposals by limiting the number of slots that are allocated on FOAK Board meeting agendas.

Get help. No program team can have a broad-enough view to find all the potential ideas. They need to do more than promote; they need to network with a variety of clients, sponsors, and organizations and make it clear that their help and input are essential to the program's success.

Choose the Right Projects

The first few projects for an innovation program (indeed, for any ongoing program) need to fulfill promises of the value propositions to stakeholders. Therefore, project selection is critical. In such cases, obvious, available assets may provide a strong starting point. This was true for FOAK. Even though some basic approaches needed to be reformulated later, the FOAK program had momentum in its support by the time these changes needed to be introduced.

So there is a trade-off in going after the "low-hanging fruit." This can provide some quick successes, but these will not necessarily provide the mechanisms for a sustainable program. On the other hand, a clear understanding of the mechanisms that work within the context of a specific enterprise might be difficult to derive from the start. And support doesn't always last long enough to survive trial and error. So the program team must consider both the organization's flexibility and patience.

If it hasn't been considered already, the program's scale needs to be taken into account. A number of factors are involved. How long should projects take? This may be determined by sponsor needs, available funding, and the length of budgetary cycles. How much should be spent on each project? Depending on what is being done, there will be a different critical mass of funding. The program team needs to find out how much was invested in similar projects, both within the enterprise and, because partners will be involved, externally. How many projects will the program take on each year? What's the funding cycle?

After the pilot stage, there probably will be very few projects in the works, so the program team needs to decide what a sustainable number is—that is, how many projects the program can support year in and year out. This involves not just attention to the investment available on a year-to-year basis, but also the team's own time investment in analysis and oversight. In addition, the program team needs to think of the program in terms of its relative impact. The larger the organization, the larger the program needs to be so that it doesn't escape notice. And, of course, for innovation programs that intend to be ambitious, enough projects must be going on so that the ratio of successes to failures is high enough to avoid creating significant doubts among sponsors.

Select the Best Partners

When the innovation project includes the aspect of collaboration, internal as well as external, the process of partnering needs to be looked at very closely. As you have seen, FOAK develops internal partners at the proposal stage but does not settle on (although it may explore) external partners until proposals are approved. What are the fundamental concerns here? The biggest one has to do with creating options.

What this points to is the need for any program to work to develop trust between constituents. And if the relationships can't be deepened within the organization, it may be difficult to partner externally. For IBM, the partnering with external clients came only after years of experience in moving progressively outward from IBM Research.

It may be that some innovation programs will face too many challenges and will not be mature enough to partner even internally to the extent that they need to be successful. Conversely, there may be innovation teams that are so skillful at developing trust and good working relationships that they can easily reach out to a number of partners when the opportunity for collaborative innovation begins to emerge, at any stage of the process.

A thoughtful and honest assessment of partnering capabilities needs to precede the design of an innovation program. If the program's goals cannot be met, either a plan must be put in place to improve partnering capabilities (such as by creating contract templates to facilitate contract negotiations), or the program's goals need to be scaled back (such as by limiting the projects to one client versus multiple clients).

Once the whole idea of partnering has been well explored, a process needs to be put in place. The lessons of FOAK suggest the following critical success factors:

- A variety of persons, working in a strong network, need to work cooperatively to identify potential partners.

- The innovation program needs to be protected from accepting inappropriate partners. For some executives and some sales people, innovation is like a magic charm. They see it as a way to draw in new business and repair relationships. But there are limits to what a program can accomplish, and choosing the wrong partners only leads to disappointment and failure. If the program is forced to accept partners strictly for political reasons, it is not likely to be successful.

- Partners need to have skin in the game. Even if a financial commitment is not required, *some* substantial contribution should be. The message sent by providing a free ride is that the trip has no value.

- Partners need to share the vision. They must buy into the program's value proposition. In FOAK's case, that means valuing the ability to work with researchers. It means wanting the asset to be put to work repeatedly in the real world. It means demonstrating a willingness to take a risk and to come to nonstandard agreements.

Overcome Legal Hurdles

Having the right partner reduces legal problems. A good relationship and knowledge of the administrative requirements of participating organizations go a long way toward avoiding the real problems of misunderstandings, internal rules, and bureaucracy.

The biggest challenges FOAK has seen are in making sure that the partner organizations recognize that an innovation collaboration has different needs than other types of partnerships. Some departments, like purchasing, cannot use their standard processes and may need to be educated about the program before they can contribute to the collaboration. The best practice for moving forward is engaging with an active and informed client sponsor.

One more point: While it is usually good to engage with all stakeholders early and often, some innovation groups take this too far. If you scour the entirety of each participating organization, looking for potential stakeholders, and then you work to get approvals from each one, you are likely to find someone who is happy to maim the project or veto it. It is better to ask key executives for the list of essential stakeholders and then leave it at that.

Make Sure the Plans Are Clear

The more heterogeneous your innovation team is, the more likely you are to move into new areas and discover hidden value. However, this happens only if the barriers to communication are overcome. Naturally, the normal sort of documentation—project descriptions, agreements, instructions, mission statements—needs to be produced. In addition, legal documents need to be made available. These need to go beyond the contracts and intellectual property (IP) agreements if there are local laws, security requirements, and government requirements.

Documentation, while essential, is insufficient. Many people do not read all the documents they are sent. Therefore, it is always good to go over everything in a discussion (face to face, if possible) where people can ask questions, learn about the context of the work, and get clarification.

Beyond receiving the information aurally, discussions (or, even better, workshops) get people personally engaged with and committed to the project and to each other. This socializing of the project is important throughout any attempt at innovation, but it has to start with the team that will execute the project. People need to feel they have input, even though the decision might not go their way. They need to understand why some aspects, which they might not see as ideal, are included. Over time, they will come to understand how they can contribute beyond what is explicit in their roles and assignments.

Support Effective Execution with High Expectations

Sandbox research has its place. If no one is allowed to follow their dreams and satisfy their curiosity, many new opportunities will be missed. However, innovation has ambitions that go beyond exploration and invention. The whole point is to create something of tangible value. And, although an innovation project takes advantage of research and, at times, cannot deliver more than new knowledge, a healthy program demands results.

For FOAK, the mission is explicit, communicated often, and not compromised. If a brilliant idea does not deliver on the FOAK mission, the advocates are sent elsewhere. This usually is good for them, because it puts them into a framework that is more appropriate. It is always good for FOAK, because it allows the FOAK Program Management

Team (PMT) to reuse its tools and expertise. In addition, having high expectations and ensuring that these are fulfilled is healthy for the program, because sponsors repeatedly get what they are paying for.

It is only fair, once expectations are set, that project teams get the support they need. This means that the timescale, although challenging, must be feasible. Likewise, the resources—people, funds, equipment— must be sufficient. For FOAK, this is handled primarily through proposal review, where the project's scope is questioned. There is no substitute for experience in appropriately scoping a project to fit the available time and resources. However, new innovation programs would be well-advised to expect everything to take longer and cost more than estimates. Heading into new areas always leads to surprises. And the more adventurous the innovation program is, the more likely it is that a budget will be stretched to its limits.

Prepare for the Next Phase

FOAK explicitly works toward commercialization and reuse. To do this effectively, participants need to make contacts with commercialization and delivery organizations and nurture them throughout the process. This requires knowledge, planning, and action.

The innovation team needs to understand how the delivery organization works, what its critical success factors are, how long they can wait for their investments to pay off, what their operational limits are, and more. The closer they can get to living in the commercialization and delivery worlds, the more they know what to say and how to say it. This will improve their chances of influencing those organizations to support their projects. The plan must include specific opportunities for communication, questioning, and relationship building. It must include assignments and measurements. Since this approach is often at odds with the training and interests of "idea people," the program team may need to provide training and support, especially in the early days. Of course, knowing what to do is not the same thing as doing it. Taking specific actions to make the plan happen is part of the job.

For IBM, this has meant bringing communications people into the loop and making sure that partners are on board from the beginning and willing to tell their stories. An important point here is thinking ahead far enough to make sure post-project resources are in place and possible impediments are cleared. It is a real challenge just to bring an innovation project to a successful conclusion, and that is often the complete focus of an innovation team's attention. Thinking past the delivery date—to the next use of the innovation and how it will be adopted by the marketplace—is essential for those who want to consistently get full value from the investment. In addition, FOAK is used for thought leadership—a goal that is often a selling point for an innovation program.

The goals of your innovation program may be different. IBM has some innovation programs that are geared toward attracting and keeping talent. Others are directed toward improving internal processes. Some are aimed more at getting an understanding of a marketplace or client than at putting a new asset into an offering. But, no matter what the goals of an innovation program are, thinking ahead, providing sufficient resources, and connecting effectively with those who need to carry the work forward after a project is completed are all part of preparing for success.

Prudently Manage Investments

A project is not a program. As the leadership manages investments, in both time and money, they need to think about the good of the whole program. For those who contribute their time (board members, reviewers, allies), this means that projects cannot be allowed to disproportionately take the attention of volunteers or damage relationships between different players (external and internal partners, researchers, support folks). And since money is always limited, projects cannot be allowed to go over budget, and checkpoints must alert the leadership to stop funding when a project can't deliver on its goals.

This last point is perhaps the most controversial part. Stopping work on a good idea, one where participants have passion and dedication, is difficult. It always looks like a bit more time or a small amount of resources will turn things around. FOAK leaders face difficult discussions on cancellations every year. Every FOAK IBM Project Team has a story about why their project is an exception and should be granted extra time to secure a client partner. Saying no is difficult, but it's essential to maintaining the program's fairness and integrity. In some cases, cancelled projects have even proven themselves in another incarnation. But the program's overall health depends on having a standard for stopping a project and sticking to that standard.

Part of managing a program is delivering the promised value (and delivering more than what is promised, if possible). Over time, any innovation program has to set expectations about what acceptable risk is. By implication, this means that a number of projects must succeed each year. Canceling projects that are higher-risk releases funds to support new projects that are more likely to provide the level of achievement that is required.

Look to the Future

Once the program has been running projects for awhile, there are two main things to look toward. First, the program owners need to make sure that over time the portfolio is balanced in a way that makes it relevant and valuable. Second, they need to develop new supporters, new allies, and new participants in a systematic way.

A balanced portfolio will look different for different organizations. Ultimately, this is about answering three questions:

- Does this program reflect how this enterprise creates value?
- Is this program looking toward the future and opening new opportunities to create value?
- Is this program exploring engagements with new participants who can provide vitality?

With regard to developing supporters, allies, and participants, this is something that doesn't just happen naturally—at least to the extent that it should. The only way that new supporters are developed is by regularly researching what matters to them and having opportunities for discussions with them on the calendar. The same sort of approach is needed to develop allies, who may extend beyond the enterprise. And with regard to new participants, this means that any program must have a level of promotion, mentoring, and training to excite and then enable new employees.

Tips on Getting Started

The guidelines just discussed may make sense, but this sequence of activities isn't the only possible one, and it might not be the best one for your organization. After all, innovation is not just a series of steps or a formula. Often, an "X factor" keeps the creative people involved and helps make the timing just right. For instance, engaging earlier than planned in a conversation with a researcher who asks a good question may lead to his or her imagination's spending downtime to come up with fresh answers. Promoting the program to an executive when you are sitting next to each other on a plane might not fit the budget cycle, but it might lead to sponsorship from a new source.

In addition to shuffling the order, not every step needs to be explicit. Some innovation teams may seem to skip steps, especially in communications, because the common culture makes them understood and assumed. In some organizations, steps that normally might be taken on by a project team member, such as quality control, might be done by a separate team. (As an example of the converse, some work done by the FOAK PMT in supporting meetings with the FOAK Board or engaging with communications for promotion would be done by a project team elsewhere.)

Determining the Best Sequence

Some activities, such as open-heart surgery, need to be done in a tightly controlled, step-by-step manner. Innovation is not one of these activities. The guidelines just discussed provide a map, not a flow diagram. Taking alternate routes, as long as you avoid getting lost, may provide a more interesting and effective way to do collaborative innovation. Sometimes you start with the idea, sometimes you start with the people, sometimes you start with a great question, and sometimes the starting point is an unexpected boon. Each of these shapes the process, and each is valid.

Along the way, opportunities—say, to build a relationship with a potential sponsor—may emerge out of circumstances. It would be a mistake to waste these. And some work might be done in parallel or even simultaneously.

Skipping Steps

Ultimately, all the pieces need to come together. But some steps will be taken care of *en passant* because they are just part of how things get done. Other steps will be handled by the larger organization. The important thing is to be sure that the work that is necessary for success is getting done.

If the work is just part of how things are done and never has been made explicit, it may not be needed for any of the goal setting or planning. For instance, most FOAK proposals benefit from the advice of people in different parts of IBM who are happy to help. Picking up the phone (without a chargeback) is part of IBM's culture. It would be surprising to IBMers to see that practice called out and defined within FOAK documentation. So, if a step is spelled out that should be assumed for your organization, leaving it out might be the best choice. (On the other hand, if something essential, such as the picking-up-the-phone example, is not assumed, it may need to be documented for your program.)

Looking at the steps, it may be apparent that some are the responsibility of other departments. Different organizations split up jobs in different ways. How these other departments are engaged can vary, but it is worthwhile to help them understand their roles and see the big picture. This will help them make the best choices as projects proceed. One caution: Large organizations tend to be too focused on whose job is whose. This can delay the work. Even worse, it can lead to inappropriate abrogation of responsibilities. For some researchers being introduced to FOAK, requirements to socialize ideas and cooperate on publicity have come as a surprise. It is easy to imagine arguments that allow them to skip these parts and stick with invention. But their participation is really essential to the idea's becoming a real innovation.

Making Innovation Part of the Job

Socialization is essential to innovation. Therefore, it isn't surprising that making innovation part of the job, instead of a separate activity that's done by folks working "over there" in research or development, is the easiest path to value. People who are doing the work and who make changes they see as valuable are natural advocates and implementers of innovation.

Involving the Workforce in Innovation Every Day

Nothing brings about innovation more than making it a day-to-day activity. In his book *Ideas Are Free*, Alan Robinson makes the case that people who are closest to an activity are most likely to understand what is needed, to have ideas on which solutions are feasible, and to be able to communicate the ideas to peers who can take action. Even better, as the title of his book says, the ideas are free, because the payoff for the people in the trenches usually is simply seeing their ideas put into practice.

While the ideas are free, their execution is not. To start something new, resources must be committed (or, often, some resources need to be decommitted). In addition, people need to see that time and money have been carved out to work on the ideas.

Perhaps the toughest part of the job is setting the expectations, especially in organizations where innovation is "someone else's job." To do this, people must know what is meant by innovation and understand what the organization requires of them. The way to approach this may be through starting conversations around problems, opportunities, and how things might be done differently. To get people engaged, it is essential to actually listen to their answers and show people through actions that their input matters. Ultimately, innovation—appropriately expressed—becomes part of how workgroups are measured, as much as their productivity and adherence to required processes.

Much of making innovation a day-to-day activity is tied to appreciating, even reveling in, small improvements. But what about bigger stuff? How do major changes, new offerings, and organizational reinvention become part of the job? A maxim says that you only get a quality organization if you have quality people. Similarly, you only get innovation if you have people who delight in being innovative. This may require new approaches to hiring, but it may just mean turning your innovators loose. Most organizations have more innovators than they imagine, but the culture gets in the way. Some of the cultural requirements—and ad hoc innovators in particular—are discussed in Chapter 13, "The Future of Collaborative Innovation."

Applying Lessons from FOAK

What does FOAK tell us about organic approaches, where innovation is part of the job? After all, FOAK is itself a program. Chiefly, lessons can be applied regarding partnering, identifying opportunities, resources, communications, and engaging with a variety of people:

- **Find the right partners.** This is important even if the endeavor is more localized and not part of a separate program with its own processes. An advantage of innovation as part of the job is that it is likely that knowledge of the participants' interests, skill, and commitment will be put to use. A disadvantage is that there will be pressure to include people in the name of being fair and maintaining good relationships. Yielding to the pressure and including the wrong people will certainly harm a project.

- **Identify real problems and opportunities.** Here again, there is a real advantage to having innovation be part of the job. Inevitably, people know the problems that are around them. Anything that is accepted for action will have the possibility of paying off. The caution here is finding a way to get the broader view. In FOAK, the greater value has often become visible only when new people with different perspectives have become involved.

- **Commit the necessary resources.** This is essential. FOAK has its own budget, and it is allocated in a way that provides the IBM Project Teams with what they need to do the job. Once innovation becomes part of the job, there is a real danger that it will drop on the priority list or that sufficient funds will not be set aside to get the job done. If this loss of funding isn't solved by executive leadership or a culture that truly values innovation, it needs to be taken care of explicitly through checkpoints and rules.

- **Communicate effectively and often across organizations.** Innovation is a social process. While FOAK's survival depends on this, more localized innovation efforts are likely to persist even if this skill is not well developed. After all, many of the people who come up with the ideas are exactly the same people who need to execute them. The problem with this is that many great ideas are likely to stay within their departments. Finding ways to explicitly reach out with innovations and demonstrate their value more broadly can provide a multiplier effect across the organization. This has value in and of itself, but it also helps reinforce a culture of innovation. Shared success stories can be a powerful way to expand innovations and nurture potential innovators.

- **Communicate well.** Even the best written document or crafted chart doesn't communicate to everyone. Good communications rely on different media and approaches, as well as repetition. This is why FOAK does not depend on only one way to explain the mission, assign responsibility, or tell the story. Text, conversations, demonstrations, tours, videos, Web pages, workshops, and more are used because people learn in different ways. FOAK participants also work against schedules with milestones to ensure that stakeholders hear the messages repeatedly. And through all of these, listening is part of the process. Innovation is a step into the new, even when it is part of the job. The elements of good communications—using different modes, repeating the messages, and listening—can make the difference between success and failure, even within a small team with a common purpose.

- **Make people a part of it.** This is the most difficult. FOAK has had to deal with stakeholders who had a lack of confidence in innovation or in their own ability to contribute to innovation. This is not solved by the slogan "Everyone's an innovator." Helping people who are not used to innovating by giving them support and providing opportunities to participate and succeed can get them engaged.

Summary

Every plan is specific—specific in terms of goals, the resources available, and the culture and relationships that dominate its execution. However, the same basic steps seem to be part of most programs—at least implicitly. These include coming up with the mission and goals, defining critical success factors, evolving an appropriate governance model, repeatedly getting great ideas, selecting the right projects, choosing the best partners, handling the legal aspects, executing, preparing for the next phase, prudently managing investments, and keeping the program fresh. Interpreting these steps within innovation programs is probably fairly straightforward, but deriving the lessons may require a closer look for those who are working to make innovation part of the job.

Of course, approaches to innovation collaboration will not stand still. In the future, the depth of collaboration, the participants involved, and the role of management will create new pathways and options. This is the subject of Chapter 13.

13

The Future of
Collaborative Innovation

Talking about the future could take us anywhere. We'll confine ourselves to near-term perspectives in three key frontiers of collaborative innovation: virtual teams, deeper innovation, and open approaches. Each of these is exquisitely sensitive to changing views on intellectual property (IP) and the emergence of more powerful technologies supporting collaboration. In addition, while they are developing more or less separately, they are likely to overlap to an increasing extent as time goes by.

Although we are looking beyond FOAK with the thoughts here, they reflect what we've learned from one particular experience of collaborative innovation. And rather than attempting to create a single scenario, this chapter provides descriptions seeded with questions and then leaves it to you to fit the pieces together.

Creating a New World, Virtually

In today's world, even common business tasks such as account planning, education, and employee reviews are difficult to do in a format other than face-to-face. At one extreme, defined, highly structured work where individuals have clear roles and responsibilities generally are successful (if less pleasant) in a virtual world. At the other extreme, creative activities that depend on moment-to-moment insights and people's pitching in as needed have a history of coming up against real challenges in the virtual world. Since the latter more closely resembles innovation activities, those challenges deserve a closer look.

Currently, most FOAK teams have virtual aspects. Even though the FOAK IBM Project Team members may spend time at the client sites, the majority of their efforts take place at IBM facilities. So immediately, challenges arise with regard to clear communications, trust, sequencing work, and ensuring quality. In addition, it is not unusual for the IBMers themselves to be located in different facilities, sometimes many time zones away.

Several aspects of FOAK projects enable virtual teaming:

- Experience with working on virtual teams (at least on the IBM side)
- Common computing and communications platforms
- Face-to-face project workshops
- Active involvement of project managers
- Relatively high (for innovation) structure and definition of milestones, goals, roles, and responsibilities

In today's FOAK program, virtual teaming is not a major obstacle to success. However, in the future, FOAK and innovation collaborations in general are likely to need to deal with teams that are increasingly dispersed and fragmented. Face-to-face meetings already stretch funding and challenge calendars, and that is likely to become more of an issue in coming years for FOAK, as well as for other innovation programs. Creating a well-designed structure and clear definition for projects will probably continue to be a priority in a results-oriented program like FOAK, but these may be too limiting for innovation programs with different goals. For instance, those pursuing more open-ended, curiosity-driven research may miss important opportunities if the structure is too restrictive. And even FOAK may find the emerging requirements of virtual teams challenging as the rate of social and technical change continues to accelerate.

Any group that intends to work toward innovation with a largely virtual team will encounter difficulties. In fact, within a virtual innovation team, you will have more occasions where efforts feel like you're taking one step forward and two steps back than with traditional innovation teams. But the potential for engaging with even more participants with ever more diverse views is thrilling. And it will be interesting to see the kinds of impact that these teams can have as time goes by.

Before the full value from talent that will be available across the network worldwide can be realized, technical and social mechanisms need to emerge that can help people communicate more richly and establish trust and confidence.

Helping Strangers Work Together

Perhaps the biggest change on the horizon will be further fragmentation of the workforce driven by the change in the enterprise/employee relationship. As described in IBM's Global Innovation Outlook 2.0, work is being organized around the endeavor or job. The model seen in Hollywood—where the best people assemble around a great script or a prominent actor or director, complete the film (the endeavor), and then disperse—may become common whenever creative people define an attractive project. Talent attacks opportunity, and those with the most skill and capability are likely to behave more like freelancers than employees.

The advantage of such an approach is that no one is locked in place. The best people, not just the best people under contract, can be brought together. This also means that these relationships will offer better opportunities for mentorship and learning than traditional firms do. The environment is more fluid, and it provides more potential for people to match up with just the right advisor or work experience.

However, problems of trust, accountability, and commitment multiply when you reach an extreme where each team member may be a stranger, little more than an e-mail address, and where there may not be common social or business cultures. Virtual relationships strip away many of the natural means we have for building relationships. In a face-to-face environment, we have facial expressions, gestures, body language, clothing, and personal hygiene as cues. We have microexpressions and, as an IBM director has suggested, perhaps even smell to help us form a basis of evaluation and commitment. We also have accreditation in the form of locale (such as a corner office), badges, and possibly letters, awards, degrees, and samples. And, in many cases, we have a history as well.

A step away from the richest face-to-face experience is working with a stranger (either face-to-face or at a distance) who is vouched for by someone we know well and trust. Medical specialists work on referrals from our general practitioners. We invite plumbers and other workers into our homes based on recommendations from friends and family.

Today, virtual teams in business generally establish the credibility of team members through affiliations, such as job titles, that are well understood. And even here, where participation may be determined through a third party in the same organization working through a stack of anonymous resumes, people bring in social factors when they can. If a consultant has a choice—adding to the team someone with a stellar resume, but whom he or she doesn't know, or adding someone he or she worked with in the past who has an okay resume—whom would he or she select? Probably the person he or she has worked with before.

As the requirement for trust grows (and it becomes very large in innovation projects), the bias toward familiarity increases. Innovation is hard enough without making the teams virtual. The FOAK program has been as successful as it has, even though virtual teams are common, because of practice, organizational support, written commitments, and face-to-face meetings. Many organizations don't even try to do innovation under such circumstances.

In addition to pushing trust to the limit by bringing together strangers in a virtual space, there are other challenges to the relationships. Each participant may have his or her own favorite process, application, and platform, adding to the confusion. There is also the very practical challenge of ensuring that benefits, including future benefits derived from any IP created, are allocated fairly over time.

Will these challenges be met in the virtual world? The answer isn't clear. Optimistic projections about creating killer business-to-business opportunities via the Web foundered as the reality of weak trust and relationship support became apparent. This led firms to pay a premium to someone they knew and could count on rather than accept the best bid on a critical component from an unknown entity.

An ingredient that is found in the Hollywood model that is not found in today's online world is reputation. If virtual teaming is pushed to the breaking point, it may be able to deliver on its promises only where the mechanisms—both technological and cultural—of reputation and social networks are well supported.

Reputation Management and Social Networks

Reputation management, and especially social networks, have the potential to instill confidence in making connections in virtual worlds, perhaps at a level approaching that of face-to-face environments. "It's not what you know; it's who you 'friend'" may become the mantra for virtual teams of all types, but especially those focused on innovation, because trust is essential when you're exploring the unknown. With connections come reputation, consequences, and accountability, but today's social networks may not be up to the task. With commerce and labor come laws and regulations (such as privacy and equal-opportunity requirements)—another set of challenges that can't be avoided.

However, we already see examples of ways to qualify and credential team members in the absence of handshakes and hierarchies, including Angie's List (www.angieslist.com), tagging, and peer comments. eBay took on many of the same challenges the business-to-business auction sites faced, and it prevailed by creating an array of 20 supports for trust (ratings, comments, security for credit cards).

Of course, for virtual teams to reach their full potential for innovation, trust between members must move forward on two legs—technical and social. For the latter, reputation management systems must be at the foundation. These usually allow people to claim expertise while having peers provide ratings, recommendations, and comments. The technologies underpinning such a system are relatively simple in concept. But difficult problems can occur on a social level (with legal implications that can make the human resources folks do cat flips). Participants have legitimate concerns about privacy and fairness. Handling traditional problems such as old-boy networks, prejudice, and built-in measurement biases can be seen as insurmountable. However, there are encouraging signs that the benefits to individuals of acting in more open ways will lead to success. Ultimately, these advantages might, almost in a Darwinian sense, select for fairer networks and reduce the impact of the ones with less egalitarian traits.

But weaknesses can be found even in the best designs. No matter what systems are used, the odds of people cheating and gaming the system rise as the payoff for doing so goes up. As elegant and simple as eBay's reputation management system is, it has already fallen prey to some underhanded tactics. For instance, some people have built reputations on small sales with the explicit intent of duping people on larger offerings. Designers will need to find solutions for such flaws before reputation management systems will truly deliver on their potential.

In addition, online identities will become more important to the success of individuals. As more of their wealth and opportunities are tied to these identities, the risk of identity theft becomes much more dangerous. In fact, one can imagine a number of scenarios in which the current problems with identity theft become magnified in the environment of online teaming. While this is less a factor in the formation of innovation teams, it could be important when new capabilities need to be engaged along the innovation pathway.

Accreditation and Online Identities

Credentials have always been an important factor in building innovation teams, but this factor has been difficult to specify dependably. Credentials are important because the people on the team need to be able to trust the other participants, and they need to have a sense of which roles they will properly fill on the team. On the other hand, there is the plain fact that when you are venturing into new areas, the capabilities may be less defined, and talent may be more important than formal capabilities. A perfect example of this is the case where the chronometer was invented as a solution to the problem of longitude, but the credentials of the successful inventor, John Harrison, kept the establishment from adopting the solution for decades.

But even when all participants respect the accreditation system, difficulties occur with varying cultural expectations, legitimate misunderstandings, and inconsistencies brought about by the complexities of separating value delivered from the charm (or lack thereof) of the person delivering the value. If you are capable and trustworthy, that might not be reflected in your rating if you are unattractive in some way. If you fall short on capability or trustworthiness, but you are devastatingly appealing, you might do well.

Timing is also a factor in the quality of the evaluations that people provide. Ratings differ depending on when people are surveyed about someone's performance because of the inconstancy of memory, the impact of the current context, and the time it takes to appreciate the benefits and drawbacks of a contribution. This weakness in scoring makes even a well-thought-out ratings system questionable and reduces its value in accreditation.

When the number of participants involved in innovation is fairly small, it is less difficult to determine which people belong on the team and what their roles should be. Reputation management systems are strained (but particularly important) when the team needs to grow to continue moving the innovation forward. Once you get beyond a few dozen people who know each other in some way—or at least have given each other a chance to work together—scaling trust and commitments becomes a challenge.

However, there is good evidence that this may be managed through social networks. Open innovation—in particular, the innovation that is seen with open software such as Linux—has demonstrated that very large teams of people can, if put into the right environment, work together effectively even though they've never had any face-to-face interactions. The investment in creating such an environment will be too big for some innovation activities, at least under current constraints. Despite the difficulties, will we see some large, highly effective social networks put together that resemble open-source software communities? Perhaps. But probably only in situations that have a strong societal need for innovation.

Getting the Environment Right

With regard to environment, people are still learning the essentials of effective virtual teaming in mundane contexts. As just mentioned, things become more difficult when innovation is put into the mix. However, some rules of thumb may be useful in designing an environment for virtual teams working on innovation.

The first rule is that there needs to be access to the decision-maker or set of decision-makers. This is particularly true where inspiration is important and decisions need to be made quickly, before the passion or idea evaporates. In addition, an environment for "Fail fast and be forgiven" seems to be an essential aspect of giving people permission to take initiative. The design should allow for small changes against an overall pattern, which is clearly stated. Using the open-software example, the software's overall design and intent may be plain to the participants, and the ability to build in fixes or augment the design in small ways may be straightforward and may encourage initiative.

Another aspect of appropriate environments is sharing resources. Everyone needs access to common tools, common documents, and areas where discussion can take place. It is particularly important to be able to send questions to the group, although some attention needs to be paid to interruption management if trust and effectiveness are to be maintained. Where resources are scarce, there must be a fair allocation system that everyone understands. But for many cases of virtual teaming for innovation, the scarcest resource is the time of the people participating.

This points to another aspect of the environment that needs particular attention—a way to show the work flow so that it is transparent to all those who are involved. Nothing is more discouraging than to be involved in such an effort, often volunteering your own time, only to have the work you've done not matter to the team. It's even worse to find out that the work was unnecessary because it was already done by another team member.

Ad Hoc Innovators

Within IBM is the phenomenon of ad hoc innovators: people who spend their own time and resources moving things forward. One aspect that makes this possible is a corporate culture that encourages people to do things apart from their designated jobs and roles. And there is also a sense that IBMers can ask people outside their group for assistance (and that they *can be asked* to help people outside their groups). Any sort of virtual innovation team needs a similar spirit of sharing and involvement.

IBM has incorporated support of ad hoc innovators into its environment. The Thinkplace application is a suggestion box on steroids. Not only does it allow employees to post their ideas to a public site, it also allows for ratings, comments, and offers of help from peers. This becomes a basis for volunteers taking on an innovation and running with it. As additional help, ideas that get good ratings and lots of comments automatically have "catalysts" assigned—innovation veterans (also volunteers) who share their knowledge, advice, and contacts.

Tools for Virtual Teams

Of course, any work on a virtual team depends on all participants being comfortable with both the function of the tools needed and the social aspects (particularly the etiquette) of any communication and collaboration tools. Again, in many organizations, tools as basic as instant messaging, even today, are absent from the workplace or are frowned on in that environment. Obviously, such circumstances will result in some difficulty in moving to virtual teams, much less innovative virtual teams.

As stated in the Introduction, innovation is a social activity. Historically, there effectively have been no lone innovators. Genius happens in groups. The requirements for genius in the past, as with the Lyceum in Greece, or the Renaissance artists, or the intellectuals in Paris in the 1930s, have been difficult to emulate in a virtual space. However, mechanisms for creating trust and sharing more instantaneously and personally are beginning to emerge. While virtual worlds, such as Second Life, may not in themselves be the answer for creating a café for philosophical discussions, they do point toward new potential for achieving this. It is not difficult to imagine teams of innovators, not collocated, coming together in the future to do things on an innovative level that approaches genius.

Deeper Innovation

Increasing and deepening collaborations between enterprises and talented individuals puts into play the Medici Effect (as detailed by Frans Johansson in his book of the same name). Briefly, when people from diverse disciplines look at problems and opportunities from different points of view, great things happen. One expert, who cannot see the implications of his or her own work, is alerted by an expert in a different field. Two bits of understanding may come together to form a whole. Experts from different disciplines apply the other person's tools to solve their problems.

In addition, potential exists for synergies that come from participants' different capabilities. (It is one thing to come up with ideas that are striking and original. It is another thing to follow through on them.) The chances of successfully bringing innovation from idea to the marketplace increase as access to more capabilities increases. Increasing the number of deep collaborations between diverse enterprises—wherein people from different organizations work at earlier stages, with more shared risk, more shared trust, and fewer bureaucratic barriers—presents many challenges. But many advantages await those who can achieve deep innovation partnerships.

The future of deeper innovation is filled with possibilities:

- Partners are getting involved at earlier points in the innovation journey, where the ideas begin to connect with needs.

- Approaches to collaboration are moving beyond traditional presentations and demonstrations to take advantage of new understandings of stories and how people can become more engaged in conversations.

- Services science is becoming a legitimate focus of study in academia. It promises to create a virtuous cycle of enhancements to approaches to innovation collaboration. (This is discussed in more detail in the section "At the Frontier: Services Science.")

- Sophisticated approaches to communicating risk offer the potential to reduce the reluctance of executives to provide support for innovation.

- The roles of communities and consumers are expanding in innovation and may in some cases take on some or all of the functions of management.

Cocreation

Firms have partnered for years and have even partnered in innovation ventures. IBM has had many instances of this, as mentioned briefly in earlier chapters. But it does seem as if the need for deeper partnerships on a more general basis is beginning to become visible. This is because many of the challenges that we face are larger and more complicated. In addition, the technical platforms for attacking these problems are much richer today than they were in the past, making more sophisticated collaborations feasible.

IBM has been actively seeking ways to work with people, especially clients, in deeper ways. This is the essence of the current IBM "Smarter Planet" advertising campaign. Cocreation is a natural outgrowth where there is already a good relationship and much respect for the capabilities of each potential partner. Many times these relationships lead to follow-on collaborations and pathways that are already more or less anticipated. At other times they can lead to new and exciting levels of partnership and cocreation.

But even where people have good relationships, they may differ in their comfort with participating in larger endeavors involving innovation. And in the case where new partners must be engaged and where there is no long-standing relationship, things become even more difficult. The trick to creating relationships that foster deep innovation is finding ways to engage in deep and rich conversations (with the right people).

A number of mechanisms are available for doing this. The traditional approach is to start with informal conversations, reviews of past efforts, or more formal PowerPoint talks that provide messages on capabilities and, perhaps, show demos. All of these are valuable, and they often help create a foundation of mutual understanding and confidence.

Fostering Rich Conversations by Using Scenarios

In emerging relationships between IBM and partners, scenarios, questions, and demonstrations are being used to promote conversations that are very much shared—where all parties are on equal footing. This is the essence of what the IBM Industry Solutions Labs (ISLs), described in Chapter 9, "Telling the Story: IBM's Industry Solutions Labs," are trying to achieve. In fact, ISL programs have already led to some significant collaborations between IBM and its clients, including FOAK projects. The key here is listening, listening, listening.

The temptation is to create complete proposals, demonstrations, and scenarios, with the aim of better establishing credibility. However, this approach can get in the way of being able to listen. It sends a message of finality that discourages input and collaboration. It just doesn't give people a chance to participate. A much better approach to fostering deep innovation is to intentionally leave holes in these presentations—spaces that provide opportunities for others to jump in, critique, and explore possibilities.

This can be very uncomfortable for all involved. Many people who have been involved in partnering and working with clients are concerned about anything that gives the appearance of being half finished or, even worse, unprofessional. The temptation is to clear out all ambiguities and fill all holes. As one researcher put it, "There should not be any open switches." However, when something is finished, or perceived as being finished, it is very difficult for people to imagine the changes. And often scenarios and demonstrations that are done in such a completed manner don't encourage conversations, but instead lead to straight-up or straight-down decisions. Essentially, a potential partner sees a future that they either want or don't want.

Beyond rich conversations, there must be clarity. And this clarity must extend beyond the people you might be engaging in the conversations. So very often there has to be documentation—in particular, definition of terms—that reaches out to other stakeholders. It is especially important to make sure that people who can say no have the information they need so that they can say yes.

At the Frontier: Services Science

As part of the rationale for deep innovation, the complexity and sophistication of problems, as well as the tools that can take on these problems, was mentioned. It should also be stated that such interesting opportunities for innovation increasingly are in the services sector. Foundational science, foundational technology, and foundational software applications already have seen significant momentum for progress. And although much can still be done in these areas between partners (in fact, a consensus foundation facilitates this), service has more unknowns and is, in many ways, a new discipline. Interestingly enough, service is also the growing part of the economy for virtually every nation.

That the services sector is still not well understood and that so few services sciences courses are taught in universities is surprising in this day and age. But the services sector—where human elements are so important and the dynamics of action, and even the essential questions are still being explored—will certainly be a realm where deep innovation will be the best route to answers. IBM is investing in building curricula that teach a new science of service systems. That science aims to apply scientific understanding, engineering discipline, and management practices to the design, improvement, and scaling of systems that support the services environment. This should enable service businesses to be more efficient and scalable.

Other interesting areas for exploration that are key to innovation and the services sector include experience engineering, understanding how priorities are set, aspects of developing trust, and mechanisms to support a more effective bridging of different cultures.

As deep innovation helps answer some questions about services science, some of the services science answers will better enable deep innovation. For instance, much work needs to be done in services science around creating an effective and useful taxonomy of collaboration. Today collaboration is a very large, vague, catchall term. And more useful terms, with more specificity, will certainly allow people to be more effective in their collaborations, such as by helping them choose the correct tools to use to do a specific collaboration job.

Assessing and Managing Risk

Risk assessment is another area where, although good science under-lies the concepts of managing risk, the communication is weak. Within organizations, it is often the case that the guidance based on the use of innovation risk-assessment tools does not effectively reach decision-makers. (Not long ago, it might have been important to mention finan-cial institutions as an exception in the use of risk assessment, but there seems to be some proof of the inadequacy of the use of these tools in that sector.) In most businesses, an amazing number of important decisions are made with risk being assessed by the gut instincts of executives.

How can risk analysis be made consumable to nontechnical people, including executives? Perhaps the best example of a popular sort of risk assessment is tracking calories when dieting. Most people understand how much a 200-calorie candy bar pushes their risk of obesity, and they weigh that risk against the benefits of consumption. The decision may be difficult, but the risk is clear. It would be beneficial if what is learned from tools of risk assessment could be presented to executives on such a simple basis. It would be especially valuable to opening more opportuni-ties in innovation collaboration, since risk, particularly executive aver-sion to risk, is often cited as a major obstacle to innovation.

Communities and Consumers Take Over Management Roles

Of course, partnerships between corporations don't represent the only kind of deep innovation that's possible. It is certainly conceivable that deep innovation based on a community of interested people would be possible. At times, they may even move to the center and assume the governance role that is usually taken by management (of firms, nonprof-its, and government). Certainly we see such activity in the social realm, where political and humanitarian efforts are driven by individuals who come together with passion and trust to successfully create change. This will not overwhelm traditional management, but it provides a model that may be effective for deep innovation in some new areas.

It is also possible to conceive of deeper relationships between busi-nesses and their users and consumers. Getting them more deeply involved in the process of innovation at an earlier time is likely to be beneficial. We see some movement toward that with beta testing of soft-ware applications and some consumer-driven/company-sanctioned Web

2.0 activities. Again, this is not to say that consumers will take over management functions at Fortune 500 companies. But consumers may take over *some* management functions in a *limited* way.

Perhaps even more exciting is the prospect of hybrids of deep innovation collaborations. These might include firms working with communities or consumers or all three working together to create striking new offerings, social programs, and approaches to problem solving. A notable advantage of creating such hybrid deep innovation collaborations would be that new ideas would be more easily socialized from the very beginning.

Open Approaches

As discussed earlier, 20 years ago, IBM did not really need to look outside to find experts or new ideas on silicon. Most of the best minds and best knowledge around chips could be found within the walls of the corporation. (Or, at least, that was the accepted view.) Today, it's fair to say that for most every area of endeavor, no one organization has a lock on the talent and the essential concepts. For significant innovation, it has become absolutely necessary to reach outside. In the 2008 IBM Global CEO Study (www-935.ibm.com/services/us/gbs/bus/html/ceostudy2008.html), 71% of the CEOs surveyed said they planned to focus on collaboration and partnerships.

This sort of reaching out is apparent in Figure 1.1 in Chapter 1, "A Program That Works." It shows how IBM Research went from splendid isolation, to working with internal groups in IBM, to, ultimately, working directly with IBM's clients. This process has not come to an end. Henry Chesbrough's book *Open Innovation* shows how corporations and other organizations are looking toward people outside for collaboration or even to take on the tasks by themselves. The milestone site Innocentive (www.innocentive.com/) actually puts out the specifications of what is needed to create a solution, such as the characteristics of a chemical compound, and asks the world to provide the answer.

Open approaches are showing themselves in a number of ways. The most obvious is the open-source software movement, which has been enabled both by richer and broader conductivity and by the evolution of a social milieu that encourages sharing and participation. Eric Raymond's *The Cathedral and the Bazaar* describes this "gift culture" well. (In fact, many of the same aspects were apparent within IBM in the days of green screens through internal forums. The excellent dissertation *Medium as Process*, by Davis Foulger, details this.)

One benefit of working more openly is the engagement of more perspectives. This not only provides for creative new ways to look at an opportunity or problem, but it also provides knowledge that might otherwise be inaccessible. But, under the right circumstances, when the participants are truly diverse, an opportunity exists for the wisdom-of-crowds effect. Of course, under the wrong circumstances, when the group is too homogeneous, a wonderful opportunity exists for the foolishness of crowds.

Within open theoretics, probably the most notable and controversial perspective is the emerging view that IP is not something that serves the public when it is kept under lock and key. A whole spectrum of arrangements for IP use, distribution, and sharing is beginning to be developed. Everything is there, from the idea that information is free to restrictive licenses to cross-licensing to the traditional strong IP protection, as is seen with patents in the pharmaceutical industry.

However, there are powerful drivers for a more open approach. These are tied to the reality of the digitization and easy access of property, no matter how it's protected. And as the world becomes more complex and moves faster, there is a need to put things together in new ways, and there are people who won't wait for a property owner to become enlightened about potential uses.

Mash-ups (user-created Web application hybrids) probably carry the flag for revising views on putting potent IP into new contexts. They bring along all the concerns about fairness to original content producers. The growing availability of processing power and data provides people with a need or an idea, with the power to pull things together in a new, unprecedented way.

The mash-up aesthetic takes on a special life as operations become more transparent. For instance, it's easy for taxpayers in California to track their representatives' votes against contributions from specific lobbyists, thanks to a site that is a mash-up of those sources of data. (This probably was not envisioned when those data were made public.) The transparency expands the ability of the person on the street to see the inner workings of firms in a number of ways. Some years ago there would have been great concern about revealing a corporation's internal workings. But it was a competitive advantage, at least initially, for FedEx to show you where your package was at any given time.

The fact is that the environment of ideas has changed. Even IBM, which used to be very careful about what information went out externally, has reached a comfort level with its employees blogging without any internal review. (However, IBM provides comprehensive guidelines on blogging.)

Openness means being open to a good number of things: open to new ideas and perspectives, to the needs of others, and to the risks inherent in sharing values, contents, weaknesses, and strengths.

BUILDING A NEW IP MARKETPLACE

In 2006, IBM's Global Innovation Outlook explored the area of IP. It discussed the issues, defined the characteristics, and established a baseline for an effective IP Marketplace in the future. It brought together a worldwide group of 50 subject matter experts from law firms, academia, governments, and corporations who were all seeking a balance between yesterday's traditional proprietary invention practices and tomorrow's open collaborative invention models. A set of guiding principles emerged regarding the creation, ownership, and exchange of IP:

- Inventors file quality patent applications for novel and nonobvious inventions of certain scope.
- Patent ownership is transparent.
- Market participants act with integrity.
- IP value is fairly established based on the dynamics of an open market.
- Market infrastructure provides flexibility to support differing forms of innovation.

Realistic introductory levels of global consistency exist for all these principles.

A manifesto was created that discusses in detail IP quality, transparency, integrity, value, and flexibility based on these guidelines. To learn more about building a new IP marketplace, read the report, or request a hard copy at www.ibm.com.

Summary

The world does not stand still. Participants are becoming more dispersed, but luckily tools and social approaches can help pull them together again. In fact, these virtual teams may provide advantages that a face-to-face team could not.

At the same time, partners need to be involved more deeply and earlier. The tradition within FOAK is to focus on technology that is already in a good and useful form. However, it is becoming clear that, to meet some objectives, partnering will need to occur at an earlier state. In fact, some of the efforts toward workshopping for cocreation already are demonstrating the promise of attacking problems and opportunities in new ways.

In addition, we are seeing that the cast of characters involved in innovation is becoming more eclectic and more interested in sharing. The open innovation, even mash-up, aesthetic points toward a new view of how to conduct innovation in an environment with fewer boundaries and lowered obstacles.

How all these pieces will come together in the future remains to be seen. And for each of them, social forces resist and oppose their adoption. However, it seems that any innovation program that intends to be relevant in the world that is emerging will need to keep these in mind.

Afterword

Fourteen years of experience have provided FOAK with processes, guidelines, and tools that address many of the challenges associated with collaborative innovation. And even though the program has a cadre of FOAK veterans to draw on for advice and mentoring, no one can project how collaborative innovation will evolve in the future.

We began this book with the statement that innovation is a social activity. Even the best ideas can provide value only if they are shared with others who can contribute to their adoption. Throughout this book, we've tried to illustrate how FOAK socializes ideas, and we hope that some of the approaches that are used can be adopted by others. At a minimum, we hope that our examples will stimulate thought about how relationships around innovation might be formed.

Relationships, discipline, flexibility, and patience may take people who are participating in innovation well out of their comfort zone. But comfort often is related to knowledge and expectations. The challenge of the unknown is always more frightening and appears more risky than a challenge where a person can identify trade-offs and touch points. Our hope is that this book, through its examples and lessons, has expanded the comfort zone of those who want to participate in innovation. And although elements of the unknown always exist in programs aimed at innovation, we hope that the lessons provided here will expand options for innovation and provide more opportunities for delivering benefits to individuals, businesses, and communities.

First and foremost, FOAK has proven the benefits of looking broadly for stakeholders. Too often, teams involved in innovation look to themselves and perhaps to one specific sponsor, only to falter when someone outside these groups objects or when a sponsor walks away, leaving no alternatives. Looking broadly for stakeholders helps innovation teams learn what can help or hinder the adoption of their idea or invention. It also creates more options, in particular with regard to sponsors and paths to commercialization. With more options in play, the decisions about whom to include begin to come to the fore.

FOAK has a bias toward engaging with people who have a passion for and commitment to innovation. Given the challenges that all innovations face, it is difficult to proceed without this sort of enthusiasm and dedication. So, looking toward socialization, this emotional factor actually has emerged as a key criterion for FOAK. For instance, one key test for sponsors is their financial investment in the project. This was one of the hard and early lessons of FOAK. Participants (internal and external) need to have skin in the game.

Innovators need to be able to communicate in terms that matter to different constituents. This means that they need to take the time to learn about other people's goals and needs, and they need to find ways to gain their input. Primarily, this involves actively listening to them, really hearing what they have to say. FOAK has made a point of developing forms and procedures for getting input and maintaining good communications. Often, FOAK innovators use specific techniques, asking good questions and engaging in rich discussions. The program has also helped those involved, especially researchers, build their skills in speaking, listening, demonstrating, and persuading.

In our experience, innovation programs need to include boundaries and discipline. Creative people tend to react against this and can be unhappy about restrictions. However, it's very difficult to get results without a level of structure. Certainly, FOAK has benefited from taking a rigorous approach to socialization of ideas. Many checkpoints remind innovators to contact a catcher, or a sponsor or partner. There is a process that makes feedback and oversight mandatory at specific points. There are even rules to follow, milestones to meet, and forms to fill out. All of this has to be done with a gentle hand. Those managing FOAK have learned that they need to review all the bureaucratic elements from time to time to make sure that their overall effect is positive. In particular, FOAK has project managers, and there are hard deadlines for delivery, irrevocable commitments, and strict limits on funding. These provide a level of structure that might be inappropriate for more speculative innovation projects.

Finally, an innovation program needs to have the right resources, and its participants need to have appropriate skills. This may seem obvious, but because of compromises or the use of inappropriate models for innovation, it is often in the skills area that programs are challenged. Different flavors of innovation require different skills and different participants. For instance, if an innovation program is primarily aimed at incremental improvements to established offerings, it is inappropriate to have people try to exercise blue-sky, curiosity-driven approaches. And although it's essential to develop skills in communications and build relationships, these steps often are not even considered part of the mandate of an innovation program.

FOAK has been continuously developing, evolving, and changing over the years. Against its own criteria, it is getting the job done, with many publicized examples that demonstrate effective collaborative innovation. This has not occurred without challenges, however. The kinds of assets piloted and enhanced via FOAK projects have had to change over the years. Sponsoring organizations, both internal and external, have undergone reorganizations or have been refocused in the middle of projects. And moving from a project that delivers value in FOAK to making a key contribution to the portfolio of offerings from an IBM delivery organization has proven to be elusive: Innovations need to compete for attention and continued investment, and that requires its own processes. The program of today, while it has the same central vision, is significantly different from what it was in the early days. If an innovation program does not find ways to renew itself and can't change with the times, it probably won't last.

If you're trying to form an innovation program from scratch, we offer this advice: Be patient. FOAK has the benefits today of having worked through problems in its growing-pains years. It also has a pool of people who have extensive experience in using the program to get their innovations to market. These experienced professionals not only have advantages in taking things forward themselves, but they have become excellent mentors to those who are new to the program. Getting the process right and giving people experience in innovation is not something that just happens overnight.

Looking forward, the FOAK program will continue to explore new ways of partnering, including partnering across entire ecosystems. This will require FOAK partnerships to evolve from one-to-one to many-to-many. And learning to nurture and manage those relationships will force the FOAK leadership team to develop new approaches, tools, and roles to manage those partnerships in both the real and virtual worlds.

Currently, FOAK is facing a number of specific changes. IBM Software Group, a key partner, is doing a review of the FOAK asset transfer process to see if opportunities for improvement exist. FOAK asset catchers will become Asset Commercialization Owners (ACOs) who will become more inspective of FOAK proposals before offering their sponsorship. Business partners, and perhaps even venture capital firms, will become as pervasive as ACOs and client partners. New sources of funding are being explored, driven by major changes in the world economy. New ways to pull projects together thematically are being revisited because many problems that society faces today are bigger. But as FOAK continues to transform, its essence will remain consistent: to accelerate the delivery of innovations from IBM Research into the marketplace.

Looking back over the history of FOAK, we believe the program's biggest achievements have been in finding new ways of listening, in learning to appreciate differences in needs, values, and even vocabularies of partners. In the future, FOAK will continue to collaborate with people based not just on their titles and checkbooks, but on their enthusiasm and commitment. And the heart of the FOAK program will continue to be communications and partnering. It is our recommendation, based on the FOAK experience, that however collaborative innovation evolves, those who want success put the focus first on communicating broadly, regularly, and rigorously.

Appendix

FOAK Process Overview

The FOAK process has 29 separate steps over three distinct phases. It is difficult to take in all the details in one sitting, so the process descriptions are covered in Chapters 2 ("The FOAK Process: Phase I") and 6 ("The FOAK Process: Phases II and III"). However, it may be helpful to describe all the phases and steps in brief, in one place. Therefore, the whole process is described here. We hope this appendix provides a quick reference and an easy way to compare the FOAK innovation process with other innovation processes. Not all steps occur in this order for every project, and projects are enhanced by a measure of iteration, especially in steps such as Refine the Scope, Select the Client, Negotiate the Contract, Facilitate a Project Workshop, and Create a Project Plan. Some steps, such as Create Joint Publicity and Facilitate a Project Workshop, may be done in parallel or at different points in the project.

Phase I

Going from the original concept to the approved proposal is about both fleshing out an idea and building relationships around it.

- **Generate Ideas:** Ideas can surface from multiple sources, both within and outside of IBM. Capturing those ideas and developing the best of them into proposals that have business value is the spark that ignites the FOAK program.

- **Identify Assets:** Each FOAK project has at its heart a core set of IBM Research assets. Providing clarity on which assets the project will use and their anticipated level of maturity helps the FOAK Board and the catching organizations understand how developed the innovation already is and what level of effort is required to commercialize the assets.

- **Identify the Appropriate Market Segment:** FOAK is a purpose-driven program with a very practical point of view. While ideas emerge around the lab, it is more common that FOAK participants look toward marketplace needs. IBMers involved in FOAK actively work with clients and IBM's client-facing teams to set ideas within specific market segments.

- **Engage the Industry Research Relationship Manager (RRM):** An Industry RRM does this by ensuring that FOAK ideas not only have technical merit, but also have an industry purpose. With over 3,000 researchers working on thousands of technologies and solutions, and with thousands of client-facing teams searching for innovative new solutions to client challenges, a focal point is needed. This is the role of the Industry RRM, which is described in Chapter 2.

- **Translate into Market Terms:** In this step, FOAK Proposal Teams create an outline of the project's intent. They also look to see that the stakeholders (clients, IBM partner organizations, key executives) value it. Promises are defined in enough detail to show how the project meets FOAK goals, how it compares to alternatives, and where adoption is likely.

- **Gain IBM Industry Support:** In order to have business impact, an idea needs to have an industry purpose. The idea must be more than just interesting; it must address a need that is a priority to the client-facing teams that will motivate them to promote the FOAK project in the marketplace.

- **Test with Existing Clients:** Networking is key to any innovation process. Discussing pre-FOAK ideas with clients with whom FOAK participants have a good rapport gives IBM's researchers and client-facing teams insights into how and if a particular client segment is ready to innovate.

- **Refine the Idea:** No idea is born with all its components well-defined and in place. An iterative process of capturing inputs—concerns, facts, contextual information, perspectives—from internal and external sources is needed to mature the idea into something that is compelling to the marketplace. In addition, this socializes the idea, increasing the owner-ship and commitment among stakeholders.

- **Gain Catcher Concurrence:** For each FOAK asset, the Proposal Team must determine which organization will provide the greatest level of hardening, enhancements, maintenance, support, and market exposure for their assets. The FOAK Board calls these organizations asset catchers. In this step, internal brand partners are oriented to the FOAK program, introduced to the project, and taken on as collaborators. Ultimately, these organizations will be responsible for ensuring that the innovation pro-vides value over time.

- **Develop a Structured Proposal:** This is a delineation of the what, how, who, when, and why of the FOAK project in the form of a document and chart deck.

- **Submit to the FOAK Board:** Only the best of the best ideas make their way to the FOAK Board for review. These ideas need to make it through the Industry RRM, Industry Team, and FOAK Program Management Team (PMT) filters before going to the FOAK Board. Those with clarity of purpose and business impact, coupled with strong industry and catcher sponsorship, rise to the top.

Phase II

A proposal is not a plan. Phase II is about bringing together the right people to spec out the work, take assignments, and work out the dead-lines. Then the IBM Project Team must do the work while, at the same time, creating the circumstances for the innovation to be adopted in the real world.

- **Approve the Project:** After analysis, questioning, and discussion, the FOAK Board approves selected projects. Only ideas that have articulated their technical and industry merits gain approval. The successful FOAK Proposal Team's reward is the opportunity to test their idea in the marketplace.

- **Convene the Internal Project Kickoff:** Here, IBM participants define the roles and identify what needs to be done. In addition, they ensure that the IBM Project Team, as well as those supporting the IBM Project Team, are all singing out of the same hymnal.

- **Identify Target Clients:** The Industry Team works with researchers to identify a pool of potential client partners and begin the process of qualifying them as potential partners.

- **Refine the Scope:** Through a series of client discussions and workshops, the IBM Project Team defines the effort in more detail and puts limits on its goals, based on the time and resources available.

- **Select the Client:** After interview-quality discussions with multiple clients, the IBM Project Team selects the most appropriate partner based on the criteria described in Chapter 4, "Getting the Most out of Partnerships."

- **Negotiate the Contract:** This step ensures that each party knows what their roles and responsibilities are and that the appropriate legal approvals are secured before they share valuable intellectual property and begin working together.

- **Facilitate a Project Workshop:** Now the real work begins! All the Joint Project Team members, along with the executive sponsors, are convened in a face-to-face discussion to chart the project's course. That is, they identify the project's specific processes, business units, resources, and time frames.

NOTE

The project workshop can be convened either just before or immediately after contract negotiations.

- **Create a Project Plan:** Roles, assignments, responsibilities, and deliverables are specified by taking into account the differences in capabilities, commitments, measurement systems, and practices across the participating organizations. Sometimes this project plan is created during the project workshop. At other times, it is created after the workshop and reviewed at the first project status meeting.

- **Implement the Project and Track the Progress:** The discipline of project management is applied to FOAK projects. Participants are expected to meet deadlines, deliver results, and provide documentation.

- **Maintain Catcher Relationship:** Nothing comes easy. To ensure that the assets from each project are successfully transferred, someone on the

IBM Project Team must take responsibility for keeping the targeted catcher organization engaged so that they appropriately plan to invest in the assets.

- **Create Joint Publicity:** Market recognition of innovation leadership is one of the values FOAK delivers. FOAK partners explore and agree upon one for more of the following: creating publicity in the form of a joint press announcement, direct client-to-client discussions, participation in analyst briefings and industry conferences or joint publications. The partners also negotiate the timing of any publicity (at contract signing, midway through the project or upon project completion).

NOTE

Publicity can be generated upon contract signing, during the project, or at project completion.

Phase III

Many innovation projects end with the delivery of a prototype or report. FOAK IBM Project Teams are not done until their work is adopted for use and reuse in the real world.

- **Reconfirm Catcher Responsibilities:** As FOAK projects progress, the IBM Project Teams gain more clarity on the state of the assets and the level of effort required to truly commercialize them. This added level of understanding provides tactical details to the commercialization agreements and enables the building of product and offering plans.

- **Determine the Path to Market:** IBM's broad reach and range provide many different paths (such as IBM sales teams and services practices, business partners, systems integrators, and resellers) for FOAK IBM Project Teams to get their innovations to the marketplace. To identify the optimal path, the IBM Project Team needs to explore various options for each asset used in the FOAK project.

- **Convene a Nine-Month Checkpoint:** FOAK IBM Project Teams have quarterly checkpoint meetings with the FOAK Program Management Team. These checkpoints are designed to keep the project on track and surface potential issues that might need to be brought to the attention of the FOAK Board. The Nine-Month Checkpoint is specifically targeted for a detailed discussion of asset transfer.

- **Complete the Project:** When the project is finished, the Joint Project Team comes together to discuss what transpired, the lessons learned, and the next steps for each organization.

- **Create a Pipeline:** To keep the catchers interested in commercializing their FOAK innovations, the IBM Project Teams must promote reuse. Much of this can be done even before the project with the first client is completed. Having a rich and credible pipeline of opportunities can greatly accelerate the time to market for FOAK assets.

- **Cross the Asset Chasm:** The process of taking an asset out of the back end of a FOAK project and getting it embedded into the catching organization's plans is fondly referred to as crossing the "asset transfer chasm." Crossing the chasm enables IBM Project Teams to keep their assets alive while tidying up the odds and ends that might preclude them from fully transferring the assets to a permanent home.

- **Transfer Assets:** Once a plan is agreed to, the researchers need to work with the catching organization to formally transfer the assets, knowledge, and support of the FOAK deliverables.

Many of the Phase III steps are actually initiated in Phase I and are continuously worked on during Phase II, such as Reconfirm Catcher Responsibilities, Determine the Path to Market, and Create a Pipeline.

Index

 FREE Online Edition

Your purchase of *Innovation Passport* includes access to a free online edition for 45 days through the Safari Books Online subscription service. Nearly every IBM Press book is available online through Safari Books Online, along with more than 5,000 other technical books and videos from publishers such as Addison-Wesley Professional, Cisco Press, Exam Cram, O'Reilly, Prentice Hall, Que, and Sams.

SAFARI BOOKS ONLINE allows you to search for a specific answer, cut and paste code, download chapters, and stay current with emerging technologies.

Activate your FREE Online Edition at
www.informit.com/safarifree

> **STEP 1:** Enter the coupon code: DAJIPXA.

> **STEP 2:** New Safari users, complete the brief registration form. Safari subscribers, just log in.

If you have difficulty registering on Safari or accessing the online edition, please e-mail customer-service@safaribooksonline.com